Praise for *7 TOOLS TO*

"In *7 Tools to Beat Addiction*, Stanton _____ take-charge message—one that is co _____ evidence—for how to overcome add _____ has influenced my professional work and changed my personal life for the better."

> —ANNE M. FLETCHER, M.S., R.D., L.D., author of *Sober for Good: New Solutions for Drinking Problems—Advice from Those Who Have Succeeded*

"Readers of this book will find Dr. Peele's tools resonate with their inner sense of themselves, and his words offer encouragement and optimism unavailable in other approaches. Mental health professionals and the loved ones of addicts can gain a completely new perspective filled with insight, compassion, and genuine understanding."

> —MITCHELL EARLEYWINE, PH.D., associate professor of psychology, University of Southern California, and author of *Understanding Marijuana*

"Dr. Peele combines knowledge, compassion, and common sense to create a book that will surely bring hope and help to all people suffering with alcohol and other drug problems."

> —PATT DENNING, PH.D., coauthor of *Over the Influence: The Harm Reduction Guide for Managing Drugs and Alcohol*

"Stanton Peele's book, *7 Tools to Beat Addiction*, will prove invaluable to people trying to cope with any type of addiction. With an engaging writing style and many examples, Dr. Peele provides the necessary tools to show each reader that ' . . . you are the primary agent of change.' I strongly recommend the book."

> —FRED LEAVITT, PH.D., professor of psychology, California State University, Hayward

"Dr. Peele illuminates for the newcomer the absurdities of the traditional U.S. recovery approach. This book will be a beacon of common sense, backed by solid science, for those struggling to make sense of their addictions and their lives."

> —TOM HORVATH, PH.D., A.B.P.P., president, SMART Recovery, president, Practical Recovery Services, and author of *Sex, Drugs, Gambling & Chocolate: A Workbook for Overcoming Addictions*

Also by Stanton Peele, Ph.D., J.D.

Love and Addiction
with Archie Brodsky

How Much Is Too Much

The Science of Experience

The Meaning of Addiction

Visions of Addiction
(edited volume)

Diseasing of America

The Truth About Addiction and Recovery
with Archie Brodsky and Mary Arnold

Alcohol and Pleasure
(edited volume) with Marcus Grant

Resisting 12-Step Coercion
with Charles Bufe and Archie Brodsky

7 Tools to Beat Addiction

Stanton Peele, Ph.D., J.D.

THREE RIVERS PRESS
NEW YORK

Published by Three Rivers Press, New York, New York.
Member of the Crown Publishing Group, a division of Random House, Inc.

www.crownpublishing.com

THREE RIVERS PRESS and the Tugboat design are registered trademarks of Random House, Inc.

Printed in the United States of America

Design by Susan Hood

Library of Congress Cataloging-in-Publication Data

Peele, Stanton.
    7 tools to beat addiction / Stanton Peele.—1st ed.
    1. Addicts—Rehabilitation. 2. Self-help techniques. I. Title: Seven tools to beat addiction. II. Title.
    HV4998.P44 2004
    616.86'06—dc22   2003023765

ISBN 1-4000-4873-7

10   9   8   7

FIRST EDITION

To my children—Dana, Haley, and Anna Peele—who have developed into the strong, nonaddicted people their mother and father wanted them to be.

Acknowledgments

As he has been for decades, Archie Brodsky was my most capable and most assiduous helper. Building on his long familiarity with my ideas and writing, his inputs were critical in the planning, writing, and editing of this book. For all of this, I express my deep gratitude. He also commented on book design issues with the assistance of Vicki Hochstedler, who was likewise an ever-willing and able helper. John and Kathy Ziga, Rich Fromberg, Kathy Treleven, and Alice Rogers-Pearlman provided needed practical and moral support at critical stages in the production of this book. I also thank my three children—Dana, Haley, and Anna Peele—for their love and support. And, finally, my colleague at New York University's Ehrenkranz School of Social Work, Lala Straussner, who sustained and supported me in my work.

This book had the unusual advantage of profiting from the contributions of three terrifically energetic and skillful editors. Whereas usually the prospect of changing editors in the course of writing a book is an author's nightmare, in this case, almost miraculously, Stephanie Higgs, Mollie Glick, and (last but not least) Caroline Sincerbeaux seamlessly responded with needed help and resources, and each made tremendous contributions to the final product. Caroline in particular never said no when asked for aid. My agent, Nancy Love, was always there with support and assistance throughout the process.

As anyone who writes a book knows, tracking down and identifying information is always a crucial, sometimes maddening, enterprise. Among those who helped me find critical sources were Linda Langscheid at Rutgers University's Alexander Library, Penny Page of the Rutgers Center of Alcohol Studies Library, Leigh Hallingby of the Open Society Institute Library, and Jennifer Johnson-Spence and Ed Kirtz of the Drug Policy Alliance Library.

America's two leading journalists on drug-related matters—Maia Szalavitz and Jacob Sullum—also helped me with key references. Jacob was not only terrifically forthcoming with such information; he also graciously read and critiqued several sections of the book. For his always ready assistance, he deserves special thanks. Tom Horvath, president of SMART Recovery, has been another helpful colleague. Christopher Wagner of Virginia Commonwealth University also offered me key insights and ideas, although neither he nor any other helper is responsible for the ideas I express in *7 Tools to Beat Addiction*.

—S.P.

Contents

7 Tools to Beat Addiction

Introduction

Probably you've picked up this book because you or someone close to you has a problem with an addiction. Perhaps you (or they) smoke, drink too much, eat too much, gamble or shop beyond your means, or maybe even take drugs. Undoubtedly you've been told, as we all have, that this problem is a disease for which you must seek medical treatment or join a support group—something that perhaps you have resisted doing. You see and hear this message in so many places— in school, in the media, from government organizations, and from treatment providers—that you may not even ask yourself whether it's accurate. But if you thought about it for a few minutes, you'd realize it just isn't so.

People quit addictions on their own all the time. We all know this is the case. How many people do you know who quit cigarettes, the most common and the most powerful of drug addictions? Did you do so? In the United States, tens of millions of people have quit smoking without treatment, about half of those who have ever smoked.[1]

Surprisingly, the percentage of former heroin, cocaine, and alcohol addicts who have quit on their own is even higher. Yet an enormous treatment/recovery industry, backed by a large government bureaucracy, tells us that it is virtually impossible to quit an addiction—and completely impossible to do so without the use of all their services.

Of course, private treatment centers have a vested interest in this debate. These are the ones that treat Robert Downey Jr., Charlie Sheen, Ben Affleck, and their ilk, often repeatedly. It's obvious why they insist that quitting addictions takes repeated, expensive stays at their facilities. Even the services of Alcoholics Anonymous (AA) can come with a price: Many claim that no one can succeed in overcoming alcoholism unless they remain in AA or another twelve-step group.

Less well known is that the government has invested millions to get an "addictive disease" message across. The National Institute on Drug Abuse (NIDA) is the government agency responsible for getting to the root of drug abuse. The NIDA was headed by Alan Leshner from 1994 through 2001—a period during which its annual budget doubled to $781 million.

Leshner is best known for his color slide show presentation, which "proved" how addiction to certain drugs, such as cocaine, occurs because these drugs stimulate certain parts of the brain. His PowerPoint presentation featured brain scans and diagrams.[2] Leshner was replaced as head of the NIDA in 2003 by brain researcher Nora D. Volkow, M.D., who has indicated that she will extend this vision of addiction.[3]

According to Leshner, stimulation of certain parts of the brain causes it to adjust so as to become hooked on the drug that stimulates it. After a certain point, addiction becomes inevitable. In making this case, Leshner insists that addiction is a medical illness that mandates treatment. According to Leshner, "It's a myth that millions of people get better by themselves."[4]

But this former NIDA chief is misinformed. Research, including studies funded by the United States government, shows that it is untrue. Numerous cases we all know about, and in our own lives, show that it is not true.

That industry, government, and faith-based organizations unite on the point that people cannot quit addictions independently makes this one of the few areas of unanimity among them. It seems ironic that all sectors of American society should be so concerned to drive home the same erroneous point.

Some other countries take a very different stance on addiction. For example, the Swiss government conducted a public information campaign to inform smokers and heroin addicts that the idea of addiction as inevitably a lifetime burden is a myth. Posters were displayed around the country with the message that most drug users succeed in quitting their habit. Swiss public health officials recognize that most addicts don't seek treatment, and many nonetheless overcome their habit. Yet they want to encourage even greater numbers of addicts to overcome addiction—and they want them to do it sooner rather than later.[5]

It is important for you to know that an independent, self-motivated cure for addiction, called natural remission, is possible. You can fight your own addictions, whether to drugs, alcohol, cigarettes, shopping, gambling—you name it. Following are major examples of this phenomenon that you can keep in mind when confronting your destructive habits.

The Vietnam Heroin Experience

Heroin is one of the most intimidating addictions, but the general public knows next to nothing about it. For most of us, what we know about heroin addicts comes from what we see on TV: ravaged users who live on the streets or who have reported to treatment centers. However, this is only a small minority of all heroin users.

How would we find heroin users who are not in treatment centers? After all, people who are breaking the law generally don't like to call attention to themselves. On the other hand, we can't do experiments in which we take average people and give them heroin until they are addicted, then see what happens to them.

Except that several decades ago the United States did do something very much like this. The government sent a bunch of young men to an isolated and scary place where they had ready access to plentiful supplies of pure heroin. This experiment was called . . . the Vietnam War.

Not surprisingly, many average youths became addicted to narcotics in Vietnam. Conditions were alternately harrowing and tedious, the soldiers were young and on their own for the first time, and heroin was cheap and easily available. This situation so scared the government that the Defense Department created a special program to deal with what they anticipated would be the masses of ex-GI heroin addicts roaming the streets of American cities. Administering this program was an assistant secretary of defense, Dr. Richard S. Wilbur.

Wilbur discovered primarily that what he had learned in medical school—"I was taught that anyone who ever tried heroin was instantly, totally, and perpetually hooked"—was wrong.[6] Of course, Leshner today teaches that once people, like the Vietnam soldiers, become addicted, they cannot quit.

The U.S. government conducted an intense research program with returning drug-using veterans. Two researchers—sociologist Lee Robins and psychiatrist John Helzer—led a team that tracked American soldiers leaving Vietnam. After screening heroin users by urine-testing them, they determined which soldiers had been addicted by asking which had undergone withdrawal when they weren't able to access the drug.[7]

Heroin users in Vietnam did not resemble the typical addicts seen on television programs or in treatment. For starters, the investigators determined that 45 percent of all soldiers in Vietnam in 1970–71 tried heroin, and almost half of these (or 20 percent overall) became addicted. Among all the men who used a narcotic in Vietnam, only *2 percent* received treatment.

"One of the original motivations for the study was the VA's concern that returning addicts would overtax their services; but the anticipated large demand never occurred," according to Lee Robins.[8]

Yet of all the men studied who were addicted in Vietnam, only one in eight (12 percent) continued to be addicted or became readdicted anytime in the three years after their return. (Remember, only about half of smokers have quit.) This was not because the remainder were abstinent. In fact, six in ten of the men who had been addicted in Vietnam used a narcotic after they returned. However, only one in five of those former addicts who used a narcotic after they got home became readdicted!

Robins and her colleagues were shocked by these results. Among other startling findings, they determined that the relapse rate was higher for veterans who were treated for their addiction than it was for those who were not.

In 1993, twenty years after the original research in the Vietnam War era, Robins was asked to reevaluate her findings in the prestigious British journal *Addiction*. Here is her summary after two decades:

> These then were the major conclusions: narcotic use and narcotic addiction were extremely common in Vietnam; availability was the main explanation; those with a history of deviant behavior *before* Vietnam were particularly at risk; addiction was rare and brief after return even when men continued to use narcotics; veterans re-addicted and entering treatment had as high a relapse rate as civilians [and higher than the untreated soldiers].[9]

What was the reaction to these remarkable findings? According to Robins, they were attacked by the research community. The Defense Department "was pleased with these findings, because they showed that Vietnam veterans had not been consigned to a life of unrelenting dependence on drugs." But Robins discovered great resistance to the results among researchers who had studied heroin addicts and found they rarely recovered.

In assessing the results of her study, Robins noted that "addiction looks very different if you study it in a general population than if you study it in treated users." The Vietnam veterans were very different from the addicts who researchers and recovery specialists were used to seeing in treatment programs, but they weren't so different from other addicts who caught themselves before their problem was bad enough to enter treatment. Robins explained:

> Their readiness to recover from addiction did not differ from that of other users. The reason that the press and scientists alike were surprised was because studies of the general population's drug dependence were and continue to be so rare. Their expectations were based on the rates of relapse found in patient populations, made up of addicts who tried but failed to get themselves off drugs.[10]

If heroin addicts such as the Vietnam vets can get over their addictions, clearly you (or someone you care about) can attempt to tackle your unwanted habits and addictions.

What Really Happens to Alcoholics

Just as with heroin addicts, we really know little about what happens to the average alcoholic. This is because only a quarter of alcoholics ever enter treatment or go to AA.

This leaves substantial gaps in our knowledge about alcoholics. Besides the three-quarters of alcoholics who never enter treatment or go near AA, do we really know what happens to treated alcoholics after they leave treatment? Take the example of Joan Kennedy, former wife of Senator Ted Kennedy. After years of drunk-driving convictions and repeated treatment, Joan Kennedy finally "got sober" in the early 1990s and was promoted as a successful treatment graduate. Almost ten years later, in 2000, she was rearrested for drunk driving.[11]

Bill Clinton's brother, Roger, supposedly recovered from his cocaine addiction after serving a prison sentence of more than a year in 1985–86 (when he entered a treatment program). President Clinton credited this jail stint with saving his brother's life. Fifteen years later, Roger Clinton, too, was arrested for drunk driving.[12]

In other words, these highly touted examples of successful rehabilitation were not rehabilitated at all, or at least their rehabilitation was shakier than was portrayed. We would find similarly surprising and disappointing results if we tracked all the less well known people who have been treated.

We might thus want to have the following questions answered: Do many treated alcoholics drink again? Do they drink the same as or differently than they did before treatment? And what happens to all the untreated alcoholics? Is it true, as we are told time and again, that there are only three possible outcomes for untreated alcoholics—jail, the hospital, or the cemetery?

In 1992 the U.S. government's National Institute on Alcohol Abuse and Alcoholism (the sister organization to the National Institute on Drug Abuse that Alan Leshner headed) carried out a massive survey of over forty-two thousand randomly selected Americans. The government agency sent trained Census Bureau interviewers to conduct face-to-face interviews with people about their lifetime drinking and drug use.

This study—called the National Longitudinal Alcohol Epidemiologic Survey (NLAES)—presented a picture of Americans' drinking problems unmatched in research history.[13] Of the over forty-two thousand Americans interviewed, more than forty-five hundred were "alcohol dependent" at some time in their lives, according to the diagnostic manual of the American Psychiatric Association (called *DSM-IV*).[14] This means that they suffered from chronic alcohol-related problems (family, legal, work, and health—including increasing use and withdrawal) that they were unable to curtail. Alcohol dependence is more serious than the other possible *DSM-IV* diagnosis, alcohol abuse, which is defined as a less severe and more transient drinking problem.

Only about a quarter of these alcohol-dependent Americans had ever been treated for alcoholism (the treated group included those who simply attended AA). Amazingly, of those who were ever treated, more (33 percent) had a drinking problem in the year prior to the interview than those who went untreated (26 percent). Such results certainly contradict claims by the alcoholism industry (for example, those made at www.alcoholismtreatment.org) that "alcoholism is lethal: Ninety five percent of untreated alcoholics die of alcoholism," and that only "four percent of alcoholics stay sober for the next year if they try to quit on their own," while "fifty percent of alcoholics stay sober for the next year if they go through treatment."

What actually occurs in regards to treatment, according to NLAES, is that although over time most of both treated and untreated alcoholics continue to drink, those who don't enter treatment are less likely to continue abusing alcohol. In NLAES, more than half (58 percent) of untreated alcoholics were currently drinking without abusing alcohol, while slightly over a quarter (28 percent) of ever-treated alcoholics were doing so. This is not quite a fair comparison, because those who entered treatment tended to have more severe drinking problems. Nonetheless, *all* of these subjects were clinically diagnosed with what we would call alcoholism, and all would have been told that they required treatment and needed to abstain.

It is surprising in the first place that so many (more than a quarter) of alcoholics who were ever treated or attended AA are currently drinking without abuse or dependence problems. Nonetheless, more than twice that percentage of untreated alcoholics were able to moderate their drinking. Taking all alcoholics together, according to the government's best research, half of all Americans who have ever been alcoholics currently drink without seriously abusing alcohol!

What remarkable results. More onetime alcoholics currently drink nonalcoholically than abstain. More people who are treated for their alcohol dependence continue to drink abusively than those who are not treated. Remember that these terrifically radical results were published by a government agency—the National Institute on Alcohol Abuse and Alcoholism—that swears to this day alcoholics can recover only by abstaining.

Why Do Those in Treatment Relapse More Often?

Of course, some people benefit from alcohol treatment; it may even save their lives. But the NLAES snapshot of treated and untreated alcoholics tells us such treatment is not a cure-all. In fact, according to this comprehensive study, alcohol treatment in the United States is not particularly effective. People treated in conventional programs not only regularly relapse, but in some cases display worse problems than those they had when they entered treatment.

Kitty Dukakis, for example, went to Minnesota's Hazelden program in the early 1980s for a diet pill habit. In 1989 she entered the Edgehill-Newport Hospital in Rhode Island for alcohol treatment. Kitty's husband, former presidential candidate Michael Dukakis, said at the time that she had had too much to drink "two or three times" following his losing 1988 presidential campaign.[15] *After* alcohol treatment, Ms. Dukakis was rushed to the hospital when she consumed rubbing alcohol for its alcoholic content—life-threatening behavior.

In 2003 sixty-year-old Calvin Klein, a corporate executive in the fashion company named for him, tried to talk to New York Knicks basketball player Latrell Sprewell while the player was throwing the ball inbounds during a game. Security guards escorted Klein back to his seat.

Two weeks later, Klein reentered substance-abuse treatment. (In 1988 he had attended the Hazelden program for alcohol and prescription-drug abuse.) Klein released a statement to explain his bizarre behavior. It occurred, he announced, because he had "recently stopped attending meetings regularly," leading to his "setback."[16]

If we accept Calvin Klein's logic—that he could never succeed without continually attending support groups—we see why he was so primed to relapse. Treatment convinced him that he could not carry on successfully without group support.

Kitty Dukakis received a similar self-fulfilling message in treatment at Edgehill-Newport: if she ever touched alcohol again, she was doomed to disaster. Whereas she had throughout her life drunk alcohol moderately, with a few episodes of abuse, she now believed that she had a permanent compulsion to get drunk, an urge that she quickly demonstrated once she left the hospital.

Is this the way to free ourselves from addictions?

People All Around Us Quit Addictions

In spite of what the government and treatment programs tell us, we all know that many people escape addictions without treatment. How do we know? Because so many of us, our friends, and our loved ones have quit addictions, including the most common drug addiction, smoking.

You have heard, and no doubt believe, that smoking is an addiction. But you may feel it's not an addiction like heroin addiction or cocaine addiction or alcoholism. However, those in the best position to know—alcoholics and drug addicts who smoke—rate smoking at or near the top of the list of hardest addictions to quit.[17] This isn't surprising. Think about it—smokers draw a steady stream of the drug directly into their lungs on the hour or even more frequently. Almost no one drinks or takes drugs as constantly as any smoker, unless he or she is a caged animal in a laboratory study.

Nonetheless, by the 1980s, after the health threats of smoking became widely publicized, about half of Americans who had ever smoked addictively quit. Most remarkable of all, more than 90 percent of them quit without any kind of treatment.[18]

This percentage of smoking self-quitters has gone down slightly since the 1980s, since so many medical treatments for quitting (i.e., nicotine gums and patches) have been made available. But treated smokers are *still* a small minority of ex-smokers. You can prove this by asking any group of middle-aged Americans if any of them have quit smoking, and then asking how many did so through a support group or any form of treatment (like a nicotine patch).

I regularly lecture to groups of alcoholism/addiction counselors, people who believe that the only way addicts can recover is through going to treatment and joining AA or another twelve-step group. First I ask them, "What is the toughest drug addiction to quit?" The audience, virtually in unanimity, shouts out "nicotine" or "cigarettes." "How many of you have quit?" I inquire. Often a majority raise their hands. Then I ask, "How many of you quit smoking because of treatment or joining a support group?" In rooms of hundreds of people who work in the treatment field and have quit smoking, never more than a handful say they quit with formal assistance.

"Wait a minute," I deadpan. "You people are too radical for me. You tell people all the time that they can't quit addictions on their own. Yet you—a group of highly experienced counselors, many of whom have quit more than one addiction yourselves—tell me you quit the toughest addiction without treatment."*

---

* Lest you think that nicotine patches have revolutionized smoking cessation, a 2003 study followed up smokers who were randomly assigned to receive a nicotine patch or a placebo. A little over one in ten (11 percent) quit smoking for a year using the patch, a slightly larger percentage than those quitting with the placebo (8 percent). After eight years, this difference was reduced to only 6 percent of those who wore the patch who were still not smoking, compared with 4 percent in the

How Uncle Ozzie Quit Smoking

How do so many people quit the toughest of all drugs? Let's examine the remarkable story of my uncle Ozzie. Ozzie was born in Russia in 1915 but came to the United States as a small child. As a teenager he developed an addiction to smoking.

Outwardly calm, Ozzie did not have obvious reasons for smoking. Nonetheless, he continued to smoke into the early 1960s. But Ozzie quit smoking in 1963, the year before the surgeon general's 1964 report on the cancer-causing nature of cigarettes gave many people a reason to quit.

I didn't actually notice my uncle had quit until years after the fact, when I saw him at a family gathering when I was home from school, after I had become interested in the question of addiction. I asked him, out of nowhere, "Ozzie, didn't you used to smoke?" Ozzie then told me his story.

He began smoking at the age of eighteen and continued smoking for thirty years. Ozzie described his smoking as "a horrible habit"—he smoked four packs a day of unfiltered Pall Malls. He kept a cigarette burning constantly at his workbench (Ozzie was a radio and TV repairman). He described how his fingers were stained a permanent yellow. But, he said, until the day he quit, he had never even considered giving it up.

On that day the price of a pack of cigarettes rose from thirty

---

placebo condition. P. Yudkin, K. Hey, S. Roberts et al., "Abstinence from Smoking Eight Years After Participation in Randomised Controlled Trial of Nicotine Patch," *British Medical Journal* 327 (July 2003): 28–9.

These figures for both smokers with real patches and those with fake patches are disappointing. This could be because (1) subjects who volunteer for such studies are less able than average to quit, and/or (2) the experience of being given a patch for the purpose of curing your craving for nicotine actually retards the impulse to quit permanently. Of course, these minuscule remission rates cannot be compared with the half of all smokers (in the United States) who have quit, because the latter figure counts people who have quit at any point in their lives, not after just one try.

to thirty-five cents. While eating lunch with a group of fellow employees, Ozzie went to the cigarette machine to purchase a pack. A woman coworker said, "Look at Ozzie—if they raised the price of smokes to a dollar, he'd pay them. He's a sucker for the tobacco companies!"

Ozzie replied, "You're right—I'm going to quit." The woman, also a smoker, said, "Can I have that pack of cigarettes you just bought?" Ozzie answered, "What, and waste thirty-five cents?" He smoked that pack and never smoked again. As this appears, Ozzie is ninety years old.

Why did my uncle Ozzie quit? To understand that, you'd have to understand what kind of person he was. Ozzie was a union activist and shop steward. Adamantly left-wing, he was a man who lived by his beliefs. It was Ozzie's job to stand up for any worker sanctioned by the company. As a result, he believed, he was punished for his activism by being sent out to the worst parts of the city on television repair calls.

Why did Uncle Ozzie quit smoking that one day, after thirty years of constant, intense smoking? He had never previously considered quitting, but less than twenty-five words thrown out by a blue-collar coworker somehow caused him to drop the addiction. We will return to this question in the next chapter, but for now it is enough to recognize that he did it. Without the aid of a support group or medicated patch, Ozzie overcame his smoking addiction. And fifty million other American ex-smokers have done the same thing.

Where Did Leshner Go Wrong?

Millions of heroin addicts haven't quit their addictions on their own, like smokers, because there aren't millions of heroin addicts in the United States. However, a majority of heroin addicts, as well as most cocaine addicts, have recovered from addiction without treatment. Millions of people with a drinking problem—including a majority of alcoholics—have quit their addictions, more than have been treated out of a drinking problem. And tens of millions of people have quit the toughest drug addiction of all—cigarettes.

So how can Alan Leshner, the head of the most prominent drug research agency in the world, claim, "It's a myth that millions of people get better by themselves"? Leshner's misunderstanding of addiction and what people do to fight it stems directly from the kinds of research his agency, the NIDA, does.

For example, researchers can't habituate human beings to drugs in a laboratory—only animals. A caged animal with no other options for animal society or recreation, if it is able to get a diverting drug by pulling a lever fewer times, will often continue to take more of the drug.

This is not the case with human beings, whose lives are impacted by such outside influences as societal values, other people's opinions, a desire to be better, and other personal and social factors. Unlike caged animals, people have a slew of options. This book deals with these factors, while NIDA researchers cannot, or will not. And as a result, their models of drug use, addiction, and quitting addiction are incomplete at best. At worst, they are diametrically opposed to the reality of addiction and the reverse of what we need to help us quit.

How Do So Many People Quit Addictions?

How do so many people leave addictions behind? The answer, we will see, does not involve a magic bullet. Rather, we all understand what the building blocks for living are, what it takes to lead a full and satisfying life.

The same building blocks are needed to overcome addiction, whether on your own or through treatment. Only we have been intimidated from focusing on them by the idea that addiction is a special medical condition that, say Leshner and other researchers who approach addiction as he does, we will one day have a drug to cure.

Major interest was aroused by the publication (in December

2001) in the *New England Journal of Medicine* of a study that examined alcoholics given the one drug approved for treating alcoholism in the last twenty years—naltrexone. This drug supposedly eliminates alcoholics' craving to drink. Naltrexone is also used as a cure for heroin addiction. Yet alcoholics receiving a placebo (sugar pill) in the study succeeded in cutting back their drinking (they were actually told to abstain) as much as did those receiving the drug.[19]

Addiction will never be cured by a pill. Indeed, when you understand addiction, the idea of a pill for curing it makes no sense. That is because addiction results when people's lives are unbalanced. It cannot be remedied by a pill, just as a pill cannot balance people's lives. But people, including you, can achieve remission by creating the fundamental building blocks that form nonaddicted lives.

This book will provide readers with these basic building blocks, which can be regarded as tools to overcome addiction. These seven tools are (1) values, (2) motivation, (3) rewards, (4) resources, (5) support, (6) a mature identity, and (7) higher goals.

What Is Addiction?

In helping you beat addiction, let me first make clear what I mean by addiction.

ALL ADDICTIONS ARE ESSENTIALLY SIMILAR

Given his view that addiction is a special product of the way some drugs impact the nervous system, Leshner made a startling reversal near the end of his tenure at the NIDA. In the November 2001 issue of the prestigious journal *Science*, Leshner indicated: "More and more people have been thinking that, contrary to earlier views, there is a commonality between substance addictions and other compulsions."[20]

The view of the essential similarities in all compulsive behavior underlies my approach to addiction. I believe that all addictions—whether to substances, people, or activities—operate according to the same principles. To see that addictions are similar in their patterns, causes, and solutions, think of addiction as a powerful, sometimes overpowering involvement to which you turn for security and gratification when you fail to find better gratifications in the rest of your life. The more you turn to the addiction, the more primary it becomes as the bulwark of your life. Yet the more you rely on it, the more negative experiences it produces in your life and the more you *need* to return to the addiction.

In 1975 I wrote (with Archie Brodsky) a book entitled *Love and Addiction*. In an earlier *Psychology Today* article, we wrote, "People can become addicted to other people in the same way they become addicted to drugs. We are not using the term addiction in a metaphorical sense; we mean it literally."[21] When people turn to an experience, any experience, for solace to the exclusion of meaningful involvements in the rest of their lives, they are engaged in an addiction.

ADDICTIONS CANNOT BE DISEASES

What Leshner and others are striving to establish is that, indeed, all compulsive involvements are like drug addictions and that they *all* can be dealt with as diseases. But Leshner's model of addiction emphasizes the special power of drugs such as heroin and cocaine and their effects on the brain, so the similarity of excessive involvements of all types seems to make no sense from his point of view.

The research of the new NIDA director, Nora Volkow, concerns dopamine, the supposedly pleasure-inducing neurochemical. One suggestion is that all addictions operate through the dopamine system. In the future, we may have brain images showing how shopping, gambling, or eating potato chips all similarly stimulate the brain, leading to addiction. There is no limit to the number of such potential images, just as there is no limit to the sources of addiction.

But the fact that many things cause pleasure offers no

greater clue to why only some people come to rely on this pleasure addictively, or to why most people eventually can overcome these addictions. What *is* valuable to take away from the idea that all addictions function the same way is that the same processes must therefore be involved in overcoming all addictions.

If all compulsions are as irremediable as Leshner believes cocaine to be, then this new view holds that compulsive sexuality, gambling, eating, and shopping are just as inescapable as cocaine and heroin are reputed to be. This view will not help people overcome these addictions.

Contrary to the NIDA's message, I stress that addiction is more malleable than you know. When people come to me for therapy, they often ask me whether their behavior constitutes a real addiction (or whether they are really alcoholic, etc.). My answer is that this is not the important question. The important questions are how many problems is the involvement causing you, how much do you want to change it, and how can we go about change?

To turn your life—or to help turn someone else's—in a positive direction, it is essential to understand that addiction is changeable and that people often are able to escape addictive behaviors and attitudes as their life circumstances change. This is because they use the addiction as a way of dealing with life, as a response to stress that is both internal and external.

ADDICTIONS AND HABITS

I refer to addictions, addictive or destructive habits, and compulsions more or less interchangeably in this book, unless there is a specific reason to differentiate them. I am aware that clinical distinctions are made between these terms—for example, diagnoses frequently distinguish between abuse of and dependence on a substance. Nonetheless, addictive problems occur along a continuum from the less to the more severe, anchored at one end (the severe one) by addictions. And although severe problems deserve different, and greater, attention than less severe ones, most of the principles governing how you improve your life and conquer destructive habits apply to any level of habit or addiction. I assume that people with all different levels of problems will read this book and can benefit from the ideas in it.

Why This Book?

At this point I have told you several things about getting over addiction that might seem contradictory. First, most people do it on their own. Second, I work with people to overcome addiction (giving both lectures to treatment personnel and therapy to individuals). Why work with people on overcoming addiction—why write this book—if they can do it on their own?

This book offers you a hand across the bridge of recovery. The fact that some people outgrow addictions without formal help does not mean you're deficient because you want or look for some help. And you should seek help if you are in the midst of an acute addictive episode. You may seek help—and benefit—from traditional treatments and twelve-step groups. But help can come in many forms, like simply seeing how others have done it, or identifying barriers you have to cross or steps you need to take. I will also discuss therapies that make the most sense in terms of this book's perspective—and that have in fact been shown to be the most helpful to alcoholics and other addicts. One such therapy is called the Community Reinforcement Approach, and another Motivational Interviewing.

This book is an aid so that you can mature out more quickly, more surely, and/or more completely by examining your life from the perspectives presented here and following the self-help guidelines provided. Reviewing data that tell you the odds favor your overcoming your problems and gaining greater mastery over your life, reading informative and inspiring stories that describe how others have done it, and learning about therapies, techniques, and exercises that work on the needed skills and attitudes—all these can help you get to where you want to be.

More than anything, this book makes it clear that *you* are the primary agent of change. Obviously, this book is not in tune with most American addiction theory and therapy, which overwhelmingly favors the twelve-step philosophy. These treatments insist on the premise that the individual is powerless over an addiction. In reviewing the extensive research on alcohol and other addiction treatment, however, we actually find that self-efficacy therapies, which focus on the individual's power and self-reliance, succeed the best.

How to Beat Addiction

This book contains many actual stories of recovered addicts, virtually all of whom did it on their own. These cases come from all walks of life, and from all of my many activities. That is, some are based on interviews I have conducted with addicts or former addicts, some come from my therapy practice, some come from e-mails from my highly active Web site on addiction, some are cases described in the research by other investigators, and some are well-known ones drawn from history and literature. But many others come from people I have known and observed. The point of this is to show ordinary people overcoming addictions without professional assistance, in the normal course of their lives. In cases I have observed or been involved in myself, of course, I disguise all names, locations, and identifying details, and create composite cases.

The reason for this variety, and the inclusion of "ordinary" lives, is that this book is not about therapy. It is about people, many of whom have not sought and will not seek therapy. Even if they turn to therapy, their attacks on their addiction will occur mainly outside the therapy experience.

Of course, I don't mean to tell you that you shouldn't seek

other kinds of help for your addiction in addition to this book, including therapy, and even AA and twelve-step therapy. There always remains a role—often a crucial one—for helpers, professional and otherwise. (While people in and out of AA do not consider AA a therapy, and instead call it a "self-help group," it is actually a support group whose members assist one another in attempting to quit drinking.) Therefore, this book is offered as information and assistance to would-be helpers as well as to addicts.

I am a psychologist and addiction therapist. I see my job as helping people build the foundation that must be in place before they successfully quit addictions. From the standpoint of would-be helpers, including therapists, friends, and parents, it is essential to get people attached to life in as many ways as possible.

People with strong values, and with the motivation to change, succeed better at quitting addictions. People with friends, intimate relationships, and families; people with stable home and community lives; people with jobs and work skills; people with education; people who are healthy—all do better at getting over addictions, just as they do at avoiding addictions in the first place.

When you have such assets, you are helped in overcoming an addiction by focusing on what you have and what you may lose. Some therapies (such as Motivational Interviewing) help you to do this. When you don't have these things, you may need help to acquire them. This may involve counseling or remedial steps, including job training, practice at relationships and intimacy, gaining an education, working at a job, developing a healthy lifestyle, and so on. Some therapies (like the Community Reinforcement Approach) help you to develop such skills. And to support the change process, you will need to focus on the rewards you experience when you rein in your addictive behavior. Therapy may help in this area, too.

In addition, you are assisted in quitting addictions by things larger than yourself and beyond your own life. One of these things is the support of those around you and your community. Another is to have and to seek higher goals in life, to commit yourself to be good to other people and to make positive contributions to the world.

I will detail how you may accomplish these things, and how you may assist others to do so if you see yourself more as a helper than as an addiction sufferer. This book provides a road map to cure, and to self-cure. It is a tool that you can use in searching your life, noting what you have and what you lack, in terms of gathering the resources you need to beat an addiction.

Finally, and perhaps most important, you should find this information encouraging and empowering. Addiction can be beaten—people do it all the time! There is no reason for you to take the government's, treatment centers', and Alcoholics Anonymous' word that people are lifetime slaves to addiction. It simply is not true.

1

Values: Building on Your Values Foundation

Values play a critical role in addiction—and your values are likely to be the key to your escaping addiction. This is a matter of both considering what your values are and sometimes refocusing on dormant values or even developing new ones. When you can truly experience how a habit is damaging what is most important to you, the steps out of your destructive habit often fall readily into place.

While you can utilize any of a wide range of values in your fight against addiction—and to a certain extent you can go with whatever works for you—it is not true that all values are equally useful in this fight. Some values even support continued bad habits and compulsions.

In this chapter we will examine values that are the most antiaddictive and that support your independence, and how you can use your own values as a tool to fight addiction. Exercises geared toward identifying and utilizing your values are provided at the end of the chapter.

What Are Values? Do They Really Matter?

Your values are your beliefs that some things are right and good and others wrong and bad, that some things are more important than others, and that one way of doing things is better than another. Values are usually deeply held—they come from your earliest learning and background. Values reflect what your parents taught you, what you learned in school and religious institutions, and what the social and cultural groups you belong to hold to be true and right.

It is impossible to maintain that values don't matter in addiction or its cure. The best predictor of whether college students will have an alcohol problem is their attitudes toward drinking—that is, whether it's okay, even good, to binge.[1] On the other hand, what makes some people join AA and quit drinking? It is because they have decided their drinking is wrong, even beyond its negative health impact for them. For people in the United States who have a drinking problem—or are told by others that they have one—treatment consists mainly of convincing them that their drinking is bad and harmful, and that they should quit.

Values are important to all addictions, and not just addictive drinking and drug taking. If you compulsively gamble, shop, or have affairs, then your values are on display. Many people feel good and get a boost to their self-esteem from shopping. However, most of these people don't consistently spend beyond their limits. They refrain from overspending because they don't think it's right. They recognize that overspending would keep them from upholding other important values, like paying their debts or providing for their children, and so they curtail their expenditures.

The same principle applies to pursuing sexual opportunities to the exclusion of productive activity. Most people enjoy sex, but they avoid compulsive or random sex because they feel it's wrong. If you engage in indiscriminate sex, then you are signaling either that you see little wrong in it or that the other values in your life are less important than the good feelings you derive from such sex. If you are willing to accept this picture of your values, then so be it. If, on the other hand, you have other values that run against compulsive sexual activity, eating, or shopping, then these values can serve as an important tool with which to root out your addiction.

Many people find that alcohol is tremendously relaxing, sexually exhilarating, or provides some other powerful, welcome feeling—but they do not become alcoholics. They simply refuse to go there. Have you ever heard someone say, "I know that when I have more than one drink, I throw all caution to the wind"? Most people who react so violently to alcohol say, "That's why I limit myself to a single drink" or "That's why I don't drink." But alcoholics regularly override this realization about their reactions to alcohol and continue to drink.

Some people who are tense by nature find that smoking is one way to relax. Yet many such people still refuse to smoke. Many simply rule it out of their lives for any of a variety of reasons—health, appearance, or their general feeling that it's bad.

Values do not simply dictate whether you do or don't try a drink, a cigarette, or a drug. They also influence whether you continue to indulge in an activity or substance and how much you will allow your indulgence to affect your life before you limit or quit your involvement. Finally, at a deeper level, values determine how intensely and how irreversibly you become addicted. They also play a major role in whether or not you choose to quit after you become addicted.

Constructive Involvements

Some values directly contradict addictions. If you have these values, they help you to fight addiction. And if you don't, developing such values is potentially a critical therapeutic tool. (This occurs through involvement and success in positive activities, which I describe in later chapters.)

Values can be expressed by statements about what you think

is right and wrong, or about your preferences, such as "I value our relationship," "I value my health," "I believe in hard work," "Nothing is more important to me than my children," or "It is embarrassing to be out of control of yourself." All of these values oppose addiction. Other values, or an absence of values, can reinforce addiction. For example, if you don't think that it's wrong to be intoxicated or high, if it's not important to you to fulfill your obligations to other people, or if you don't care whether you succeed at work, then you are more likely to sustain an addiction. The exercises at the end of this chapter will give you a chance to explore how your values contribute to or oppose addictive involvements.

VALUING THESE THINGS HELPS COMBAT ADDICTION

- *ACHIEVEMENT*—accomplishing constructive and socially valued goals, such as participating in athletics, running for office, getting an education, succeeding at work, or providing for your family
- *CONSCIOUSNESS*—being alert, awake, and aware of your surroundings; using your mind to make sense out of your life and experience
- *ACTIVITY*—being energetic in daily life and engaged in the world around you
- *HEALTH*—eating well, exercising, getting health care, and choosing an overall healthy lifestyle
- *RESPONSIBILITY*—fulfilling your commitments as well as doing what the law obliges you to do
- *SELF-RESPECT*—caring for and about yourself and, by extension, all people
- *COMMUNITY*—being involved in the communities of which you are part (your town, school, work organization, religious group, neighborhood, political party) and contributing to the welfare of these groups—and the larger world

---

How Do Values Fight Addiction?

To say that your values influence your desire and ability to fight addiction is to say that you act in line with what you believe in and what you care about. Such values can be remarkably potent. For example, I heard a woman say, "I used to smoke, and sometimes I think of going back to it. However, now that I have small children, I would sooner cut my fingers off with a kitchen knife then start smoking again." Even if this woman fell to temptation and smoked one cigarette, it is highly unlikely that she would relapse entirely.

In her memoir, *Room to Grow*, actress Tracey Gold described her life-threatening anorexia. When she appeared on the *Today* show to discuss the book, host Matt Lauer asked her the standard disease question: Was she over the disease, or was it still with her? "It's my Achilles' heel," she said, "but I have two small children, and I could never fall all the way back."

Observing this new sense of identity and resolve in new parents should make you think, quite sensibly, "This person couldn't be an alcoholic or a drug addict; she cares too much about herself and her family." But in the alcoholism and addiction field, we are told that if we believe these people have really become much more resistant to addiction, we are deluding ourselves. Likewise, when you observe some rock star, actress, or athlete enter a drug or alcohol treatment center, you are discouraged from thinking that you could never let yourself go wrong like that. It *is* always worth maintaining your empathy and humility. At the same time, it is also valuable to appreciate that you wouldn't put yourself in a position like that, not when you have kids, satisfying work, and basic self-respect.

As a society, and as individuals, we need to grasp that there is no more important facilitator or antidote to addiction than our values. For example, people who value clear thinking will shy away from regular intoxication. Likewise, a responsible person highly concerned for his family's well-being would not allow himself to shop or gamble away his family's money. People who are focused on their health will be reluctant, or refuse, to drink excessively or to take drugs.

A prime example of a person whose values helped him to overcome an addiction is my uncle Ozzie. As you will remember from the introduction, Ozzie quit smoking forever based on what seemed like a chance statement by a coworker that Ozzie was "a sucker for the tobacco companies." We are now prepared to answer the question of why Uncle Ozzie quit.

Remember that Ozzie was a committed union activist. The most important value governing Ozzie's life was the desire to maintain his integrity and independence from his employer, who symbolized for Ozzie the entire capitalist system. As a shop steward, he regularly demonstrated the strength of his convictions by pressing worker complaints and defending fellow union members, even though he felt he was punished by being sent out on service calls to the worst neighborhoods.

Intentionally or not, Ozzie's coworker's statement that he was a sucker for the tobacco companies hit Ozzie in his value solar plexus. This colleague made Ozzie see a connection between his anticorporate values and his smoking, producing the revelation that smoking ran counter to his overwhelming desire to be free from company control. When Ozzie realized that smoking compromised the most important element in his self-definition . . . well in that moment smoking didn't stand a chance. After finishing the last pack he purchased, Ozzie never smoked again.

Where Do Antiaddiction Values Come From?

Children learn values from the people around them. Most importantly, they learn values from their parents or the people who raise them. But people also learn many values from their peers and the groups that they belong to. The process by which people learn values is called "social learning." And these values sometimes have a remarkable impact on people's lives—particularly when it comes to alcohol, drugs, and addiction.

Research regularly demonstrates the power of shared values in relation to alcohol. In the 1950s a sociologist noted that he had never seen anyone drunk in New York's Chinatown. Intrigued, he undertook a study of this community.[2] The sociologist perused the arrest records in the local precinct between the years 1933 and 1949. He discovered that 15,515 arrests had been recorded in Chinatown, but not one of these arrests included an observation of drunkenness. After further examining drinking styles, attitudes, and social occasions in Chinatown, the sociologist, Milton Barnett, wrote:

> The children drank, and they soon learned a set of attitudes that attended the practice. While drinking was socially sanctioned, becoming drunk was not. The individual who lost control of himself under the influence of liquor was ridiculed and, if he persisted in his defection, ostracized. His lack of continued moderation was regarded not only as a personal shortcoming, but as a deficiency of the family as a whole.[3]

Pretty powerful stuff! In this day and age, social shaming might seem outdated, ludicrous, even psychologically damaging. Nonetheless, within Chinese culture—a very large group worldwide—it has been a very effective technique for training children.

Few other communities are as unified in their values as Chinatown was in the 1950s. However, ethnic and religious groups still convey strong values about substance use and abuse.

One group long noted for its distinctive drinking style is the Jews. In 2000 an exhibit entitled "Drink and Be Merry: Wine and Beer in Ancient Times" came to the Jewish Museum of New York. The exhibit pointed out that Jews had, since antiquity, developed a ritualistic, moderate approach to alcohol consumption that contrasted with the periodic, orgiastic use of alcohol by neighboring tribes.

When the claim is made that Jews have historically been moderate drinkers, objections are always raised that this is no longer true. For example, whenever I mention this fact to an AA member in Los Angeles or New York, the person starts listing Jewish alcoholics he or she knows who attend their AA group.

Two upstate New York researchers, Barry Glassner and Bruce Berg, heard the same claims—and believed them. Both reported that they personally knew an alcoholic Jew who hid his drinking. Both had read accounts that traditionally low Jewish alcoholism rates were rising. They consulted with experts, one of whom claimed that the Jewish alcoholism rate was growing alarmingly.

However, after conducting intensive interviews designed to elicit hidden alcohol problems, the researchers failed to uncover a single Jewish alcohol abuser among a random sample of Jewish respondents.[4] Not one respondent they questioned had been intoxicated more than a few times. Only a quarter of the sample had even heard rumors of Jews with drinking problems—generally stories about distant relatives. The accuracy of these self-reports, ironically, was upheld by the very alcoholism expert who had issued an alarm on Jewish alcoholism to the investigators. The so-called expert on Jewish alcoholism reported that in a city of about ten thousand Jews, he knew of five Jewish alcoholics. Even this microscopic number was questioned by the other experts the researchers consulted, who said they knew at most of one or two Jews with a drinking problem.

All in all, the Jews and the Chinese are striking examples of how groups around the world determine behavior toward powerful intoxicants such as alcohol.[5] And although it may be true that these groups do not hold sway over their members as they did in earlier decades in America, they nonetheless demonstrate how powerful, enduring, and decisive socialization by family, religious, and cultural groups can be in insulating people throughout their lives against addiction.

How do these groups teach the value of moderation? Glassner and Berg identified four factors or techniques that enabled Jews to avoid drinking problems (and which in fact closely resemble what we saw of Chinese American techniques):

1. *Learning moderate drinking in childhood.* Jews in the study usually had their first drink as children, "in the home as a part of religious ceremonies (Jewish tradition includes wine drinking at weekly Sabbath ceremonies and holidays, notably Passover) . . . only about 5% of the sample recalled their first drinks as (occurring) outside the family and later than childhood."

2. *Insulation by peers.* As adults they associated almost exclusively with moderate drinkers, often other Jews. When they observed others drinking badly, they rejected those people. As one subject in the study said: "This one guy was making a real ass of himself. He'd had too much to drink and it made everyone uncomfortable. I guess our friends just are not heavy drinkers. . . . I think he eventually got the message, because he was one of the first to leave."

3. *Refusal skills.* Jewish interviewees were "generally unafraid to offer an assertive 'no' when they are encouraged to drink more than they wish." A typical respondent declared, "If everybody is drinking and I feel like having a drink I'll have a drink. If everybody is drinking and I don't want a drink, I don't drink."

4. *Viewing alcoholics as outsiders.* Jewish respondents associated heavy drinking and alcoholism with non-Jews. The authors noted that Jews commonly use the Yiddish expression *shikker vie a goy* (drunk as a Gentile). As one respondent claimed, "It sounds like a stupid generalization, but non-Jewish people

drink more heavily than Jewish people. That's a generalization
I've been brought up with . . . and I still think it's true."[6]

Combining Glassner and Berg's research with studies of
other low-alcoholism cultures, such as Chinese, Greek, Italian,
and Spanish, we can extract the following values taught by
low-alcoholism cultures and groups:

1. Drinking is accepted but is socially governed, and people
   are taught to behave within clear boundaries.
2. People are taught to identify good and bad styles of drinking, to place a high value on drinking properly, and to disapprove of bad drinking styles.
3. Alcohol is not seen to remove personal control, and the individual is held responsible for his or her alcohol consumption and behavior while drinking.

Think now about how you were introduced to alcohol and,
if your family drank, how alcohol was dealt with at home. Did
your parents drink regularly at dinner or at cocktail hour? Did
your parents regularly have parties where alcohol was served?
Or did they bring out alcohol on special family occasions? In
any case, was the drinking a controlled and positive experience? Were you allowed to have small amounts of alcohol as a
child on these occasions?

On the other hand, did one or both of your parents consume
alcohol alone, even secretly?

Overall, how did you feel about the drinking you observed
at home? How has this affected your own drinking experiences?

Finally, how do you treat—or plan to treat—alcohol in the
family you now have or envision having? Do you expect to
consume alcohol with your children present? On what occasions and in what manner will you drink? Do you plan to offer your children tastes of alcohol?

There are no right answers to these questions. If you come from a family of origin that did not drink or had negative drinking rituals or habits, you might not feel comfortable drinking with your own family. In any case, however, you should think through your approach to this critical question.

Exceptions and the Rule: At-Risk Children

Generally speaking, being raised in a community that instills values of moderation, health, and responsibility will help a person avoid addiction. People with these values are less likely to become addicted and, if they do become addicted, they will have an easier time fighting the addiction. However, there are exceptions to these rules. If we go to a local park and watch the people who get up at dawn to run, we would expect very few to be drug addicts, alcoholics, or smokers. And we would be right. But, as we know, some professional athletes do become addicts or alcoholics. What are we to make of such glaring exceptions to the idea that people who value their health won't harm themselves with drugs and booze?

We can provide several explanations for these exceptions. First of all, not all good, or even great, athletes value their bodies and health as much as we might think. (Mickey Mantle was a prime example.) As children, they might have learned to place a strong emphasis on their performance, but not necessarily on taking care of their bodies. Second, when we see that some professional athletes from deprived backgrounds succumb to addictions, we need to think about the many people from similar backgrounds who are not athletes—the prevalence of alcohol and drug problems among young men in these communities is far higher than it is for professional athletes.

Take the example of two children, one of whom has been well cared for, values himself or herself, feels he or she has a great future, and cares very much about his or her health. The other child has not been so well cared for, thinks that no matter what he or she does the future is bleak, has regularly seen people smoke and drink to excess, and cares little about his or her health.

Do you think each of these children is equally likely to become a drug or alcohol addict? Do you think it is important for you to raise your child to be more like the former child? Why?

Although most of us recognize that the former parenting techniques are superior, we are simultaneously given the message (via the disease theory of alcoholism and other addictions) that how you treat your children has no impact on their likelihood of being substance abusers. In fact, we know that these two hypothetical children are not equally likely to become drug addicts, and research on high-risk children, which I review later in the book, proves what you already know to be true.

Social Class and Addiction

Newspapers and experts love to warn that addiction and alcoholism strike doctors as well as day laborers, professors as well as bus drivers, politicians as well as gardeners, and so on. Data from epidemiologic research about drinking in the United States shows that this is not true. That is, the better educated a person is and the higher the person's income, the more likely that person is to drink in America, but to drink without problems. Conversely, "the highest rates of abstention, but also of problem drinking and of alcohol disorder, are found in lower social classes."[7]

The same is true in the case of drugs. Many people experiment with drugs in the United States. In fact, inner-city youths and adults are no more likely to try drugs than those in our prosperous suburbs. This is an important realization, because a disproportionate number of the people in jail for using drugs are from inner cities. This injustice results because drug enforcement is disproportionately imposed on people of color and poor people, whose drug consumption is more public.[8]

Nonetheless, not all those who use drugs are equally likely to become and to stay addicts. For example, in the early 1980s, when cocaine became highly popular in the United States, many people were said to become addicted to it. Public health efforts were launched to alert Americans to the dangers of cocaine. By 1987, the entire profile of cocaine use in the country had changed. Middle-class use dropped drastically, while cocaine use and addiction moved "down the social ladder," according to David Musto, a Yale psychiatrist.[9]

The migration of cocaine use—and addiction—down the social ladder was not surprising. It was foreshadowed by what had already happened with a legal substance, nicotine. When the serious health risks of smoking were first announced by the surgeon general in 1964, about 35 percent of adult Americans smoked cigarettes. This percentage did not vary according to people's educational level. Within twenty-five years, significant numbers of Americans had stopped smoking. But this cessation of smoking did not occur evenly across the population. In 1987, about the same 35 percent of those with a high school education or less still smoked. Yet just half that proportion of college grads smoked![10]

Over time, all people have a chance to catch up, and smoking has declined among all social groups in America (just as crack use has declined in inner cities). Whereas in 1991 37 percent of African American men and 27 percent of white men smoked, by 2001 the figures were 28 and 25 percent, respectively.[11] Nonetheless, large educational and income differences remain in smoking cessation. For example, by 2000 about half of all those who had ever smoked who were above the poverty line had quit, but "barely a third of ever smokers below the poverty line had similar success in quitting." Meanwhile, three-quarters of those with a graduate degree who had ever smoked had quit.[12]

Why are people in higher social categories superior at resisting and desisting addiction? There was a famous exchange between the great American authors F. Scott Fitzgerald and Ernest Hemingway. When told that Fitzgerald had said, "The very rich are different from you and me," Hemingway replied, "Yes, they have more money."

But there are other differences between the privileged and the underprivileged. Privileged people pay more attention to information about health—that is, they value health more. Their backgrounds and environments give them advantages in understanding and appreciating health information.

Values also explain why more middle-class and upper-middle-class people drink alcohol. They are more likely to believe that they can keep the practice under control—and they are right! This value is one of self-efficacy, or the view that it is important (and possible) to determine your own destiny.

Notice the difference between this view, or value, and that purveyed by AA. People are taught in AA that it is wrong—arrogant, unhealthy, even sacrilegious—to think you control your own existence. But for many other people, this belief is the basis of their mental health and successful adjustment. No social class is immune from problems or is inherently better at enjoying life. And, of course, poorer people do have real disadvantages to live with, making it harder for them to be self-efficacious. But middle-class values of self-control, achievement, healthfulness, self-efficacy, and responsibility are significant factors in controlling excess and addiction.

Such values are not exclusively middle-class. Some people whom we would expect to have such values on the basis of their backgrounds do not in fact have them. And many people from deprived or traumatic backgrounds do develop addiction-resistant values. Also, people change their values—most adolescents think very differently about themselves and their lives and consider very different things important than do adults. And, as we shall see later in the book, this shift is one of the most important antidotes to addiction in people's lives.

Finding a Path That Fits Your Values

In Alcoholics Anonymous' *Big Book*, Bill Wilson described how he was transformed out of alcoholism by "enter[ing] upon a new relationship with my Creator . . . I must turn in all things

to the Father of Light who presides over us all." Chapter 4 of
the *Big Book* describes how atheists must learn to believe in
God and to accept religion:

> As soon as we admitted the possible existence of a Creative
> Intelligence, a Spirit of the Universe underlying the totality of
> things, we began to be possessed of a new sense of power and
> direction, provided we took other simple steps. We found that
> God does not make too hard terms with those who seek
> Him. . . .
>
> Instead of regarding ourselves as intelligent agents, spear-
> heads of God's ever advancing creation, we agnostics and athe-
> ists chose to believe that our human intelligence was the last
> word, the alpha and the omega, the beginning and end of all.
> Rather vain of us, wasn't it?[13]

Religion is less obviously injected into AA today. But some
overtly religious values are still communicated by AA and
other twelve-step programs. For example, the view that the
best way to surmount a problem is by acknowledging one's
powerlessness over it—and "that [only] a power greater than
ourselves could restore us to sanity"—offends some people's
values. These people just don't choose to view the universe
that way; they don't feel that submission is the answer to their
problems. And these people can overcome addictions in their
own independent way.

Self-Efficacy As a Value

Powerlessness may thus be a more controversial aspect of the
AA philosophy than its roots in Christianity. Many addicted
people already believe they are powerless before ever encountering the twelve steps. In many ways, this is part and parcel of
the addiction. For example, believing that alcoholism is a disease, that no one escapes the grip of heroin or cigarettes, that
withdrawal from either is too horrible to resist, or that you are

born to be addicted plays into the power and irresistibility of the way you experience the substance (or activity) to which you become addicted.

Psychologist William Miller and his colleagues at the University of New Mexico conducted an important study in which they tracked subjects who reported for outpatient treatment for an alcohol problem.[14] The investigators' purpose was to forecast which subjects were more likely to relapse following treatment. They found two primary factors predicted relapse—"lack of coping skills and belief in the disease model of alcoholism."[15]

Think of it—treatment in the United States is geared primarily toward teaching people to believe something that makes it more likely that they will relapse! Instead, psychological theory and research indicate that it is more empowering and successful for you to believe in—and to value—your own strength. In this view, the critical element in cure is to develop your sense of self-efficacy. Yet if you express this view, or that you are uncomfortable with the value of powerlessness taught in the twelve-step approach, you will be told that you are in denial and that you cannot succeed at quitting addiction.

We often wonder why so many people decline to enter treatment or to join AA. And AA's own surveys reveal that only 5 percent of those who enter AA continue to attend for as long as a year.[16] One researcher, Barry Tuchfeld, interviewed people who strove to lick a drinking problem on their own.[17] These individuals rejected the value of AA and treatment in their lives. If you believe the AA model and treatment personnel, these statements represent denial. Contradicting this, the subjects Tuchfeld selected for his study had successfully eliminated their drinking problems for many years.

Values and Your Recovery

Here are some of the statements made by Tuchfeld's subjects in which they explain why they wouldn't enter treatment or join a support group:

"The one thing I could never do is go into formal rehab. For me to have to ask somebody else to help with a self-made problem, I'd rather drink myself to death."

"Formal treatment seemed to be a sort of a pigeonhole that I didn't want to be put in."

"I'd never consider going to a doctor or minister for help. Good Lord, no! That would make me drink twice as much. I'm the kind of person who has to do things on his own."

"But as far as I . . . was concerned, AA was absolutely of no attraction to me at all, absolutely not. And as far as a doctor is concerned . . . And preachers—boo—I'd rather go out and talk to my donkeys than a preacher."

"Who wants to get up there and listen to somebody else's problems when they're sitting there with so many of the problems on their own shoulders . . . ?"[18]

These voices clearly illustrate that some people are eager for an alternative to AA. And independent recovery is a valid option—especially when we consider that the large majority of addicts do quit on their own. It is entirely possible that the repeated alcoholic or addictive relapses of people such as Joan Kennedy, Robert Downey Jr., Calvin Klein, Kitty Dukakis, and others are due at least in part to their continuing reliance on someone or some group outside of themselves to solve their problems. If they were counseled more about self-reliance, they might be more successful in fighting addiction.

Nonetheless, it is not for this book, or anyone else, to determine the best path for you. Undergoing treatment, attending AA for a brief or extended time, selecting a nontraditional treatment, alternating treatment and going it on your own—these and other paths have succeeded for many and could succeed for you. What is important is to be clear on and to respect your values and preferences.

Regardless of whether you seek treatment or make efforts to

change outside of formal treatment, you and others dealing with you must respect your values. True, you may need to learn how to do things in a new way, or to value new ways of looking at the world. However, in order to decide what recovery path to take, you must first understand what is important to you, what you believe, and what you consider to be right. (Exercises at the end of this chapter will help you to identify such values.) Otherwise, your energy will be wasted in an unacknowledged values war between you and your would-be helpers or, worse, in a war with yourself.

Helping Someone Else Find the Right Path for Him or Her

Quite often, when addiction therapists say that they are practicing a scientific approach in addiction treatment and claim they are rejecting a values approach, they are misrepresenting what they are doing, which is actually to impose their values on their patients. They assume that people are unable to harness their own value systems and therefore need a therapist to infuse them with the "right" values and directions.

Think back to the experiences of my uncle Ozzie, whose coworker inadvertently harnessed Ozzie's *own* values as leverage in influencing his innermost mind. A helper using this technique generates far more power than can be gained by simply berating people about their failures and the need for them to believe what the therapist tells them. This therapeutic technique is called Motivational Interviewing, and in Chapter 2 I will show specifically *how* therapists practice this and how you can do it for yourself and others.

The first step in this approach is to remain open to the other person's own insights. People want to be respected, and if they feel they are not being judged, they will express themselves fully.

Since denial is said frequently to characterize people who

are confronted with their problems by a therapist or group, why didn't Ozzie display this trait at the moment that he changed? Because it was in his own interest to align his behavior and his values. He made all the crucial connections for himself. His "helper" didn't have to discuss the problems Ozzie had with smoking. Ozzie, more than anyone else, was well aware of these problems. In fact, when Ozzie now describes his former habit, he talks about how his fingers were yellow with nicotine that he could never wash off.

Virtually everybody cares deeply about some value. Everybody has something important to him or her. Just visualize the principle that in trying to force people to recognize their problems, a helper will encounter more and greater resistance. If, instead, the would-be helpers can "go with the flow"—following in the direction of the addict's own values—they are far more likely to help the addict move forward.

Conducting a "Values Intervention"

In order to help someone figure out which of that person's own values will help him or her fight addiction, you can conduct a values intervention. Start out by asking what factors in the person's life are important to him or her. Family? Health? Religious beliefs? Or being a good person? Be as open as possible in conducting such questioning—you are an explorer trying to learn about the map of another person's mind.

After eliciting an addict's primary values, you may not have to do much more in order to get that person to see how his or her habit is in conflict with basic values he or she holds. The very process of interviewing that person can serve this purpose. However, sometimes you may need to push a little further, perhaps by gently saying, "I don't quite see how your behavior fits in with those values."

The important thing about any such statement that you make is that it be nonconfrontational. You are expressing genuine puzzlement, not a condemnation. You only want to clarify a contradiction in the person's values that you are confused about. I will examine such motivating techniques more fully in the next chapter.

Teaching Values

In an environment bereft of positive values, people will be more likely to be addicted and find it harder to escape addiction. One group of addicts—criminal addicts—is particularly resistant to intervention. Criminal addicts are rapacious individuals who view life simply as a smorgasbord for them to grab whatever they want. Drugs and alcohol just become one more way to rip off the world. This is very different from hapless individuals arrested for use or possession of drugs or low-level drug trades, whose crimes are defined entirely by their involvement with substances that have been made illegal.

If we can't teach people, starting in childhood, to have core values of achievement, self-awareness, productivity, healthy habits, responsibility, self-respect, and respect for the greater community, then we will have more addiction no matter how many drug education programs we force on children.

And we can teach children about legal drugs—especially alcohol. By demonstrating moderate drinking ourselves and exposing children to social drinking in positive, multigenerational family settings, by explaining that alcohol is meant to be enjoyed but not abused, and by holding people responsible for how they drink and how they behave when they drink, we re-create the positive drinking cultures established through the generations in many parts of the United States and the world.

When we don't express such attitudes and values—about addictions and about life—then children learn very different values from advertising, from fraternity parties, or from former alcoholics who lecture in their schools that alcohol is a poisonous, uncontrollable, devouring substance. Values can be a powerful tool for fighting addiction, but it is up to addicts attempting to recover (as well as parents of children who want to prevent them from becoming addicted) to determine which values are most important to them.

So don't be afraid to express when you think something is wrong in the world, or when people behave in a way of which you disapprove—even if sometimes these are people you and your children know and care about. Don't shy away from values in your own mind or in your dealings with others, particularly young people. Embrace and relish what you think is important and right—or in cases where you recognize consciously that your values are wrong or harmful, work on changing them. Publicize your values as primary indicators of who you are. And harness and use your values.

■■■■■

Exercise: A Values Mind Experiment

Think of something that you at one time in your life were addicted to, or else that you were (or are) very much tempted by. For example, did you at one time smoke or gamble compulsively? Did you ever drink excessively? Do you now very much enjoy having several drinks? Do you sometimes really pig out on chocolates or some other sweet?

Now reflect—why did you give up the addiction or not take the excessive habit further? What keeps you from indulging in your current pleasure/vice continuously, or excessively?

These things are core values of yours—values toward yourself (i.e., self-respect), health, appearance, work, family, consciousness, and so on. First, simply appreciate that you hold these values. Second, see if you can utilize them in some other way, to change an area of behavior you have a less firm grip on than the one your values currently curtail.

■■■■■

Exercise: Values Worksheet

To further assist you in identifying your core values, list the three *worst* losses you could suffer in life, such as:

Your health
Your family or life partner (or their approval)
Your appearance
Your relationship to God
Your intelligence
Your standing in the community
Your self-respect
Your job/profession/work skills
Your friends
Your ethical standards
Something not mentioned above

Make a list of how your worst habit is affecting these three things.

Now describe a way that you can keep focused on each of these values as leverage to change your addiction.

■■■■■

2

Motivation: Activating Your Desire to Quit

The simplest answer to the question "When do people change?" is "When they want to." No amount of science, therapy, and brain scans is ever going to change this truth. This chapter shows how critical motivation is in overcoming addiction, and reviews the best methods for energizing you to change, even when dealing with the most severe addictions.

Placing so much importance on motivation in changing addictions is controversial. In order to appreciate the role of motivation, we need to get past some of the standard treatment techniques that you have heard about that not only are unnecessary, but can actually do more harm than good.

In place of these unhelpful ideas, you will learn therapy techniques that have been shown to be the most effective for combating addictions. These therapies offer significant pointers for self-cure as well. They can help you not only to motivate others, but to focus your own motivation to change and to convert it into action.

The Role of Motivation in Change

AA considers willpower to be utterly ineffective. The idea that people have the commitment and power to be able to change on their own (without the help of AA, a "higher power," and other AA members) is anathema to the group. According to Frank Keating, the governor of Oklahoma and an avid supporter of AA, "what 66 years of AA experience has confirmed was that willpower, desire, and intellectual knowledge won't keep a drunk sober."[1] Yet what is it, if not willpower or motivation, that makes some people join, stay with, and succeed in AA?

Wanting, seeking, and believing that you can change do not necessarily translate into immediate success. The fact that Uncle Ozzie could do it in one shot does not mean that you will do it that way. It is much more common for people to make several attempts before successfully quitting their addictions. Indeed, this persistence is a sign that you really want to quit.

It is true that repeated failures are demoralizing and may signify that you need to try something new. It can also mean that you are simply not in the right place in your life to change, and that you need to do more groundwork.

But while these setbacks can be discouraging, don't get down on yourself for your inability to instantly transform into the person that you want to become. Addictions have roots deep in your lifestyle, outlook, and personality, and beating them will naturally take a concerted, complex effort. Demoralization is much more harmful to the recovery process than being overoptimistic. In fact, pessimism is hurting you at least as much as what the AA terms "denial" (believing that you are doing better than you actually are).

On the other hand, if and when you finally succeed, don't conclude that what you are doing at that moment must be the best kind of cure. It is not necessarily proof that this one technique works for everyone or even that it will always work for you. The addiction sections of bookstores are filled with testaments to the approaches that may have worked for one person, who then turns his or her success into a worldwide movement. Some of these programs might work for you—but if they do, then it will be because they have tapped into your own powerful drive to change, not because of any magical process that they have prescribed.

Stages of Change

The motivation to change takes different forms, depending on where you are in your addiction cycle. Some people have to be introduced to the idea that they need to change. Others have spent a lifetime fighting to change. One widely used scheme for organizing the stages of change was devised by psychologists James Prochaska and Carlo DiClemente:[2]

Prochaska and DiClemente's Stages of Quitting
1. *Precontemplation*—you haven't thought about changing
2. *Contemplation*—you have begun to muse that your life might be better if you did change
3. *Preparation*—you make a decision and start planning to change
4. *Action*—you take steps toward changing
5. *Maintenance*—you have had some success and now need to keep it in place

According to Ozzie, he was actually at the precontemplation stage—he had never actively thought about quitting—and he jumped to quitting. If you have bought and are reading this book, you have probably already decided you want to change, and are at least at stage 2 of Prochaska and DiClemente's list. Alternately, you may be concerned about someone who appears to be still at stage 1, and want to make them aware they *should* want to change. Different motivational techniques may be helpful at different stages of the change process, as we shall see in Chapter 3.

Stories of Sudden Change

Some people, like Uncle Ozzie, are capable of the most re-markable, instantaneous transformations. Since they have never before tried to change, they can readily believe that their efforts will be successful.

Such stories of sudden change abound in AA groups. AA calls these stories "hitting bottom," after which, according to AA lore, the person joins AA and succeeds. And that's just great. But there are actually more stories like this where peo-ple quit without AA, treatment, or any other official thera-peutic activity. Here is one such story from a woman interviewed by a researcher who studied individuals who quit a drinking problem without treatment or AA:

> [In the house's] hallway was a fan of some sort. I had to use the head, so I proceeded to squat down on the fan to use it as a commode . . . What really shocked me, what made me con-tinually think about it, was that supposedly my daughter . . . was up and saw me in that condition.[3]

What does hitting bottom mean? Peeing in a vent where your daughter might see is certainly bad, but there are plenty of people who have done worse and kept right on drinking. These stories are essentially value statements, expressing that "I did something so bad in terms of what is most important to me that I just had to change."

Here is another story from the same study. A pregnant woman was drinking a beer in the morning in order to ward off a hangover:

> I was drinking it, I felt the baby quiver and I poured the rest of [the] beer out and I said, "God forgive me, I'll never drink an-other drop," and from that day to this, I haven't.[4]

This story shows just how subtle and personal hitting bot-tom can be. It is also a story about the power of motherhood.

Feeling that it is important to be a good parent is a value that drives many women to quit addictions while pregnant—even if after giving birth, as one woman told me, she resumed her heroin addiction.

Fathers, perhaps more so recently, are also frequently driven to quit addictions by images of parenthood. One man who had grown quite overweight in his forties slipped while carrying his small child. He was convinced he had endangered his son because of his obesity, and he immediately went on a diet and exercise program, losing almost fifty pounds. One psychologist described a man who was picking up his children in the rain but stopped to get cigarettes first. The psychologist concluded: "The view of himself as a father who would 'actually leave the kids in the rain while he ran after cigarettes' was . . . humiliating, and he quit smoking."[5]

Professional goals can also provide the motivation to fight addiction. One man described to me how he kept drinking even after he started attending AA meetings regularly. While on a business trip, he waited until after successfully completing a sale to go to the hotel bar. As he was about to take his first drink, he spied someone he had been negotiating with and whom he admired. This man seemed to be eyeing him disapprovingly. The first man got up, left the bar, and quit drinking for good.

Of course, this other man probably wasn't even thinking about the drinker, who he certainly didn't know was an alcoholic. But, reflected in this admired person's eyes, the alcoholic saw himself in a light he could not tolerate. Only with this image in mind could he finally give up the booze. Also, notice that in this story, as a member of AA, the man had already been trying to quit drinking. In fact, when people claim such miraculous moments, they usually represent the *end* of a process of at least contemplation. They may even take place after several failed efforts to quit.

AA hitting-bottom stories are about moments when people decide to enter treatment or join AA or a similar group. Many of these individuals actually enter treatment—and have such moments—repeatedly, before they finally decide to stop the cycle. Think of all of the celebrities you've heard of who experience several "awakenings" and relapses into addiction before finally cleaning up their lives. Unlike the AA rock-bottom stories, which focus on the decision to seek external help through AA, the examples I have provided are about becoming committed to change and pursuing the path that is most likely to succeed. This might involve entering treatment or a support group; or it might mean changing on your own.

For some people, such moments can mean quitting treatment as a precursor to success. Consider the following letter from a reader:

> Dear Stanton:
> Just a little note to let you know that six years ago I coincidentally came across your book whilst in the middle of my ninth or tenth try with outpatient alcoholism treatment. This was in addition to the nine or ten detoxes and four or five thirty-day rehabs I'd gone through. Well, I started reading your book and your insights caused such a massive change in paradigm to the point that I have never drunk since. I owe a lot to you for taking the time to publish such a breath of fresh air in the field of alcoholism. Reading your books had given me the ability to look at the treatment I was going through from the outside looking in, rather than being caught up in the closed loop of inside looking out.
>
> Don

Don's resolve and his ability to change were crystallized through the opposite of the AA approach. He suddenly decided that it was his responsibility to change, that it was up to nobody but himself, and that he had the power to do it. When he placed this burden squarely on his own shoulders, it made the task more manageable for him.

Can You Really Quit Drugs?

Although many people claim to see all addictions in a similar light, others find it hard to believe that real drug addicts can quit. They think drugs must be the exception to the rule, due to the chemical hold drugs have on users. Indeed, the arguments of the NIDA and ads by the Partnership for a Drug Free America convey the idea that even a brief flirtation with drugs sends the user off on a one-way trip that cannot be reversed.

Nothing is farther from the truth. As usual, it is the government's own data that tell us that at some point most drug users decide that they have had enough. Consider the National Survey on Drug Use and Health, conducted periodically by several agencies of the U.S. government (including the NIDA). This survey reveals that although many Americans have at one point or another used drugs, few of them progress to becoming heavy users or addicts. Very few continue to use drugs over a long period of time.

According to the 2002 survey, 46 percent of all Americans over age twelve have tried an illicit substance. However, only 15 percent have used one in the past year, and only 8 percent have used in the past month. The survey does not even report weekly or daily use of most substances, because the percentages are simply too microscopic.[6]

Consider the statistics on marijuana use. Forty percent of Americans have at some point used the drug—but only 6 percent have used it in the last month. More than 14 percent of Americans have tried cocaine, but fewer than 1 percent have used it within the last month. And about 1.5 percent of Americans have ever used heroin, but just one-tenth of 1 percent have used it within the past month.

In other words, of all people who have ever used cocaine or heroin, just over 5 percent continue to use it currently (the same holds for crack cocaine). The idea that if you (or your child) ever try a drug you will soon become addicted is a myth—a very popular one, but a myth nonetheless. If this book were only directed to those who are addicted to or even currently use the most potent drugs, there would be little audience for it. Remember, only one-tenth of 1 percent of Americans—one in a thousand—currently use heroin, and fewer than 1 percent currently use cocaine (including crack). According to the National Survey, 3 percent of Americans abused or were dependent on *any* illicit drug (out of over 46 percent who have ever taken an illicit drug). But the majority of these abused marijuana. In 2003, when the 2002 data were released, what had formerly been the National Household Survey on Drug Abuse changed its name to the National Survey on Drug *Use* and Health. The term "drug use" provides a far more accurate picture of the data.

Since marijuana is the most commonly used drug, there are more people abusing marijuana than other drugs. Many debate whether people can be genuinely addicted to marijuana. Of course, from the perspective of this book—that becoming addicted means being involved in an engrossing experience that diminishes a person's ability to focus on and cope with other parts of life—the answer is yes, marijuana can be addictive. According to the 2002 National Survey, those abusing or addicted to marijuana represented 1.8 percent of Americans (60 percent of those who depended on or abused any illicit drug).[7] Yet we must always keep in mind, as with other illicit drugs, that most of those who have ever used or abused marijuana have ceased or control the habit.

And so we know that drug users can and often do quit on their own. Saying that drug use is just another category of human experience that people can handle is not to minimize drug abuse. Noting this reality is simply a way to make you realize that you can change this area of your life, like any other, both before and after you become addicted (although after becoming addicted, of course, it is harder).[8] It is also to tell you that if you find your gambling, sexual or love relationships, or purchasing to be overpowering, these experiences may be as addictive as the most powerful drug. But this need not discourage you from summoning your motivation and licking your addictions, as drug users often do.

The Most Effective Therapies and What They Have to Tell You

Much research has been done on the most effective treatments for addiction, particularly for alcoholism. The two best treatments for alcoholism rely on putting the ball on the alcoholic's side of the court, helping the addicted person channel his or her own motivation into successful change. These therapies are called Brief Interventions and Motivational Interviewing (or Motivational Enhancement). Incorporating the results of every clinical trial of alcoholism treatment available, William Miller and colleagues at the University of New Mexico found that these treatments had shown by far the most evidence of effectiveness. In addition, alcoholism treatment consisting of providing and encouraging use of a self-change manual was in the top five in these investigators' ranking of effectiveness.[9]

The successful therapies described in this chapter take a different approach to how you change from most traditional addiction therapy. These therapies place responsibility for changing your addictive behavior on *you*. They do this by (1) minimizing the time you're in therapy, (2) expecting you to establish your own goals and methods for change, (3) working from your individual value framework, and (4) checking your progress over time, but not forcing the desired changes on you. In other words, effective therapies believe that you are capable of change, and in fact conveying this belief is the key ingredient in creating change.

The only problem is that these effective therapies are only irregularly used and are often slighted in favor of traditional treatments. The underlying principles of Brief Interventions and Motivational Interviewing, which enlist people's own inherent motivation to overcome drinking problems, contradict the principles of AA and the style of traditional treatment, which is confrontational. There are signs that the traditional treatment monolith is beginning to crack, but it is still by far the dominant approach in the United States. For example, Motivational Interviewing has become so popular that many treatment centers advertise that they practice it. Yet most such programs continue to rely on the confrontation-of-denial approach, in which therapists and groups insist that every patient has a disease and must abstain—and that those who refuse to accept these views are in denial. But this approach cannot be made consistent with Motivational Interviewing.

In any case, we can take from these two effective therapies ideas, techniques, and principles that you can use on your own to attack your addiction. At some point during your personal recovery process you may decide to seek therapy or other external help. If you do so, keep the key elements of these successful treatments in mind, so that you can recognize whether the therapy you select is utilizing effective principles.

Brief Interventions

When you have a physical exam, your doctor might ask you, "How many drinks would you say you have in a week? Do you drink about the same amount each day, or do you drink mostly on weekends?" This physician is initiating what is known as a Brief Intervention (BI). Brief Interventions (BIs) are often built into an ongoing medical relationship or regular health screening. They are a flexible way for a health care provider to address a potential substance problem with patients. (BIs are also used in nonmedical settings, such as family service agencies.) In a medical setting, a BI begins with an assessment by the doctor. The physician will ask how often you drink and how much you consume at one time, and then may compare this with typical or healthy drinking levels for someone with your characteristics. The doctor in addition may use one of several brief questionnaires that measure drinking problems. If you have substantial drinking problems, you will be assessed to see whether you are alcohol-dependent and if so, how severely. A medical test of liver injury—which can indicate a serious alcohol problem—may be used.

The screening and assessment would be followed by feedback: "You know, for most men your age, the healthy limit is two or three drinks a day," or "You have identified several problems stemming from your drinking," or "You are having some difficulty with your liver; let me show you on this test." As in any health care encounter, a doctor would discuss your general life and health problems, and pursue their relationship to your drinking.

The procedure is conducted neutrally, like any other impartial medical assessment. The physician or other health care worker then initiates a conversation about steps to lower risk, which, in Brief Interventions for alcohol, usually means reducing your drinking from an unhealthy level. If you are more severely alcohol-dependent or have other serious medical or psychological problems, you will be flagged for referral to a specialist. Since only a small percentage of all those screened are severely alcohol-dependent, however, BIs reach a wider range of people for whom conventional alcoholism treatment would be inappropriate.

Your spouse may also participate in the discussion. Following the feedback from the assessment, the physician may simply advise you to cut back. Alternately, the physician may say something like:

> We meet again in ＿＿ months, on ＿＿ (there may be more frequent visits to a nurse). What goals do you hope to achieve when we meet again? How many drinks do you plan to be having daily/weekly at that time? What do you need to do to make sure this happens?
>
> Here are some of the services this office can provide for you. Do you feel any could be helpful to you? I also have some brochures for you that contain information about ways people

go about reducing their drinking and other information on alcohol. Are there ways you feel your wife can be helpful, without shifting the burden to her?

Note that the doctor provides suggestions, options, and self-help material for the person to follow through with. Although the doctor provides structure and feedback for change, the manner in which you decide to tackle the problem is up to you.[10]

We are used to intensive hospital programs for people with drinking and drug problems. So the simplicity and self-reliance that underlie the success of BIs—and the approach of this book—can seem strange to us. Yet no alcohol treatment has shown more consistently effective results than BIs. The World Health Organization conducted an international evaluation involving ten countries, both developed and developing. BI therapy resulted in substantial reductions in drinking across the wide variety of cultures this study encompassed.[11]

The success of Brief Interventions reflects a broader finding, one that surprises most people: Nearly every systematic comparison of two or more treatments for alcohol problems has found that the less intensive treatment is at least as successful as the more intensive one. In the mid-1980s researchers Bill Miller and Reid Hester compiled the available research comparing hospitalization of alcoholics with outpatient programs. None of the studies showed that hospitalization yielded better results.[12] Because of such research, most insurance companies and HMOs, along with treatment providers, shifted their emphasis to outpatient treatment. Unfortunately, although the format of the therapy changed, usually the content of the therapy remained as it was—along with all the unhelpful beliefs and practices that characterize traditional treatment. But you do not have to rely on poor treatment practice, because you can apply the principles of Brief Interventions to your own life.

How can you harness the assets of a BI in your own recovery process? The critical elements for change in BIs are (1) a nonjudgmental atmosphere where you can focus on your problem in a calm, nondefensive way, (2) your acceptance of the need for change, (3) provision of suggestions and options, which you can choose among and combine into your own course of action, (4) the unintrusive support of the adviser or health care worker, (5) a process that engages your commitment to and responsibility for change, and (6) regular follow-ups when you know your progress will be monitored. The sidebar provides a mnemonic, FRAMES, developed by William Miller and his colleagues, for remembering the key elements in Brief Interventions.[13]

THE BRIEF INTERVENTION PROCESS (FRAMES)

F: *Feedback* about risky behavior is given
R: *Responsibility* for change is placed with the individual
A: *Advice* is given to change
M: *Menu* for change options and methods is presented
E: *Empathy* is expressed
S: *Self-efficacy* is encouraged

One powerful aspect of the BI process is the continuity of contact. That is, the regularity and extent of follow-ups may be the most effective aspect of a treatment. Remaining in touch with a concerned third party who provides you with objective feedback focuses you on your behavior and your desire to change it. It is very helpful if you have someone you can rely on, who wishes the best for you, but who is not as emotionally involved as a spouse usually is, and so can objectively record your successes and failures.

The BI model has also been used for weight control and smoking cessation. It can be applied successfully to any behavioral or addictive problem. With weight control—for example, in Weight Watchers—the helper provides menus, nutritional information, and self-help guidelines, then reviews success and failure on a weekly basis. This kind of therapy contrasts with most drug and alcohol treatment, where counselors are so intolerant of slips and backsliding that it is impossible for those seeking help to be honest about how they are doing.

Think also of shopping or sex addictions. You know when you are doing the wrong thing, like remaining in a relationship in which you are abused. It does no good for others to discourage you further by pointing out your failures. But sometimes people have trouble finding the motivation to change. The Brief Intervention approach emphasizes that the counselor will keep in touch to encourage and respond to appropriate behavior, even when it takes you a while to activate the behavior you know is better for you.

If you wish to address your own problem, the efficacy of BIs tells you that, first, intensive therapy may not be necessary to change. It is more important for you to devote continuing attention to your problem, seeking, trying, and selecting from a variety of techniques. It is continuity—meaning repeated contacts (even if not that close together in time), nonjudgmental feedback, and review of your goals and the efforts you are making and their success—that culminates in distinct progress for many people, and that can help you. As we review in the exercises at the end of this chapter, you can conduct your own Brief Intervention by enlisting a caring helper to participate in this process.

Overcoming Denial

Standard American addiction therapy often sees as its goal the confrontation of the addict's denial, as if you need to be shaken into an awareness that you have a problem. But this does not provide an accurate description of an addict's reality. If your addiction has led to divorce, job loss, or being arrested, then you are already aware that something is wrong. And if your addiction is, in part, an attempt to assuage bad feelings about yourself and your world, then you surely realize that something in your life needs to improve.

It defies common sense to believe that when you overeat

(and are obese and incur health problems such as diabetes), smoke (and develop chronic bronchitis or emphysema), or gamble or shop compulsively (and are in hock) you are totally unaware that something is wrong. When you hear the term *denial*, alarms should go off—particularly when it is used to explain why you or someone else needs to participate in therapy that is being imposed against your will. It is not that you may not need encouragement and prompting to change. But unwelcome efforts from a therapist or loved ones to change you often actually make you *more* resistant, so that you spend more energy fighting their efforts than fixing your problem.

This conflict and waste of effort are particularly apparent when therapists persist with analyses and treatment plans that you reject. When therapists say that you are in denial under these circumstances, they are really saying that you are not thinking about your problem (or trying to change it) in the way they want you to. You may then feel that your supposed "helpers" are seeking to dominate your thinking or that they are attacking you. If, on the other hand, therapists or would-be helpers demonstrate some subtlety and patience, they can encourage you to explore your problem fully. Motivational Interviewing, as we shall see, is an important technique for accomplishing this.

Motivational Interviewing (Enhancement)

Motivational Interviewing (MI) is a successful therapy technique developed to take advantage of psychological knowledge about how people can most effectively help others reconsider and change their behavior. People respond best to therapeutic inputs when they are approached with respect and empathy. This simple truth is often lost in therapy. Think about it: How do you react when someone bombards you with feedback that you're completely off base and all wrong in your approach to something? Most often you won't react well. If, on the other hand, people begin by respectfully considering your point of view and accepting your sincerity, you will most likely respond to insights and suggestions they offer you.[14]

Consistent with the stance in this book, MI shows that there is often not a sharp line between successful therapy and self-help or helping people informally. What works in the therapeutic setting works in your own life. Thus the techniques involved in Motivational Interviewing are applicable when you are acting as a parent or friend, and when you are considering your own situation and your need to change.

People overcome addictions when they realize that it is in their own best interest to do so. The goal of Motivational Interviewing is to get people to examine their habits in terms of their own values and goals. Likewise, you are most likely to change when you can see yourself and your own actions in this light.

Suppose a high school student wants to be successful, to make money, and to achieve high status—like most people. Yet his or her behavior, including drinking and drug use, is making this goal less likely. A parent or helper could give this child a standard lecture: "If you think you're going to be a success, think again. Don't you see you're headed down the road to nowhere?"

What if, instead, the parent asked the teenager about his or her goals—"What do you want to achieve in life?"—and then examined the child's progress in this direction in a non-accusatory way? The parent could ask the child to think about the kinds of people he or she admires—probably high achievers who didn't create roadblocks for themselves.

A person conducting such a motivational interview should keep the following elements in mind:[15]

1. Express empathy ("I accept that you are a valuable person")
2. Explore values/goals (e.g., "What do you want for yourself?")
3. Develop discrepancies ("How are you going about this?")

4. Roll with resistance ("I accept everything you say")
5. Support self-efficacy ("You *can* achieve what you want")

If you are concerned about someone and would like to try reaching out to that person using the MI approach, the aim in this kind of questioning is never to place yourself in direct conflict with the target. Whenever you sense resistance, back up. The key to this approach is to push the ball back to the other person (generally by asking questions), even when you feel you know what the truth of the matter is. And, despite your deeper purposes, you should mean it when you make these into questions. You must leave the answers up to the person you are questioning.

Suppose a man has come to speak about his wife's objections to his drinking. Instead of immediately assuming the man has a problem and taking the wife's position about the man's drinking (whether or not this ultimately turns out to be true), the questioning might go like this:

Man: My wife is always griping that I drink too much.
Questioner: And how does her griping affect you?
Man: It's a real pain.
Questioner: So you want to do something about that. And what makes her think you drink too much?
Man: She just doesn't like me drinking. So when something happens—like when I fell asleep on the couch and spilled my drink—she freaks out.
Questioner: Do you think you drank too much that time?
Man: Well, yes . . .

Follow-up questions could include: "Describe any other times you may have drunk too much." "Did an interaction with your wife spur that episode?" "How does your wife generally react when she thinks you've drunk too much?" "Do you anticipate she will react this way when you start to drink?" The goal of this questioning is not to judge the man, but to understand the link between his drinking and his relationship with his wife. Exploring this link through questions may well reveal patterns in his relationship that make sense to him, as well as ways to change and improve it and his drinking, without putting him on the defensive.

Motivational Interviewing and Adolescents

Motivational Interviewing takes a good deal of skill, based in self-restraint. In order to inspire someone through use of this technique, you must place your own values on the back burner, at least for the time being. Perhaps you cannot be this detached when it comes to a member of your own family. Nevertheless, it is worth your while to try this technique as a way of improving your communication skills. I have seen some parents adopt the technique beautifully. And if you reach the limit of your skills (and patience), then seek a therapist or counselor who practices this way.

Young people often offer the most resistance to therapeutic treatment. Therefore, techniques that overcome patient resistance have much to tell us about dealing with adolescents. An important reason to employ such techniques with your adolescent, rather than relying on traditional therapies, is that traditional therapies may force teenagers to view their substance abuse as a permanent condition. It is standard practice in many drug and alcohol treatment programs for therapists to insist that adolescents act out because they have a disease. In this way, therapy can transform a temporary problem into a lifetime stigma.

Brief Interventions and Motivational Interviewing do not demand self-labeling. Instead, the addiction can be treated as a temporary condition, while the therapy allows adolescents to realize how their actions are putting them at risk, and that they have the power to change their behavior. When you seek a therapist for yourself, a child, or another loved one, question the professional on his or her approach, on his or her views of whether addiction is a disease, and about Motivational Interviewing and Brief Interventions. Don't let the therapist simply assert that he or she practices these therapies, however. Rather, ask specific questions such as "Do you think my child can outgrow a youthful drinking problem, like bingeing on weekends?" "How intensively do you feel you need to treat someone in order to overcome an addictive behavior?" "Do you feel that people often bring important insights to resolving their own problems?"

Motivational Interviewing, like Brief Interventions, can help you address your own as well as others' addictions. The key to Motivational Interviewing is confronting your own contradictory impulses and harnessing your own values and motivation in the service of rejecting your addiction. We will devote some exercises specifically to helping you do this at the end of the chapter. However, keep in mind in what follows that the skills needed to talk with other people constructively about their problems not only will help your relationships with others, but often can cast light on your own unexamined habits and behavior patterns.

CONDUCTING A DRUG/ALCOHOL INTERVIEW WITH A TEENAGER

People often seek tools—lie detectors, urine tests, and telephone bugs—to find out whether children are using drugs and alcohol. Here is a twelve-question checklist, involving no electronic or other intrusive devices, for figuring out how likely it is that a teen is abusing substances, and if so, how severe the abuse is.

These questions can be utilized, with modification, by parents or counselors. Note that these questions are not about determining whether a child drinks or takes drugs. Instead, they are geared toward exploring how badly a child's life is being disrupted by drugs, alcohol, or some other involvement. If as a parent, on examining the questions, you feel you cannot carry out such an interview, seek a counselor or therapist who uses this kind of approach.*

Background Setting

• How do you get along with your family? (A parent may ask, "Can you identify some good aspects of our family? Which aspects need improvement?")

• Who are your friends? What kinds of things are they interested in?

• What grades did you get? How have these changed recently? (For a parent, of course, the goal is to explore the feelings and behaviors surrounding poor school performance.)

• What extracurricular and organized activities do you do? (For a parent: "How are you feeling about these? Do you still like them and participate fully?")

Use and View of Drugs and Alcohol

• (If the teenager uses drugs or alcohol) What does the drug/alcohol do for you?

• How do you define a drug addict or alcoholic?

• What for you is an example of a drug/alcohol problem?

• Has anyone you know ever had a drug or alcohol problem? Have you?

Life Goals and Achievement

• What is important to you? What do you hope to achieve in life?

• How does your drug/alcohol use affect your reaching your goals?

• Do you want to be a healthy person? How do you act on this concern?

• How do you feel about yourself?

---

* Serious substance abuse problems require professional assessment utilizing tools that measure their severity. See W.R. Miller, V.S. Westerberg, and H.B. Waldron, "Evaluating Alcohol Problems in Adults and Adolescents," in R.K. Hester and W.R. Miller, *Handbook of Alcoholism Treatment Approaches: Effective Alternatives*, 3rd ed. (Boston: Allyn and Bacon, 2003), 78–112.

Counselors and parents also need to address certain additional questions. This must be done not to score points against the child, but to identify major risk factors that need to be dealt with practically. Two of these issues are the impact of substance use on sex and driving. If these topics do not emerge immediately, they may come up during a second or third conversation. Children should be given a chance to express their own ideas about what kinds of problems are at stake. If they do not themselves raise the issues, the kind of interviewing described here will still offer natural lead-ins to bring the topics up.

Whenever addressing these points, it is critical to remain nonconfrontational. Of course, parents usually don't want their children to have sex too early. And they don't want kids getting stoned or drunk in the first place. But parents, despite their best efforts, cannot always prevent these things from occurring. The best a parent can do is to eliminate fundamental dangers to the child's well-being, things that can derail teenagers' lives permanently. Pregnancy and car accidents, both of which are associated with drinking, are two such things that can be guarded against by providing information on contraception and by making available safe transportation alternatives (like those endorsed by Mothers Against Drunk Driving). Acknowledging the dangers of pregnancy and drunk driving does not connote approval of teenage sex or drinking. But if, as a parent or counselor, you refuse to accept that sex occurs or that kids get drunk or take drugs when we know that they do, then you may lose any chance to work with children to prevent the very worst outcomes.

All the Best Therapy Together Can't Beat Your Own

I attended a small conference of leading researchers in addiction therapy. One described an ongoing study he was conducting of behavior modification for smoking. A number of techniques had shown some success—his study bundled all techniques that had shown any success together into one grand treatment protocol. But, he said, thus far the control group—which received no therapy—was doing better than the treatment group in staying off cigarettes! In fact, what seemed to be taking place was that the experimenter was conducting a Motivational Interviewing session.

Of course, a control group of subjects must be equally interested in quitting smoking as those receiving the experimental therapy and must interact (in this case minimally) with a therapist. Otherwise it would not be a fair comparison, since experimental subjects have regular meetings with a therapist that might influence their outcomes even aside from the treatment they receive, while the control group would have no such contact.

The researcher described an interaction with a control subject in the study: "A man who had recently quit smoking told me he was having lunch with his former wife's mother. Not only was he intensely anxious, but she smoked the same brand of cigarettes that he used to. And he knew she would offer him her cigarettes."

This scientist continued, "I wasn't able to recommend any techniques to him, since he was in the control group. But as we sat there with me smiling, he rehearsed a number of techniques he came up with himself in preparation for this risky meeting to prevent him from relapsing. When he left the office, he was feeling good about himself and optimistic about being able to resist this challenge to his cigarette sobriety."

This chapter is intended to enable you to do the same—to harness your own motivation and figure out your own set of coping strategies—whether you meet with a therapist or not.

Motivational Interviewing Exercises

Before examining Motivational Interviewing techniques through a series of exercises, let's first get a feeling for what MI actually is and does.

MI is built on the fact that people typically change on their own, and that, fundamentally, all change occurs because of decisions people make for themselves. The most powerful techniques for bringing about change, therefore, allow people to follow their own values and preferences. Only in this way will they genuinely accept the goal of change and pursue it with the means at their disposal.

At the same time, people often behave self-destructively. Various events, the passage of time, and maturity can make them realize and change this. The question is whether helpers can facilitate this process by making it quicker and surer. Motivational Interviewing is a way of holding a mirror up to people so that they can see that they are defying their own feelings and values. This helps them to bring their behavior in line with who they want to be.

Although the goal in Motivational Interviewing is to enable people to change, the therapy does this through greater understanding. You help someone gain understanding by understanding them better. In order to do this, you need to understand the fundamental motivating principles in their lives, what they value most and consider most important, and what in their lives will enable them to change. You as the interviewer are in a learning mode yourself.

But, as I have said, you can at the same time be performing this service for yourself. Holding up a mirror to others' thought processes and motivations can also hold a mirror up to your own. While you are assisting them to see into the self-defeating contradictions that often characterize human thought and action, you can simultaneously become aware of these conflicts in yourself and move to change in a positive direction.

■■■■■

Questioning Exercise

Tell a family member that you want to ask them some questions. Set an allotted time period, as short as fifteen minutes and up to a half hour or forty-five minutes. Then pick a topic you are concerned about or interested in with regard to this person, and ask them questions. *Make no statements of your own.* Make sure that these are real questions—that is, designed to elicit information, not to convey your own feelings (you wouldn't say, for instance, "Do you really believe that?" but would ask instead, "Why do you feel that way?"). At the end of this discussion ask the loved one this: "How did you like this discussion?" On your own, take ten minutes and write down your impressions and what you learned. You may show what you wrote to the other person.

Improving your understanding of and relationship with a family member will help you as well. In later chapters, we will specifically describe, for example, how improving marital interactions lessens the impulse to engage in addictions and offers support for curtailing them.

■■■■■

Reflective Summarizing

People are often happy to talk about themselves at length. But you need to respond to them to facilitate further sharing. In motivational interviewing, particularly early on, your responses should reflect the person's comments, and not impose your own views and judgments. You are following their lead, almost as if you were dancing. Or you can think of your task as acting like a focusing mirror that sharpens the returning image.

As you listen to people, you are culling from their statements the critical elements of what they are saying. While they may talk for several minutes, your responses will typically take seconds. Practice this in your next conversations. Here are the rules:

1. Respond to the person you are talking to, but speak far less.
2. The content of your comments is determined entirely by what you are told.

3. Make no judgments, but simply try to understand the essence of what you are hearing.
4. Your feedback consists entirely of restating the meaning you have gleaned from the other person.
5. You may follow your feedback with a query about whether you understood the other person correctly.
6. Pay attention to how the person responds to your reflective summary. If the person argues or rephrases, try again. Never argue. Smile, make eye contact, and nod affirmatively.

This type of communication is effective for many purposes: It shows people that you are really paying attention to them, it clarifies for you what in fact they are saying, and it also causes them to sharpen for themselves what they want to say. Ultimately, the skill of reflective summarizing sharpens your ability to listen and understand others.

Developing Discrepancies

Of course, you are not really a neutral listener when you are encouraging someone to quit an addiction. You have a direction you want to go in and a goal for the interaction. Some of what the person comes out with will strike you as wrong and harmful, even self-deceptive. But you are not simply to bellow out, "You're full of it."

Developing discrepancies means presenting to people, in their own terms, the disconnects between their utterances. That is, they claim they want one thing (such as intimacy) while they pursue a course of action (going to singles bars) that produces the opposite. The advantage of Motivational Interviewing over providing an expert psychological analysis is that it's not your job to ferret out the source of people's conflicts; that's *their* job.

Thus you simply lay out for people, leaving as few fingerprints as possible, the contradictory things you heard them

say. You begin, "I'm a little confused" or "Could you clarify
something for me?" Then present the person's contradictory
statements or sentiments: "You say the thing you want most is
intimacy, yet you go to singles bars to find dates, when you
say that only leads to transient relationships."

You may delve deeper to ferret out these discrepancies.
"Help me with one thing. You say that you can't stand other
people controlling you. Yet after every time you get drunk,
you end up making amends to people. Isn't this really placing
yourself under the control of other people?"

You may even have to repeat the same discrepancies several times to have the person focus on and deal constructively
with his or her contradictory impulses and actions. As the interviewing progresses, you may give your genuine views or
express facts about the case as you see them. This, if done respectfully, is one more way to advance the MI process.

While you are performing this exercise, examine how people deal with such contradictory thoughts, values, and behaviors. As the other person struggles to make sense of these
discontinuities in their thinking, reflect on how you might be
avoiding resolving your own discontinuities, and how you
might profitably confront these conflicts in yourself.

■■■■■

Motivationally Interview Yourself

Consider why you are not able—or refuse—to change a habit
that is harming you, or that others complain about. List *all*
the reasons you are not able to quit.

Examine your reasons, now, as though you were a doctor or
a psychologist.

Consider how you might explore with a person why each
reason is really no excuse for not changing the behavior.
Remember that the person (i.e., yourself) needs to reach this
conclusion inwardly, with guidance but without pressure.

Consult with that same "client" about how to turn these
negatives around so they no longer serve as excuses.

Propose methods to overcome each reason in your initial list.

Remember the old *Pogo* cartoon: "We have met the enemy [or in this case a potential client for change] and he is us."

■■■■■

Brief Intervention Exercise

Set up your own brief intervention program with a friend, family member, or other person concerned about your progress (perhaps they, too, want to work on an addictive problem or make changes in their lives, and you can assist them as they in turn help you). After an initial meeting where you discuss steps you each plan to take, schedule a fixed date within the next month to meet again. At that meeting, come prepared to assess the behavior or its consequences—for example, conduct a weigh-in, review a drinking diary, evaluate your success at reducing or eliminating smoking, consider if family relations have improved, and so on. Whether you are successful or not in your enterprise, review the actions you have taken and assess which steps hold the best promise (either from among those you have tried or new ones you want to explore). At the end of your discussion, schedule a fixed date to meet again.

■■■■■

3

Rewards: Weighing the Costs and Benefits of Addiction

If motivation is the force that drives you to act, then rewards are what you gain from that activity. People quit their addictions when they begin to get more rewards for living without the addiction than they got from feeding the addiction. Put into economic terms, you relinquish your habit when you believe that its costs exceed its benefits.

Of course, the nature of rewards is highly subjective. You incur all sorts of costs from an addiction—health, financial, legal, interpersonal, and so on. However, you also are getting benefits from it—rewards that often loom larger than life because they are so immediate and familiar to you.

The Rewards of Addictions

The disease model regards addiction as an unfortunate genetic inheritance. You are unlucky enough to have been born with an intrinsic urge to drink, to take drugs, or even to shop—or perhaps your brain is wired in such a way that these activities create unmatchable "reward impulses" for you. Conventional therapy is only interested in the negative consequences of your addiction. But in this chapter we are going to explore the *reasons* behind your addiction. Excessive alcohol consumption, eating, and sexual activity provide you with feelings and sensations that you desire and need.

Some of these essential feelings are a sense of being valued, of being a worthwhile person, or of being in control. It is critical for you, or anyone trying to help a person with an addictive problem, to understand the needs that the addiction fulfills. This understanding is necessary in order to root out the addiction.

In fact, as you're no doubt aware, addictions don't really provide the addict with positive experiences or benefits. Although they provide short-term or illusory rewards, addictions ultimately lead to negative feelings and life outcomes. In the long run, you are *worse* off as a result of your addictive behaviors.

Moreover, over time, addictions take on their own momentum. Once you get used to relying on your addiction, your whole life begins to revolve around it, and your indulgence in overeating, drinking, smoking, or shopping becomes the first place you turn when you are under stress or simply looking to please yourself. You lose focus on how the addiction is damaging you—you begin to take the sensations and rewards it offers you as a given, as though you had no other way to obtain them.

It is these short-term and habitual rewards in your addiction to which you are attached. And people are simply not ready to give up these benefits until they find an alternative source of satisfaction. No one wants to jump off into space, leaving behind the habits that they have relied on for years, until they can find another source of positive feelings and gratification on which they can rely.

The task for you, in order to overcome any destructive habit, is first to get a handle on why you turn so regularly to the same sensation or experience—what you get from the addiction and the role it serves in your life. Examining what underlies the addiction will help you to get your automatic responses under control. Only then can you identify how you can find superior, nonaddictive rewards to take the place of the addiction.

The Pros and Cons of Drinking

The idea that an addictive habit provides the addict with benefits may initially seem puzzling. When people are ruining their lives, how are they gaining something from the behavior? A study of heavy drinkers provides data on the kinds of benefits that addictions confer.

In a 2002 study, British psychologist Jim Orford and his colleagues interviewed heavy drinkers about their drinking experiences.[1] (Heavy drinking was defined for men as more than fifty drinks a week and for women more than thirty-five—although standard drinks contain somewhat less alcohol in Britain than the United States.) They found that 91 percent of heavy drinkers experienced relaxation, 88 percent found that drinking provided them with fun/humor, 81 percent thought that it stimulated their social life, 65 percent fostered friendships by drinking, and 67 percent felt more self-confidence when they drank.

In other words, as far as heavy drinkers are concerned, alcohol allows them to have more fun, improves their dealings with other people, and makes them feel better about themselves. A typical statement expressed by a heavy drinker in the study was "If I've got something on my mind, then I have a few drinks, and everything doesn't seem as bad as it did before."[2] Social motivations are expressed this way: "I mean I love my wife and children, but it is nice to get away and relax down the pub when you can just sit and have a drink, talk to people you've known for years and years about football, work, or whatever."[3]

This is not to say that heavy drinkers see only a positive side to their drinking. Orford's study also found that they perceive disadvantages to their heavy consumption. The primary drawbacks reported were a decline in physical well-being (72 percent) and financial/business matters (71 percent). However, drinking affects different people in different ways—and many people both positively and negatively. For example, while 81 percent listed social benefits of drinking alcohol, 23 percent reported social drawbacks. Although a large number of heavy drinkers (72 percent) reported that drinking hurts their physical condition (mentioning headaches, stomach upset, feeling sick, etc.), a small minority (23 percent) actually said it improves their sense of physical well-being. The areas where benefits and drawbacks were listed in close to equal numbers are sleeping (61 percent benefits versus 48 percent drawbacks), eating (37 percent benefits versus 55 percent drawbacks), and marriage/close relationships (42 percent benefits versus 56 percent drawbacks).

These scores resulted from people checking a box to indicate a benefit or a drawback in a certain area. But subjects also offered open-ended comments about their drinking. For example, becoming argumentative was a drawback often mentioned in connection with their relationships. One characteristic of the drinkers that the authors noted was that they focused on immediate consequences, whether positive or negative, rather than long-term effects of drinking. The drinkers were particularly likely to ignore long-term negative health consequences.

Some of the alcoholics in Orford's study also noted that the positive consequences of drinking tend to tail off into negative ones:

> It gives you a warm feeling, I suppose really. A safe feeling initially, because it heightens your other feelings . . . and, therefore, it does make you feel quite sort of comfortable with yourself, and comfortable with your life, or what's going on, and then again it's how you, where you go from there on how

many more you have, and how . . . the mood you're in . . . because you can drink so much and feel pretty OK, but then if
you go over that it can either bring down a barrier and bring
floods of tears, bring about a feeling of stupidity or emotion or
whatever it is: you silly, silly, silly sod.[4]

There are several points to be extrapolated from this research. First, heavy drinkers rate the benefits of drinking as being greater than the drawbacks. Second, they do recognize
drawbacks, even as they continue to drink. Lastly, the benefits
and drawbacks drinkers focus on are short term—they ignore,
for example, the health problems continued heavy drinking
causes. But some of the most significant drawbacks from drinking involve longer-range consequences (for example, divorce,
or job loss, or permanent health problems). These data illustrate that a major dilemma for alcoholics and other addicts is
that powerful social and emotional results appear immediately
to reinforce their drinking, while negative consequences tend
to accumulate and have their greatest impact later.

The message you can derive from seeing the benefits people
experience that make them continue their heavy drinking is
that these benefits can be replaced. It is possible for you to
evolve and develop so that you no longer need the drinking or
other addictive experience so intensely. You can find other avenues for getting the experiences you seek.

Addiction and Depression

When we are considering the potential rewards of addiction, it
is important to distinguish people who rely on their addictions
to attain positive sensations (like relaxation and fun) from people who use addiction to avoid negative feelings (like anxiety
and depression). The former group uses their addiction "to feel
good," whereas the latter group relies on it in order to cope
with their emotions, or "to feel better."

Among the most common reasons people smoke, drink, take

drugs, shop, seek sexual release, overeat, and so on is that they feel bad. Depression is a major precursor to addiction. At the same time, depression is on the increase among Americans—and, indeed, worldwide. The poet W.H. Auden characterized post–World War II Americans as being in the throes of "the age of anxiety." Although many of us experience depression and anxiety simultaneously, today the most common emotional problem for which people seek medical attention is depression.

Do drinking and other addictive behaviors relieve depression? People have been drinking for this purpose for eons, and "drinking your cares away" is an accepted motivation for drinking, even among nonpathological drinkers. (In the movie *Seabiscuit*, the narrator, David McCullough, comments that during the Depression, when you needed a drink most, you couldn't get one.) Sometimes you simply experience a bad event, and alcohol is a means for letting off steam and for recovering your equilibrium. Very normal, nonaddicted people report getting drunk at a wake, after a divorce, when they lose a job, and so on.

Ordinary drinkers may in fact be helping themselves maintain a positive outlook on life. Several systematic research studies have found that *moderate* drinkers are less depressed and anxious than either abstainers or heavy drinkers.[5] Critics have claimed that mentally healthier people are more likely to drink moderately in the first place. In one study, the researcher assessed levels of depression in subjects at the beginning and end of a two-year time period—whatever their initial level of depression, moderate drinkers at the second measurement showed less depression than others who were at the same level of depression initially.[6]

On the other hand, drinking to feel good can evolve into drinking to relieve depression. Heavier drinkers (like Orford's subjects) can become more depressed after consuming alcohol than they were initially, because of both the depressant effects of alcohol and the consequences of their behavior when they are intoxicated. As they recognize their depression coming on again, they may turn to drink again to relieve it. Thus they are caught up in the cycle of addiction.

Chronic drinking can affect people's emotions so greatly that they lose a large measure of their emotional self-awareness. William Styron, the author of *Sophie's Choice*, presents this dilemma vividly in his 1990 memoir, *Darkness Visible*. When Styron was in his sixties, he quit drinking because he suddenly found that alcohol made him nauseous. After he went dry, Styron realized that he had been abusing alcohol for forty years. Despite this, he reported that he had functioned well on alcohol over this time, and refused to "rue or apologize for my use of this soothing, often sublime agent which had contributed greatly to my writing."[7]

However, once Styron stopped drinking, he was overwhelmed by debilitating depression. He now realized that he had been using alcohol "as a means to calm the anxiety and incipient dread that I had hidden away." Depression had always been part of Styron's life, but it had been muted by the alcohol that he used to consume.

Styron's case suggests that for some people alcohol acts as a therapeutic agent. Of course, relying on alcohol over such a long time to deal with anxiety and dread is likely to be unhealthy, as it turned out to be for Styron. But the same logic could be applied to antidepressant use as well: *Any* reliance on a substance to combat depression can be problematic. (Ironically, Styron reported that antidepressant drugs were completely unhelpful to him.) Alcohol illustrates how use of a calming agent is double-edged: Although moderate use can have a positive psychological benefit, anything that is used regularly to compensate for a persistent deficiency can escalate to an addiction.

Are Addictions Pleasurable?

Most people assume that drug use is inherently rewarding—which is the position taken by the National Institute on Drug

Abuse. That is, people take it for granted that drugs such as cocaine and heroin are so pleasurable that it is almost impossible
to resist them once you have tried them. However, we have
seen that this is not the case; in fact, people resist the pleasurable effects of drugs as a matter of course. For example, most
people who at one point took heroin or cocaine no longer do
so. Even addicted users, like the Vietnam vets who became dependent on heroin, taper off when their lives permit them to
pursue a normal range of rewards.

Drugs are clearly not irresistibly pleasurable. For example,
when most people receive a powerful narcotic drug in the
hospital, they never consider the possibility of continuing to
use the drug after they have recovered their health.[8] You don't
want to be off in the ozone when you're not in pain, because
the feeling of uncontrollable intoxication isn't pleasurable for
most people. Indeed, hospitals now regularly allow patients to
self-regulate painkillers at their hospital beds (called patient-
controlled analgesia, or PCA) because patients limit their use
of the analgesia to those times when they experience pain.
Hospital patients show no inclination to experiment with narcotic effects because they find them enjoyable or rewarding.

On the flip side, consider how a typical heroin addict regards
the experience of narcosis. The following description comes
from *The Road to H*, a book about street addicts by psychologist Isidor Chein and his coworkers.[9] The first time that one
young man took heroin, he said, "I got real sleepy. I went in to
lay on the bed. . . . I thought, this is for me! And I never
missed a day since, until now."[10] Just as most ordinary people
don't want to stay in bed all day, most people don't want to
take a drug that causes them, in the words of addicts, to "nod
out."

Even when normal people find drug use pleasurable, they
don't react like the addicts Chein studied. These nonaddicts
often find stimulant drugs such as cocaine to be more pleasurable than narcotics. In one experiment, psychologists at the
University of Chicago administered concentrated ampheta-

mine to volunteer subjects.[11] Subjects found the drug highly pleasurable. Yet on subsequent experimental occasions when offered either the drug or a placebo, even though they continued to say the drug elevated their mood, they increasingly chose the placebo over the amphetamine. That is, they no longer wanted to continue to experience the elation they felt when taking the drug.

Think about these volunteer subjects, who included students and professionals at a leading university. While they found the drugs enjoyable, they really weren't in a position to continue to savor a high state while they had to go about their busy days. After the initial experience wore off, they were unwilling to immerse themselves in an artifically elevated mood, preferring instead to carry on their ordinary, involving lives. But for people whose ordinary experiences may not be so engaging and rewarding, continuing to indulge in the drug experience may be preferable to everyday life.

The Drug Use Scale

Many addiction experts argue that drug users are not capable of weighing the pros and cons of their drug use. Perhaps addicts begin using a drug because it provides them with certain rewarding effects. But in this view, by the time users become dependent on the substance, they are no longer able to evaluate its costs and benefits. This view of drug use is based on a small subset of drug users—the ones who have given up all their life connections aside from their drug habit. These are the hardcore addicts typically portrayed in the media, the ones who are invited, once they become clean through a twelve-step group or treatment, to lecture in school drug education programs.

But the experiences of these people are so uncommon that they bear no resemblance to the usual experiences of drug users. Research shows that many onetime addicts are able to cut back or quit drugs, often on their own, as their lives progress. This is because, for most people, drugs become less attractive as other things become more important and more rewarding for them. Many former users are too busy making a living, supporting a family, or maintaining a position in society to continue pursuing the rewards of drug use.

Many Americans have used drugs. This was especially true in the late 1970s and the early 1980s. At that time, the highest-profile drug was cocaine. According to the National Household Surveys, cocaine use rose steadily from the mid-1960s to a 1980 peak (when there were 1.7 million new users), then declined until 1993 (to 635,000 initiates). The number of cocaine users then began increasing to a point where it is again approaching its peak number—the 2001 survey reported 1.2 million new users.[12]

Researchers uncovered surprising information about this mass of cocaine users. Most of them did not develop significant substance abuse problems. And those who did develop problems, including dependence, generally quit or cut back on their own. This was what researchers from the prestigious Canadian Addiction Research Foundation reported in their 1987 book *The Steel Drug*.[13]

The cocaine users quoted in *The Steel Drug* described a range of positive feelings they attained from their drug of choice. The most common rewards stemmed from cocaine's effect as a stimulant:

• "I like the energizing feeling."
• "Your mind is alive, everything is intensified, everything is wonderful."
• "You feel invincible—anything is possible, you can do it all."
• "You're on top of the world."

A range of related benefits came from these stimulant effects:

• "You can function."
• "It sharpens perceptions."

- "It gives you confidence."
- "It makes you feel more comfortable with others."
- "It facilitates communication with others."[14]

Cocaine obviously provided these users with rewarding feelings. However, over time the drug also began to take a toll. For example, a third of cocaine users eventually suffered from nasal problems, a fifth of users were plagued by uncontrollable urges to use, and other users experienced a variety of downsides to the energizing effects of cocaine (including sleep disorders, exhaustion, and an inability to relax—each of which affected about 15 percent of users).

What is critical in this study is what people did after encountering substantial problems. When the negative effects of drug use outweighed the benefits for them, they typically cut back their usage or quit entirely. Thus, ironically, when people found themselves with uncontrollable urges to take cocaine, this loss of control actually *caused* more of them to quit.

Another researcher, Ronald Siegel, followed ninety-nine social cocaine users for a period of four years.[15] He also tracked fifty of them who continued to use cocaine for nearly a decade. What was most striking about the social users in the initial report was that they encountered less intense effects from the drug, both positive and negative, as the study progressed. In other words, the drug became less central to their experience and their lives. For the fifty users followed for a decade, less than a fifth (18 percent) developed more intensive usage patterns over the years. As a group, whenever these users saw the need to cut back or quit, most simply did so—and they reduced their usage without the support of formal treatment.

Discouraging Excessive/Addictive Use

The idea that drug use is commonplace and that the best prevention is to develop a fulfilling, meaningful life provides us with a whole different slant on preventing addictive drug and alcohol use. The best guarantee for avoiding addiction is to build up sufficient rewards to offset any potential addictive appeal from drugs. This approach also holds true when it comes to children. Kids who become involved in positive endeavors are less likely to be derailed by drugs, alcohol, or other addictions.

Yet consider for a moment—who lectures your children about drugs and alcohol at their schools? Drug and alcohol education programs invite recovering alcoholics or addicts to give lectures to their students. But those individuals who end up as heavy drug and alcohol abusers have other traits that have led to their addictions. The lecturers are actually more limited in their approach to life than the kids, and this is why they found the effects of drugs so rewarding in the first place. Think of it: These "helpers" will tell kids how irresistibly pleasurable drugs or alcohol are, making the substances sound extremely tempting. It really makes no sense sending people into the classroom to describe how great or uncontrollable the sensations of these substances are. The good news is that most kids will eventually find this is not true on their own, but of course only after trying the substances themselves.

Most kids will also recognize that it is important to build a successful, well-rounded life. For the most part, they know that constant use of drugs and alcohol isn't healthy because it might spoil their success at school, at work, and in their social life. Thus, the best way to discourage addictive substance use and habits is to show children that they can attain the rewards of a productive lifestyle. Children who are at risk for continued substance abuse and addiction are usually the ones who don't see a prospect for attaining these rewards.

In 1998, Congress enacted a bill banning young people convicted of drug offenses from receiving government financial aid to attend college. The Bush administration aggressively enforced this law, causing fifteen thousand students with drug records to lose their financial aid, along with another ten thousand who failed to answer a question on government loan applications about drug convictions.[16]

I was moved to reflect on this destructive policy when I spoke with a well-respected researcher in the alcoholism field about problems my daughter was having in college. To reassure me, this person told me that she had been convicted of assisting her boyfriend in selling drugs in her freshman year and had gone to prison. Eventually, this woman straightened out her life. Indeed, she is now a professor at the very school where her undergraduate education was interrupted by a stint in the state pen! Knowledge of her earlier conviction somehow never surfaced. I noted to this woman how today she couldn't have gotten any loans or grants to attend college or graduate school.

In 2002 Yale University joined a number of other schools in not only objecting to the law but offering to replace financial aid lost by students.[17] Here, at last, was an institution that spoke with its pocketbook in supporting sane drug policies. The Yale administration recognized that if it deprived these former drug users of the positive rewards of education and personal advancement, then they would be *more* likely to look to drugs for fulfillment. It makes more sense to reward those who once used drugs but are now seeking higher education, rather than punish them, which cannot help them to become productive contributors to society.

Moderation *as the Opposite of Addiction*

The ability to identify alternative sources of rewards is the superior means for avoiding addiction. A Harvard psychiatrist named Norman Zinberg was among the first to note that this was the key to understanding and addressing addiction. Zinberg began his classic book *Drug, Set, and Setting: The Basis for Controlled Intoxicant Use* with the following passage:

> The viewpoint toward the use of illicit drugs expressed in this book has developed gradually during more than twenty years of clinical experience with drug users. Initially I was concerned, like most other people, with drug abuse, that is, with

the users' loss of control over the drug or drugs they were using. Only after a long period of clinical investigation, historical study, and cogitation did I realize that in order to understand why certain users had lost control I would have to tackle the all-important question of how and why many others had managed to achieve control and maintain it.[18]

Zinberg thus examined the differences between addicted and nonaddicted heroin users. Primarily, he found that nonaddicts had alternative identities and lives other than using drugs: They knew people from non-drug-using groups, settings, and activities, spent time in those settings, and got satisfaction from them. To put it another way: They found other aspects of their lives sufficiently rewarding that they were able to keep their drug use under control.

The same logic applies to quitting an addiction. In *Cocaine Changes*, a group of sociologists studied cocaine users who had cut back or quit serious cocaine habits.[19] These researchers found something very similar to Zinberg's distinction between controlled and addicted users. That is, the recovered cocaine addicts had other people and areas of interest in their lives they found rewarding, which enabled them to tail off and eventually cease their excessive drug use.

Our image of heroin is such that we might imagine the only thing that could compete with it to be some other drug. This is the kind of logic pursued by the National Institute on Drug Abuse when it seeks a "cure" for heroin addiction. In fact, Zinberg discovered that moderate heroin users controlled their drug use in the service of the most prosaic, but ultimately the most powerful, rewards—children, daily life rituals, and work. Zinberg and his colleagues discovered that unlike compulsive users, moderate users

tend to schedule or defer their drug use so that it does not interfere with personal, social, or work obligations. One woman will not use unless she can arrange to have someone else care for her six-year-old daughter, because she feels she should not be too "high" if the child needs attention. Weekend users tend to refrain from Sunday evening use because it may leave them too tired to work effectively on Monday morning.[20]

The Rewards of Work and Family

Family and work responsibilities are two of the most powerful experiences human beings can have, and their rewards regularly outweigh the benefits provided by drugs, alcohol, and other addictions. Consider James Joyce, one of the twentieth century's great literary geniuses, who got drunk virtually every night of his adult life. Yet his biographers did not label him an alcoholic.[21] Why? Because he worked all day, nearly every day, and drank, usually several bottles of wine, starting only around 8 P.M., after he ceased his labors. Joyce's wife, Nora, resented his drinking, but she dedicated herself to him, threatening to leave only when he failed to provide for his family.

Although Joyce and Nora survived, even thrived, in spite of their difficult lifestyle, their two children did not fare well. Joyce loved them but smothered them and moved them around Europe at his whim, with no consideration for their emotional stability. His daughter ultimately was institutionalized for schizophrenia (although it can be debated whether and in what way the Joyces' peripatetic lifestyle contributed to her disorder). Joyce's son, Georgio, a good-looking and talented man, was married to two well-to-do women. But he never had a job or career. In between Georgio's marriages, after Joyce's death, supporters limited the money they gave to Nora because Georgio would spend the bulk on booze. Georgio *was* an alcoholic. While we might say that he shared with his father a weakness for alcohol, what he lacked was the life purpose, the rewarding activity that diverted his father from drinking constantly.

While you may not be a genius at work, you probably limit your addiction because of your professional obligations. Odds are that you already take steps to make sure that your addiction doesn't interfere with your livelihood. This demonstrates that you already have the means to control your habit under the right circumstances.

Tipping the Scale of Addiction

We began this chapter by reflecting on the rewards that we experience from indulging our addictions. Many of us drink, shop, or eat in order to counteract negative experiences such as boredom, depression, or self-loathing. It is important to recognize the way in which we often substitute the rewards of addiction for the rewards we lack in our everyday lives. When you think about the benefits that you receive from the addiction, think of a scale, with the reasons for using on one side. Now let's focus on the other side of that scale. What are the costs, the negatives, of your addiction?

In tipping the scale, we need to keep in mind the different stages of addictive behavior change. Some people need to be convinced that they should quit their addiction. Sometimes simply considering this idea of a scale, with its enumeration of all the negative effects of the habit, helps people gain the insight that change is necessary.

As a reader of this book, you have probably already decided that you want to change. The issue that you face is how to establish new behaviors and how to maintain them over the course of your nonaddicted life. In order to do so, it will be helpful to keep this scale of costs and benefits in mind. It will motivate you to change, and it will keep the change in place in the years to come.

For those people who are not yet committed to change, the cost-benefit balance can suddenly shift, as it did for Uncle Ozzie. When a tremendous weight is dropped onto the negative side of the addiction self-assessment scale or a large positive benefit is added to the positive side, the balance can change precipitously. However, the balance usually changes more gradually, as you find more reasons in life to change, while negative outcomes become more intolerable to you. Determining the ways in which your habit has been weighing you down, and then identifying rewards to counteract those of the addiction, can speed and reinforce this process.

Look at the Situation

In many cases the harm in a behavior is due to the situation. Behavior such as drinking, which can be innocuous in one setting, can be harmful in another (like a sexual or conflict situation). Thus, to complete your analysis of harms, you also want to look at when, where, and why you engage in a behavior. Besides helping to make clear its negative impacts, this analysis will also help to clarify your reasons for resorting to the addiction, or the functions it serves. Ask yourself these contextual questions.

THE PLACE OF YOUR ADDICTION IN YOUR LIFE

When do you resort to the addiction?

What *precedes* the addictive behavior? How do you *feel before turning to* it?

What do you *experience* when you resort to the addiction? How do you *feel as a result of* it?

What *results* from your addictive behavior?

Why do you turn to your addiction?

What keeps you coming back, despite so many negatives?

Make Sure a Negative Is a Negative

People change for all sorts of reasons. Obviously, many people who use substances regularly fall short of being addicted. In his autobiography, *"Surely You're Joking, Mr. Feynman!" Adventures of a Curious Character*, the Nobel-winning physicist Richard

Feynman described how he suddenly realized that he always had a drink at a strip club he regularly went to, even though his drinking was by any standards moderate. He quit drinking on the spot.

Of course, Feynman could decide for whatever reason he chose that he no longer wanted to drink (and in his case he was readily able to quit). If drinking is not the cause of your problems, however, giving it up is a misleading gesture. To mislabel the source of your problems, or the dangers you face, is usually not a good basis for change. If you reject alcohol, thus feeling virtuous about attending to your health, but continue smoking and overeating, you clearly haven't addressed the real source of your problems. Some behaviors, such as sex and alcohol, are often disapproved of more for moral reasons than for actual health reasons. If so, you should be sure on what basis you are rejecting them.

One divorced woman who smoked told me, "I know smoking is bad for me, but I'm not having sex! At least I'm doing one thing right." Her point was that she was making some progress in her habits. But she was mixing a health and safety risk (smoking cigarettes) with what she felt was a moral transgression (having nonmarital sex). Having sex is a healthy activity, assuming that you choose partners reasonably and you practice safe sex. But in the United States, we tend to translate personal and ethical feelings into health prescriptions. In this case, the woman believed that both having nonmarital sex and smoking were wrong. Not doing one seemingly permitted her to continue engaging in the other. But, of course, abstaining from sex does not prevent lung cancer, any more than quitting smoking reduces the risk of STDs from unsafe sex.

People often confuse moral and health concerns when it comes to evaluating the costs and benefits of drinking alcohol. Drinking moderately has been repeatedly proven to be healthy, because it reduces heart disease. Ironically, abstinence is actually a risk factor for coronary disease! Based on decades of research findings, an editorial in America's most prestigious medical journal, the *New England Journal of Medicine*, suggested a clinical trial where patients with heart disease would be given alcohol as a medicine.[22]

However, although most Americans drink, as a nation we are preoccupied with the dangers of alcoholism. So many Americans (and certainly many public health agencies and officials) reject the idea that drinking has any healthy consequences. But this denial, based on the fear of alcoholism, has the negative impact that people cannot realistically assess the costs and benefits of their drinking.

MISPERCEPTIONS OVERHEARD AT THE NEIGHBORHOOD COFFEE SHOP: "SHOULD I QUIT DRINKING AFTER MY HEART SURGERY?"

One day at the Coffee Klatch, I overheard a group of middle-aged locals, several of whom had had heart surgery, as they discussed the costs and benefits of drinking. Their level of misinformation was startling:

Wife of man who had quadruple bypass surgery: "It's okay for him to have a glass of wine, but no more shots of Scotch."

Truth is: No form of alcohol has been found to be superior to another in terms of preventing heart disease, so long as it is consumed moderately.

Man who had congestive heart failure: "That's all baloney. I've read all the research—grape juice does as much good as wine. And all alcohol hurts your muscles. Your heart is a muscle, so you shouldn't drink."

Truth is: Alcohol has been shown to have special properties above and beyond grape juice. This man had congestive heart failure, or a failure of the heart muscle, and so drinking is not good for him. But most heart disease—by the far the number one killer of Americans, men and women—is due to atherosclerosis (also called coronary artery disease, or hardening or blockage of the arteries). Alcohol reduces atherosclerosis, even in those who already have coronary artery disease.

Man with heart failure, on questioning: "Before my heart attack I had two drinks at lunch, two at dinner, and two at night . . ." (trailing off, implying he had even more).

Truth is: This man is joking about his excessive drinking in order to disprove that moderate drinking can be healthy. But his experience says nothing about the potential benefits of moderate drinking. Moderate drinking for men is defined as two drinks daily, although it could conceivably be even higher for middle-aged and older men with CAD. But certainly six or more is not recommended for anyone.

Procrastination

Many of us are waiting for just the right moment to change, when the costs of the addiction are so great that change is unavoidable. We can imagine the perfect situation for kicking the addiction; we're just not there yet. Jeff, for example, is an affable thirty-year-old smoker who would like to start a family. He expects to quit smoking after he gets married. In fact, he actually has an elaborate fantasy that this will occur because he will marry a smoker, and she will be forced to quit smoking when she becomes pregnant, dragging him along with her.

Given his intelligence and strong value system, it would seem that Jeff would have enough motivation to change on his own now. That is, if the idea of having a wife and children is so appealing to him, then Jeff should quit smoking as a way of pursuing the family rewards that he seeks. In fact, it makes the most sense for him to begin dating a nonsmoker, who would insist he begin the process of quitting smoking immediately. Instead, by setting up such an elaborate scenario in his head, Jeff is creating an out that keeps him from having to fight his addiction. This is the danger of picking your rewards so specifically that they actually stand little chance of occurring. You can get started now, and beat Jeff to the recovery path—unless he reads this book first!

Traumatic Events

Maybe you are waiting to change until you have a heart attack, you develop diabetes, you go bankrupt, or your spouse leaves you. You figure that this will resolve all your hesitance or ambivalence. Once one of these things happens, then you will *know* that you have to change. Perhaps you have seen how famous people use catastrophic situations as reasons to fight addictions, and you want to follow in their footsteps.

For example, Jerry Lewis was a heavy smoker. He made no bones about it in public, dragging on a cigarette throughout his marathon Labor Day charity TV show. But he quit after undergoing quadruple bypass surgery. "Whenever I feel like smoking," he quipped, "I pull up my shirt and look at the scars on my chest." People are often strongly motivated to change when they suffer severe heart disease or other medical traumas.

But there are serious drawbacks to waiting until you are on the operating table to decide to change. Sometimes you die. Sometimes the disease (like lung cancer) is irreversible. Rather than waiting for something awful to happen to tip your cost-benefit scale, it is more useful to visualize these negative outcomes before they occur. In this way, you can use controlled fear to modify your current behavior.

Some people speak of their doctors taking them to the cancer ward of their hospitals in an effort to convince them to quit smoking. You can do something like this on your own by going to a support group for those who have experienced the worst outcomes that you yourself may be headed for. It may provide you with a better idea of the rewards that you stand to reap by quitting your addiction—improved health, longevity, and control over the state of your own body.

Shift the Balance of Rewards from Your Addiction: Recognize, Reframe, Replace

The rewards of your addiction sometimes disappear of their own volition when you identify them for what they are. Simply putting a name on the reasons that you pursue your addiction can remove their power. Allow yourself to acknowledge, "I drink in order to feel comfortable with strangers," or "I get into love affairs because I cannot be alone." This admission may allow you to put your finger on something you know is not right or needs to be changed.

One therapy technique for problem drinkers is to videotape them when they are intoxicated. While they imagine drinking made them more attractive to others, many alcoholics don't actually enjoy looking at themselves when they are drunk.

There are a number of ways you can shift the balance of your addiction scale. Think of them as the three R's—*recognize, reframe,* and *replace*. First you can recognize and focus on the negative consequences of your addiction. Then you can redefine the benefits you feel you get from the addiction, reframing them as negatives. For example, you can start to think of an addictive habit you use to relieve tension, be sociable, or fill time instead as a way you maintain deficient aspects of your life. Finally, once you have identified the reasons that you resort to the addiction, you can replace these rewards with less harmful alternatives.

SHIFTING THE BALANCE OF YOUR ADDICTION SCALE: RECOGNIZE, REFRAME, REPLACE

Recognize: Identify and focus on the negative consequences of your current behavior.

Reframe: Recast a purported reward of your behavior as a drawback.

Replace: Replace a supposed benefit of the addiction with a less harmful alternative.

Replacing Rewards

When you examine the rewards reaped through your addiction, you will often discover that they are weak and/or illusory. That means that you should seek out healthier ways to get the same needs met. As you keep in mind the limitations of the addictive rewards—the weight gain, the cost, the intoxication and hangovers, the recriminations and guilt—look for superior ways to gain each supposed benefit of your addiction. For example, if you turn to alcohol, cigarettes, or food to help you relax, then you might try exercising, doing a guided meditation, or getting a massage.

Obviously, some gratifications provided by an addiction will be easier to replace than others. Filling an empty place because you don't feel loved or you don't have a purpose in life is going to require major life refocusing. At the other extreme, eating or drinking because you are bored is a more straightforward problem to solve.

One common problem, particularly associated with prescription drug abuse, is difficulty in sleeping. Either because the drug is used specifically to sleep (sedatives and tranquilizers) or because stopping the drug causes discomfort (as is true of painkillers, antidepressants, and some other medications), people often continue to use soporific drugs even while wishing that they could cease. And the main reason they give is their inability to sleep without the drug.

Sleep is among nature's most treasured rewards. My standard response to the many people who contact me about their inability to sleep is "Walk or exercise yourself into tiredness." It may be a mark of our times that many people get weary at work, but not because of physical exertion. In fact, they have unchanneled excess physical energy. Ironically, if they exercised, they would be more alert at work. Furthermore, most people will find it easier to get to sleep if they walk or do another form of exercise for thirty to sixty minutes a day. Really desperate people might even try doing an activity in the middle of the night. At least they'll be putting time otherwise wasted to good use.

Seeking respite through means other than ingesting a chemical is one example of taking a creative, flexible approach to counterbalancing the rewards that you lose when you give up your addiction. If you are having trouble fulfilling a specific need, then you may consult an expert or find a reference book about your problem. Just be careful to evaluate suggestions that substitute another addiction in place of the first one: for example, sleeping pills to replace alcohol for a person who is now having trouble sleeping.

Concrete Reward Systems: Providing Reasons to Quit

As we have seen throughout this chapter, rewards can be used to motivate people to fight their addictions. If we know that rewards lead to success, then why aren't more treatment programs structured around simply providing addicts with concrete rewards, like money or other benefits?

Several research studies have examined the effect of such rewards on addiction. A series of such studies was conducted at the Baltimore City Hospital by Johns Hopkins psychologists in the early 1970s. In one study, alcoholics were recruited as subjects. The alcoholics were permitted to drink large amounts of alcohol. However, their privileges for the rest of the day were determined by how much alcohol they consumed. If the subjects drank more than five ounces of alcohol, they were sent to their rooms to eat pureed foods. If they drank less than the prescribed amount, they gained access to private phones, an entertainment room with TV and pool table, the opportunity to socialize, and so on. The study found that subjects drank significantly less when they were penalized for heavy drinking and were rewarded for moderate drinking.[23]

Allowing alcoholics to drink in a laboratory is no longer permitted. However, many of the principles from the Johns

Hopkins research have been utilized in practical ways in recent studies. In one study conducted by Stephen Higgins and his colleagues at the University of Vermont, cocaine addicts were rewarded for abstinence. Each time these subjects passed a urine test, they were given vouchers for amounts that increased with each successive negative test. They could then trade in the vouchers for goods and services purchased for them by the research staff.

The individuals in the rewards program were compared with other subjects who received standard counseling based on the view that their addiction was a disease. Of the subjects who received the rewards, 58 percent completed the full twenty-four-week treatment. Only 11 percent of those who received disease counseling completed the program. And of those receiving rewards, 68 percent achieved at least eight weeks of continuous abstinence, compared with 11 percent of the disease-based counseling group who attained continuous abstinence (the rest failed either because they dropped out of the program or they used cocaine during the course of it).[24]

This research shows that concrete rewards facilitate the recovery process. The only problem with these findings is that it is unclear who would provide the positive reinforcement after the experiment is completed. In fact, the experiement is, in itself, somewhat infantalizing and continues to place the addict in a dependent position. Ultimately, it is the ability to gain rewards from real life (as we see in the next chapter) that will be the firmest bulwark against addiction.

Intermediate Rewards

What do you do until real rewards kick into play? Linda was very overweight. Like most people, she wanted companionship and true love. She was aware that losing weight would help her in this goal, and other aims she had. Yet she reckoned that even if she effectively dieted, it would be many months, or longer, before she achieved her goal weight, and who knew how long until she found a lover.

Of course, this dilemma faces every person trying to change an addictive habit. The ultimate goals of happiness, love, a healthy lifestyle, and so on may be considerably down the road. What rewards keep people on the path of behavior change?

People need to find intermediate rewards—those that reinforce their change until they achieve their ultimate goals. Linda began walking, and she soon began to feel more physically alive than she had in many years. And she was assisted by her scale. A scale is a remarkably rewarding instrument. It provides immediate feedback—and reinforcement—for people who are achieving small losses of a pound or two, which others may not perceive. Even after losing many pounds, a weight loss that is noticeable, people may still be far from a physical ideal. But the scale tells them about the progress they have made. Along with this, they can appreciate their improved mobility and a host of other gratifying reactions, including their efficacy in accomplishing change.

One of the best natural rewards is when others begin to ask a person if she has lost weight (one person asked Linda if she had had her stomach stapled). Weight Watchers, a support group for weight loss, applauds each member's announced weight loss after a weigh-in at the beginning of the meeting. Loss of even fractions of a pound receives applause, and it is buoying to anyone receiving it.

Indeed, one of the difficulties of quitting addictive habits such as drugs and alcohol is that intermediate rewards are harder to obtain than for weight loss. That is, what does achieving some progress mean for the substance abuser? AA and NA (Narcotics Anonymous) do not applaud reduced drinking or drug taking or fewer binges—they respond only to complete abstinence.

Substance-abusing individuals and their helpers should be far more accepting of various signs of progress short of complete abstinence. Otherwise, few will find the motivation to continue on what is, after all, as long and difficult a path as the one to weight loss.

After the Change, Savor the Rewards

Once you have given up or modified a behavior, you need to change your focus. Now that you have successfully attained the rewards of quitting, you have to keep these former costs and current benefits in the forefront of your thinking. It is important to remember both the negative outcomes that you have eliminated from your life and the positives that you have gained. For example, concentrate on how easily you breathe now that you have quit smoking, or how easy it is to walk now that you have lost some weight. On the other side of the equation, remember how you woke up with a raspy throat when you smoked, or how difficult it was to turn over in bed before you lost weight.

Gloat a Little

One of the greatest rewards for fighting an addiction is that you can now feel proud of your life choices. Revel in your change and in the rewards that you have attained. After Arthur lost thirty-five pounds (following very negative feedback from his doctor), he continuously told his friends about how he had lost the weight through changes in his diet and exercise routine, how good they would feel if they lost weight, and so on.

Of course, this endless boasting was annoying to many people (including his wife)—sometimes people who have quit addictions can be almost insufferable. But, obviously, this drawback was secondary to the fact that Arthur was embracing and reinforcing his new self. He had made an amazing effort, and he was cheering himself on to continue the most difficult thing he said he had ever accomplished, the thing that made him proudest about himself. As time went on, he stopped talking about his weight loss endlessly—although it

was still one of his favorite topics. As he toned it down somewhat, he actually became better at encouraging others, including his wife, to follow his example.

Summary: Rewards and Life

Psychologist Miles Cox and his colleagues summarized six factors that enabled people to "lead emotionally satisfying lives
without alcohol," and thus to sustain their recovery.[25] These
factors apply for all addictions.

1. Note more positive changes and fewer negative changes in
   their lives.
2. Express greater life satisfaction.
3. Develop substitute activities.
4. Have more nonalcoholic activities they enjoy.
5. Have fewer frustrations pursuing goals and deal more effectively with these.
6. Experience environmental changes that enhance their satisfaction with life.

This list summarizes how finding and enjoying new rewards,
and recognizing and appreciating the benefits you gain from
ceasing the addiction, are key to replacing addictive habits.

In the next chapter, we will focus on making sure that you
have, or can obtain, the resources in your environment so your
world provides the rewards you need to change.

■■■■■

Exercise: Reconsidering the Rewards of Your Addiction

List the *benefits* that you receive from your addictive behavior.
Think about the rewarding sensations and feelings you seek
from it, such as:

• It relaxes me or reduces anxiety.
• It feels as though I am taking care of myself.

- It gives me a sense of control over my feelings and my life.
- It makes me feel more attractive to others.
- It lessens my depression.
- It provides excitement or combats boredom.
- (Fill in your own.)

Now what are the negatives this habit is causing in your life?

- Legal problems
- Difficulties at work
- Health problems
- Disapproval of spouse, partner, family
- Financial problems
- Self-esteem problems
- (Fill in your own.)

Now think how the costs and benefits have shifted. Think about the benefits of your addiction when it first began, and compare these to the benefits that you seek now. How have your rewards shifted? Have they become more or less pleasure-oriented? Do you engage in your addictive activity in order to seek positive sensations or in order to drown out negative ones? Think now about how the costs have changed over time.

For every benefit of your addiction that you list, find three alternative ways you can gain these feelings, satisfactions, or experiences.

4

Resources: Identifying Strengths and Weaknesses, Developing Skills to Fill the Gaps

Overcoming addiction requires you to evaluate your strengths and weaknesses and to address your weaknesses effectively. This involves two related sets of activities. First, you need to assess what resources you already have and what resources you currently lack. Then you need to develop the skills that will allow you to expand your resources. Moreover, these skills themselves are critical in overcoming addiction.

Not all people are created equal in terms of kicking addictions. You might think, "Sure, I could lose weight if I had a personal trainer and chef like Oprah and those Hollywood stars." However, compared to someone else who can't afford a health club membership, you may be in a relatively good position to get in shape. Take someone working at a marginal job—say, a single mother who waitresses. What does she do during a break or following work in order to relax? Smoking seems like the cheapest, easiest relief she can turn to, while a better-off person might take an aerobics class.

The relationship between personal resources and addiction

was clearly demonstrated during the great cocaine surge of the seventies and early eighties. Several years after cocaine use became widespread, people started to announce that the drug was ruining their lives. Of course, not all cocaine users found the drug to be equally destructive.

In addition to managing the habit better, many stockbrokers, filmmakers, and other better-off people who did encounter problems were better able to kick their cocaine habits, whether or not they resorted to expensive treatment centers. This was not as true for many users in inner cities, where cocaine (and, later, crack) addiction continued to flourish throughout the eighties.[1] Yale psychiatrist David Musto commented on the disparity between the experiences of different groups in quitting cocaine:

> The question we must be asking now is not why people take drugs, but why do people stop. In the inner city, the factors that counterbalance drug use . . . often are not there. It is harder for people with nothing to say no to drugs.[2]

We know that being able to afford treatment at the Betty Ford Center is no guarantee of overcoming drug or alcohol addiction. Nor do wealthy people avoid other addictions. You might even say that they have more opportunities for an addiction like shopping. Hollywood stars also seem to have endless time for romantic entanglements, including self-deluding, short-lived love addictions. Nonetheless, research shows that the more resources people have and develop, the more likely they are to recover from addiction.[3]

Resources are not limited to money. Here are key assets in fighting an addiction:

- Intimacy and supportive relationships
  Marriage and family relationships
  Friendships, groups
- Employment and work resources
  Work skills and accomplishments

- Leisure activities
  Hobbies and interests
  Ways of relaxing
  Exercise routines
- Coping skills
  Practical skills
  Social skills
  Emotional resilience and ability to deal with stress

These personal assets are a better predictor of recovery than wealth. But how do you develop these resources if you don't already have them? Therapy can be helpful here.

Assessing Your Strengths and Resources

As I emphasize throughout this book, you probably already possess the basic resources required to overcome whatever destructive habit you may have. Take Chet, for example, a homeless alcoholic. One day he found himself in a shelter in an old school building. He began shooting baskets in the gym. It had been decades since Chet last played basketball, but he had actually been an excellent high school player who had gotten sidetracked from accepting the athletic scholarship to college he was offered.

A social worker saw Chet shooting baskets. She quickly rounded up some children in the shelter and asked Chet to organize a game. Chet took the opportunity to instruct the children in basic basketball skills. This began a long trajectory that ended with Chet quitting drinking and becoming a coach in a local athletic league.

When I spoke to Chet about his remarkable recovery, he described how coaching basketball reminded him of long-dormant abilities that he possessed. "I've been in treatment maybe a dozen times over the last decade and a half," he told me. "Each time they asked me about my arrests, divorces, previous treatment, et cetera. All that did was remind me of what

a failure I was. They really didn't need to do all that to determine that I was an alcoholic—I spent all day drinking from a
bottle in brown paper bag." But "in all those times in treatment, no one had bothered to discover that I had been an excellent basketball player." This resource proved to be the
foundation of Chet's recovery.

When Chet took stock of his strengths, he discovered that
he also had a gift for working with young people. Identifying
the resources that you already possess is a big part of the recovery process. The resources you command include not only
your abilities, but also the confidence you have gained from
your past accomplishments. Included in this background are
the disadvantages, setbacks, and crises you have overcome—including addictions. For example, if you have quit smoking—
the toughest drug addiction of all—shouldn't you be able to
lick just about anything? Likewise if you have lost weight.

Now look at your life and inventory your strengths. What
are your greatest accomplishments in life? What are you good
at? What do you enjoy doing? What do people like about you?
What big changes have you made in your life? What resources
do you have at your disposal? Some possible answers to these
questions are:

- I quit smoking.
- I am good at home repairs.
- I am well organized.
- I am smart with money.
- People like my friendliness.
- People turn to me in crises.
- I have always held a job.
- I have good relationships with my children.

These and other successes like them may seem like small triumphs. But none of these abilities can be taken for granted.
Some people desperately need to organize their lives. Many
need to learn how to deal with stress. Few people cannot ben-

efit from improving their communication skills, and some people have great difficulty communicating even their basic needs to other people. The fact that you're already gifted in any of these areas means that you are that much closer to beating the addiction or negative behavior that concerns you. Many people would envy your resources!

Let's Work from Here

In therapy, I spend a good deal of time exploring the resources and skills discussed in this chapter. When patients describe their strengths, I am often impressed by the depth and breadth of their abilities. Identifying existing resources can be energizing and inspiring. You, too, have strengths you should be proud of. However, I also recognize that people who come to me with an addiction problem need to expand their skills, or to generalize the abilities they possess to other parts of their lives.

Take the example of David, an older, successful businessman who came to see me because he couldn't free himself of a relationship with a younger woman who mistreated him. Although David's love relationship was in terrible shape, he had many resources to draw upon. Aside from his professional and financial successes, David had some years earlier quit smoking after decades of addiction. He described how every day when he came home from work, his young daughter had greeted him crying and saying, "Daddy, why are you killing yourself?"

David had discovered the strength to overcome a powerful nicotine addiction. However, he was unable to end an abusive relationship. During our sessions together, we examined the resources that had allowed David to quit smoking. He had confidence in his professional competency, and he had a loving relationship with his daughter. When I asked him what his daughter thought of his current relationship, he replied, "She detests it." We also focused on his pride in his business accomplishments, where he wasn't a person who let others take advantage of him. By building on his existing resources, most especially his pride and affection for his daughter, David was able to withdraw from his manipulative girlfriend.

If you are well organized, practical, or gifted at household repairs, then similar problem-solving abilities will work in other areas of your life. These abilities should inspire you with confidence and give you faith that you can accomplish more. Picture yourself in your most confidence-inspiring setting and try to maintain that confidence while working on the rest of your life. When you can see yourself in your best light, then you will be the most confident about combating your addiction.

As you chronicle your existing resources, you can at the same time assess your weaknesses. By appraising your skills, you highlight the ones that are missing. These are skills that you may need to develop in your effort to beat your addiction.

Developing the Essential Skills to Beat Addiction

Which of your coping skills require the most improvement? Which added skills would most assist you in combating your addiction? We can identify the skills that have been found to be most critical to the recovery process. These include *social skills*, which enable you to deal with people and life (communication, problem solving, and being alone); *managing emotions*, dealing with the emotional states that drive you to resort to addictions; and *resisting urges*, dealing with impulses to turn to cigarettes, food, shopping, or other harmful habitual responses when faced with stressful situations. Even after people have been clean for a time, they need to learn how to break the cycle that compels them to resort to their habit. The skills needed to interrupt this cascading series of events are collectively labeled *relapse prevention*.

In sum, essential skills for escaping/avoiding addiction are:

- Communication
- Problem solving

- Independence/being alone
- Managing negative emotions
- Resisting urges
- Relapse prevention (breaking the flow of destructive behavior)

The Community Reinforcement Approach

As I have indicated, treatment is often not necessary to overcome an addiction. Yet some treatments (such as Motivational Interviewing and Brief Interventions) are far more effective on average than others. This is because these treatments tie into natural recovery processes, mobilizing the life skills and resources most helpful for achieving remission from addiction. Since we are concerned with addiction remedies that actually work, I introduce here one of the treatments that has demonstrated the most success in fighting addiction, called the Community Reinforcement Approach (CRA). An evaluation of studies of alcoholism treatment outcomes by Stanford health psychologists John Finney and Susanne Monahan ranked CRA as the most effective program for treating alcoholism.[4] CRA succeeds because it examines the role of alcoholics' drinking in the context of their overall lives, and addresses each component of these individuals' worlds by teaching needed skills and assisting with other resources.[5]

CRA is distinctive as therapy in that it is oriented primarily toward training alcoholics to cope with their natural environments. The therapy program begins with two crucial exercises: completing the Happiness Scale and the Goals of Counseling. The Happiness Scale asks clients how they would rate their contentment on ten factors in their lives—drinking, job/education, money, social life, personal habits, marital/family relations, legal matters, emotional state, communication, and overall happiness. The Goals of Counseling then target specific improvements in the areas identified as problems, and develop plans for achieving them. Thus, from the start, CRA's method for pursuing sobriety is to improve the individual's ability to function in the real world.

CRA seeks to identify problem spots in addicts' lives and turn these liabilities into resources for the person's recovery. When addicts change how they deal with core life elements—such as their work, their family, and their leisure time—they succeed at avoiding their addictions. CRA thus modifies a person's environment so that it reinforces and supports sobriety.

CRA comes into play at many points in this chapter. The elements of CRA (in addition to the Happiness Scale and Goals of Counseling) are (1) identifying addiction triggers, (2) a job club, (3) marriage/relationship counseling, (4) recreational planning, (5) skills training, (6) resisting urges, and (7) relapse prevention—all of which we deal with in this and the next chapter.*

That the combination of these elements is so successful with severely alcoholic individuals is an indication that addressing these factors in your own life will be helpful. And, in fact, utilizing this efficacy, psychologists have begun to apply CRA in new settings. For example, one research group administered CRA to a group of homeless alcoholics, comparing it with a homeless shelter's standard treatment (AA and twelve-step counselors). CRA proved far superior in reducing drinking among this population, a very difficult one to help.[6]

CRA has been applied to other drugs in addition to alcohol. We discussed in the last chapter the success of Stephen Higgins and his colleagues at the University of Vermont in rewarding abstinence among cocaine addicts with vouchers that could be traded for goods and services. As we noted, the problem is that such experimenter-provided vouchers are the antithesis of real-world rewards. As a result, the Higgins team also employs a CRA component in their treatment. In research

---

* CRA also sometimes includes the use of Antabuse (disulfiram), which makes drinkers nauseous when they consume alcohol. The alcoholic's partner makes sure that he or she takes the drug as scheduled.

geared to assess the added benefits from CRA for cocaine addicts, the researchers found it further reduced cocaine use during treatment and led to better functioning following the treatment period.[7]

Addictive Situations

Before turning to skills themselves, it is valuable to conduct a situational analysis of your addiction—that is, to seek to identify the circumstances in your life that cause you to resort to that habitual response. These are your environmental triggers. We described such a situational analysis in the preceding chapter as a way of understanding the function your addiction serves. CRA begins with such a functional analysis. This involves asking a set of questions to determine which situations leave you vulnerable to your destructive habit. These include both external events and internal emotional states.

For example, do you frequently turn to your addiction after a fight with your spouse? Is a bad day at work, or being angry with your boss, an addictive precursor? Is loneliness the main trigger for your excesses? Just as certain work situations drive people to drink, to overeat, or to gamble, some after-work situations take a predictable negative route. Some social groups may encourage your addiction, leading you to settings and activities where that behavior is most likely to occur. Being aware of your triggers and planning ahead to deal with them enables you to minimize your exposure to harmful settings, and to control your reactions when you are exposed to unavoidable triggers.

With a recognition of these triggers in mind, let's review the range of coping skills you will need to utilize.[8]

Communication

Communication is the building block of professional and personal relationships. In these and other arenas, you need to take in information and present information to others. You need to feel secure enough to listen to things that may be unpleasant, without shutting off or striking out at the messenger. When presenting information to others, you need to want honestly to convey concrete information, rather than to put the other person down or make yourself feel good.

An inability to allow genuine feedback from one's partner is a trait of relationships with problems; often it accompanies substance or spousal abuse. To take one well-known example, John Lennon was dominated by his wife, Yoko Ono. Albert Goldman's biography *The Lives of John Lennon* described how Lennon, when he drank, verbally abused Ono. He took advantage of his intoxication in this way because he had no way to communicate his discontents ordinarily.

This in no way justifies Lennon's, or anyone else's, abuse of a spouse. But it does suggest a way around it. Learning effective communication techniques (including between partners in a couple) is a critical element in resolving addiction. Take Ed, whose drinking was fueled by his feeling that his wife did not provide for his needs at home. This, of course, could be more or less true. But when Ed learned to express in a reasonable way that he wanted a meal prepared when he got home from work, his wife was better able—and more likely—to respond positively. At the same time, of course, a better communication process allowed Ed's wife to make reasonable demands, one of which was that Ed not retreat to the sofa to drink throughout the night.

Communication skills can be taught, and you can improve them on your own. In order to communicate effectively, you must first create a positive tone. Point out positive things your partner is doing, perhaps in response to requests you previously made. Next, identify the specific problem concerning you. Don't make global criticisms, but describe how the problem affects or bothers you. Then solicit the other person's reactions. Try to imagine how the other person feels. Acknowledge how your actions feed into the problem. Ask for ways that you can help your partner to change.

GIVING AND RECEIVING FEEDBACK

1. Create a positive tone—point out a positive action by your partner.
2. Identify a specific problem rather than making global criticisms.
3. Describe how the problem affects or bothers you.
4. Solicit the other person's reaction; try to imagine exactly how he or she feels.
5. Acknowledge how your actions feed into the problem.
6. Ask for ways you can change to help your partner change.

The same communication principles apply to marital communications, those between parents and children, and those with other relatives or coworkers.

Problem Solving

Addicts are characterized by their negative outlooks; they experience life as a series of problems that they are unable to cope with. They panic, or feel depressed due to their hopelessness, and turn to their addiction as a way of coping with these negative feelings. If you don't feel up to meeting life's challenges, you may rely on drugs, food, or sex as a way to anesthetize yourself against anticipated failure.

In place of this defeatism, which contributes to the failures that you anticipate, you can learn methods of coping with problems. The essential ingredient in problem management is remaining calm and sensible. You must gain confidence that you will be able to deal reasonably with the problem. This does not mean you can always reach a perfect resolution. It does not mean that the problem will disappear. It *does* mean that you feel capable of coming up with a reasonable response. This is inspiring rather than depressing—depression is the condition that results from believing you have no avenues open to you when a problem arises.

The first step in problem solving is to identify the problem—framing it in manageable terms, so that it does not seem overwhelming and frightening. Don't let self-criticism ("I always end up in this situation") or self-defeating thoughts ("I'm not strong enough to deal with this") demoralize you. Rather, focus your thinking in a positive direction. You may say to yourself, "The last time I got into this situation, I had no idea how to deal with it. Now I have experienced and dealt with it, and understand what to do. I know I can get through this successfully."

Problems, of course, come in all sizes. Not having money to pay a bill is one problem. Having a water heater break is another. As unpleasant as these are, they are limited and you can address them specifically. Having a problem with your boss or spouse is a larger problem, one that will involve more extended thinking and changes on your part. Getting divorced, moving, or having a child with emotional problems—even quitting an addiction—are larger problems still that engage all of yourself and your life.

Making a problem manageable so that you can tackle it can mean breaking a larger problem into component parts. If you are leaving a relationship, for example, you have to see to your emotional well-being, find a place to live, find new companionship, and arrange a number of other parts of your life. Thinking globally that your life as you know it is over is not a good starting point for tackling these issues.

With a good fix on your problem, you can begin to seek out needed information and evaluate possible options. There is a desirable midpoint between deciding precipitously without acquiring enough information or considering enough reasonable options (called premature closure) and not being able actually to make a necessary decision. After selecting an option, your goal is to commit yourself to the course of action while simultaneously being open to feedback about whether that course of action is workable and successful. Finally, keep in mind your growing body of success at solving problems, a ré-

sumé that you will lengthen each time you apply this structured approach.

TEMPLATE FOR PROBLEM SOLVING

1. Identify the nature and scope of the problem.
2. Speak positively to yourself about your ability to cope.
3. Frame the challenge in manageable terms (i.e., identify specific steps to take).
4. Gather information and review options for responding.
5. Evaluate success and decide whether to continue or to change
   your approach.
6. Make your constructive approach to problem solving a habit.
7. Relish your success at dealing with challenges—you are a
   problem solver!

One man who had been hospitalized for alcoholism returned home to find his wife had moved them to a new apartment during his treatment. Opening the door, he confronted
an empty apartment with boxes piled willy-nilly throughout
the space. The man promptly went on a bender. This is one example of a habitual dysfunctional response to problems. Even
people who never go out drinking may do something equally
irrational and unhelpful, such as yelling at loved ones, when
faced with a stressful situation.

We have spoken about identifying triggers for your addiction, some of which are everyday and predictable. But others
are more unpredictable and often involve problem solving.
What will you do the next time your ex-wife refuses you the
chance to visit with your kids, or when a friend you rely on lets
you down? What about when you come up short on your
monthly expenses, or needed freelance work is not coming in?
What will you do after a fight with your spouse or child? There
are more productive alternatives than the addictive choices
you have relied on—alternatives you are able to prepare for in
your mind and to practice with each opportunity that arises.

Longer-term problems, in turn, involve greater efforts at developing coping strategies. When Joan faced problems at an unrewarding job, she went shopping. Naturally, this exacerbated the financial problems that contributed to her depression and discouragement. Joan sought a financial consultant to help her put her finances in order. But Joan had been avoiding the recognition that her problems and bad feelings at work were essential to her unhealthy shopping.

Thus, part of her effort to control her spending was for Joan to think realistically about her job situation. This included (1) negotiating a better situation at work, (2) seeking further training to increase her marketability, and (3) looking around for a new job. Even before this paid off in a better position, Joan began to feel that she was dealing effectively with her situation and that things would come out right. This is an example of self-efficacy. The feeling of being able to respond to problems is extremely rewarding and a powerful tool for change.

It is important to realize that the goal of developing problem-solving and other skills is not to eliminate life problems. That simply can't be done in normal existences, and the effort to escape all stressful encounters is in itself a motive for addiction. You need to recognize that stress and problems are a part of life that you will have to accept and cope with. The goal is to be better prepared for the problems and stress you will encounter.

Independence and Being Alone

Addiction is nearly always tied to relationship problems, to the absence of or search for intimacy and companionship. On one hand, you are most likely to turn to addictions when you are lonely and bored. On the other hand, loneliness may drive you to seek out the company of others, even if they have a negative impact on your life. When people are alone, they turn to every type of compensatory excess: drugs, alcohol, shopping, eating, TV, gambling, and so on. In order to avoid being alone, they will tag along with any group that will accept them, even if they have to indulge in destructive behavior in order to prove their membership in the group.

Thus, if you are seeking to curb an addiction, you need to learn how to spend time by yourself constructively, without desperation. This ability, in turn, requires several skills or resources. For example, in order to enjoy spending time alone, you must learn to calm yourself down, rather than look to other people to calm you. The skills to achieve calmness can be found through a number of approaches, such as yoga, meditation, and other relaxation or centering techniques. If you are not into developing techniques for being alone, then engage in ordinary positive activities such as walking, exercising, reading, selected television viewing (recognizing that using television as your main companion is itself addictive), hobbies, and writing letters or e-mails to real people in your life.

In addition to the skill of relaxing and centering yourself, you need certain resources, without which it is not possible to maintain an independent, self-respecting life. These independence-supporting resources include structure, interests, healthfulness, and contentment. Structure means having a full life—a place to stay and prepare meals, a routine for working and making a living, a family or other people to live or be with, places to go and social companionship for your recreational time. Each of these, of course, can be a large matter in itself. The Community Reinforcement Approach offers help to people who sometimes lack the most basic resources—for example, offering a job club to help people find work and a social club to give them a place to go where they can socialize without drinking.

As you develop these basic life resources, you will be better able to spend time alone and to select your company on a more positive basis. As part of these developments, you may also address your health. This includes regulating your meals, engaging in regular physical activity, sleeping enough (but making sure you are tired and relaxed enough to sleep well), and so on.

Finally, seeing yourself as someone with a respectable and responsible life, one that you can look at with pride, is fundamental to your self-esteem. Your confidence that you have created a reasonable, positive life for yourself will strengthen you even as you seek further fulfillment and larger satisfactions in life.

Dealing with Negative Emotions

Addictive behavior is often triggered by a negative event that leads to depression, anxiety, or anger. These negative events are bound to occur from time to time in any person's life, but they do not have to lead to harmful behavior. Your ability to deal with emotional upsets in a healthy, functional way is critical to eliminating addiction. Psychologists have developed therapeutic techniques to deal with emotions such as anger, anxiety, and depression. These techniques (called cognitive-behavioral therapy) involve changing the way that you think about and react to an emotion-arousing occurrence.[9]

Dealing with things that set you off emotionally is a subset of problem solving and resembles that process. The first step is to identify predictable situations that create the negative emotions with which you must cope. Does being with certain people always make you feel rejected or negative about yourself? Do certain situations always lead to arguments and anger with your spouse? Do you always have a negative reaction when a certain coworker tries to one-up you or an acquaintance jokingly puts you down? Do you drink or overeat when you have had a difficult day at work, or when you are lonely and bored? To be forewarned about these situations is to be forearmed.

In coming to grips with emotions, people are sometimes slow to identify what they are feeling at a given moment. People may need help in identifying the signs that they are becoming angry. For example, your anger may begin whenever you start feeling frustrated or slighted by others. The anger may begin as a sense of discomfort or irritation. When you can recognize these cues, you develop an early warning signal to your own emotions. The next step is to get a handle on these emotions, which can escalate rapidly.

With an emotional reaction, reframing—changing how you think about an event—is critical. Reframing in this case means defusing your immediate emotional reaction by casting it in a different light. Simply remembering that you have had strong emotional reactions before that have been unwarranted is a good habit of thought to develop. For example, when you are angered by the actions of a family member, you can keep in mind that you have responded emotionally before and gotten over it, because you realize this person loves you and is not intentionally trying to hurt you. You might say to yourself, "It's just his way of dealing with his stress—it has nothing to do with me." By activating this thinking as soon as an emotion-arousing event occurs, you can sidestep your emotional upset and avoid lashing out.

Once you have reframed the emotional event, you can then develop a new pattern for dealing with it. Rather than expressing uncontrolled anger or turning on your heel and storming out, you can develop various ways to bide your time until your anger subsides and you are in a better place to respond. This may mean simply counting to ten, or else standing in place with a smile (if someone asks you what you are doing, tell them, "I am thinking"). Or if this is too much for you to accomplish, simply say, "I am not prepared to deal with this now," and leave the situation, although try not to seem angry as you do so.

Changing your initial reactions as much as possible is followed by deeper changes in coping with your feelings and the things that set them off. Since these often involve people, such changes call into play your communication skills. That is, if a coworker or family member regularly makes you feel bad with comments that you interpret as put-downs, take a moment with that person to describe how such comments make you feel, and ask the person please not to say those things.

In addition to addressing the sources of your anger, where possible, you need to find new outlets for venting your feelings more constructively. What else could you do to let off steam after a difficult day at work or being angered by a coworker? Physical activity is one ready alternative. You could go to the gym or do a relaxation exercise. When you are bored, you can make taking a walk your patterned response. You are then killing two birds at once—dealing with feelings and gaining physical fitness.

Now that you have started to develop alternative ways of dealing with stress, anger, and other negative feelings, you can examine your coping strategies in a calm, rational way. What coping strategies have worked for you? What kinds of negative emotions are still limiting your recovery process? Research has shown that cognitive-behavioral therapies that attack problems in this way can be as effective as medications (for example, in treating depression).[10] The longer you practice your new approach to managing your emotions, the more effective this process will become. While the uplifting effect of drugs diminishes over time, your coping skills will continue to grow as you practice your ability to deal with yourself in trying situations.

TOOLS FOR DEALING WITH EMOTIONAL UPSET

1. Identify situations that trigger angry, depressed, or bored feelings.
   • *Prepare for or avoid such situations.*
2. Reframe these events to defuse your emotional reactions to them.
   • *Change how you view and label an event so it is less upset-*

ting: e.g., "He is not attacking me, but is venting his own stress."

3. Develop ways to delay or avoid an emotional reaction.
   - *Count to ten.*
   - *Employ a relaxation technique.*
   - *Leave the room (where the situation permits).*
4. Develop and review techniques for addressing your upset.
   - *Speak clearly and unemotionally to the person upsetting you.*
   - *Be clear in your mind that it is the other person's problem.*
   - *Leave the situation with dignity and pride.*
5. Find a technique to help when a person you deal with regularly is the source of the upset.
   - *Ask the person please not to act that way in the future.*
   - *Stay away from the upsetting person or provocative situation.*

Frank had recovered substantially from his chronic alcoholism, to a point where he typically went on brief binges only a couple of times a year. Each of these binges was prompted by his first becoming upset with his boss. Frank would usually try to call his wife first, but when she was unavailable, Frank's next stop was his favorite bar. He resolved not to drink when he went, and sometimes he didn't. Unfortunately, sometimes he did.

In therapy, Frank practiced saying calmly that he wished his boss would simply let Frank know what was bothering him. But it would make Frank too dependent on his boss's tempestuous nature to hook his own sobriety solely to the other man's ability to control his emotions. Thus Frank learned not to take his boss's brusqueness toward him personally. He was able to recognize, and incorporate into his reaction, that his boss's yelling was a temporary storm and would quickly pass. In addition, Frank had to develop venues other than his old bar haunts to resort to for comfort when his wife was not available.

Resisting Urges

There are many different ways to resist addictive urges. In one study, psychologist Saul Shiffman studied the techniques to resist cravings for tobacco by people who had overcome nicotine addictions.[11] He classified these techniques into three different approaches: cognitive, behavioral, and social. People utilizing each approach all managed to resist addictive urges, but each group did so in its own way.

For example, people with a cognitive approach thought through the negative consequences of their addiction. They thought through the positive benefits of quitting (as we described in the last chapter). They used techniques such as willpower, distracting thoughts, and delayed gratification to resist the addictive impulse.

Similarly, people with a behavioral approach resisted the addictive impulse by eating or drinking something else. They also turned to relaxation techniques, physical activity, and distracting or delaying activities to shore up their resistance.

In the third category, people with a social approach turned to others for support and took themselves out of harmful settings in order to resist addiction.

Shiffman discovered that each of these techniques for resisting the urge to smoke was equally effective. In fact, the only technique that he found to be ineffective was self-punitive thinking. Getting down on yourself for things you did or did not do was simply no help. But any kind of can-do approach—be it cognitive, behavioral, or social—worked to shore up resistance. In other words, any technique that appeals to you can be effective, so long as the technique is empowering and not self-denigrating.

Techniques for Resisting Urges to Resume Smoking

Cognitive	Behavioral	Social
Thinking of the positive consequences of quitting	Eating or drinking something else	Seeking social support
Thinking of the negative consequences of using	Physical activity, exercise	Escaping the situation
Willpower (no specific thoughts)	Relaxation	
Distracting thoughts	Selecting a distracting activity	
Delay ("I'll hold off")	Selecting a delaying activity	

Breaking the Flow: Relapse Prevention

Addiction, like many other problems in life, is often cumulative. That is, after an initial misstep, you become a victim of your own inertia. In an effort to recoup your losses, you repeat the behavior, but the more you resort to the addictive behavior, the more slippery the slope becomes. One clear example, of course, is gambling, where "throwing good money after bad" literally describes what you are doing. But the same is true for all addictions.

I once attended an alcohol support group where a woman described how a series of quick decisions ruined her life. Although she had not had a drink in six years, she ended up at a bar. She had a drink. She drank too much and became drunk. She got in her car and drove. She was stopped by the police and arrested. She lost her license. Unable to drive, she lost her job. Her husband then divorced her.

This woman portrayed her eventual decline as the inevitable result of her first misstep. But the truth is that at any point she could have exited from the cascade of disasters. She could, of course, have avoided the bar. She could have sat at the bar but had a soft drink. She could have gone to the bar, had one drink, and then gone home. She could even have gotten drunk but then taken a cab home from the bar. She could have developed an alternative transportation plan to get herself to work.

It is important to recognize your own power in fighting addiction. Stopping the momentum toward addiction is a teachable skill called "relapse prevention."[12] Relapse is not an unfortunate event that happens to you; it is a series of bad choices that you make. Components of relapse prevention include skills we have already reviewed, such as identifying and preparing for (or avoiding) high-risk situations—those in which you know you are likely to engage in the behavior you wish to cease. It involves developing alternative responses to situations you cannot avoid that cause you stress and that lead to other negative emotions.

Relapse prevention means developing backups to abstinence. The key is to realize that even if you slip, you do not have to descend in a free fall to a complete relapse. This can be the problem with a confrontational, abstinence-only approach. If there is no tolerance for a slip or mistake, your feeling is likely to be that you might as well go all the way after one mistake—no distinction is made between having a beer, getting rip-roaring drunk, or going on a weeklong bender. In addition, since even a small slip is viewed in such a negative light, your bad feelings about the slip magnify the transgression, adding guilt to the bad effects of your relapse.

Virtually no recovered addicts resist the urge to engage in their addiction for the rest of their lives. But a slip should not drive you to abandon all restraint. The alternative is to recognize you have the ability to immediately regain control after a slip: "I just mistakenly had a drink (or even several); I will resume my abstinence." If you are a food addict (compulsive eater) and eat a whole bag of chips, you should not take this as a signal to go ahead and binge for the rest of the day, week, or month. Or if you are a shopping addict and you bought an item that you didn't need, this should not cause you to drop the restraints you have learned and go on a full-blown shopping spree.

Your emotional and practical planning are the keys to avoiding these further steps to all-out binges. First, try not to get so down on yourself that further excess becomes your only refuge from self-loathing and despair. Second, whenever you feel yourself sliding out of control, remember that you have a choice. If you wish to escape, then you *can* pull yourself out of the maelstrom. You probably already realize these things, at least in part. Even the woman who drove drunk and lost her job was attending a group to assist her in avoiding future drinking. Thus she had avoided the last and worst step in her series of mishaps—resuming her alcoholism.

I always tell clients, "You are about to make your worst mistake." In other words, whatever has come before—and I mean *whatever*—you can always make your problem worse. This is a good reason to stop now. If you have done damage to your health, then it's time to give your body a break. If you have caused pain to a loved one, you can apologize. Even if you have committed a crime, you have options available to you—for example, getting good legal representation and taking responsibility for your actions.

Alarming as it may initially sound, knowing that your worst decision always lies ahead is actually a reassuring notion. It means that in the midst of a problem you can rescue yourself. Things are not as bad as they can seem when you are in the middle of them. It is your repulsion toward what you have already done, and the panic this engenders, that blind you to solutions. You have the ability to apply the brakes and avoid relapse.

The Community Reinforcement Approach Revisited

Throughout this chapter we have identified skills that will help you to beat addiction. In order to overcome your problems, you need to learn how to communicate, how to be alone, how to deal with negative emotions, and so forth. However, it is important to recognize that none of these skills exists in a vacuum. The reason you want to develop skills is so that you can use them to garner more resources, such as healthy relationships and intimacy, rewarding work, and a stronger sense of self. These resources, in turn, will allow you to resist addiction in the future.

As we have seen, the Community Reinforcement Approach incorporates a functional analysis of the place of an addiction in a person's life. Certain work situations drive people to drink, to overeat, or to gamble, just as some after-work situations take a predictable negative route. Some family conflicts regularly lead to addictive reactions. Beyond enabling alcoholics and addicts to recognize and avoid these triggers, and offering training in skills to counteract them, CRA provides further antiaddiction resources in every facet of a person's life. For example, CRA organizes job clubs to teach addicts to find work and to avoid job-related triggers to an addiction. CRA programs also provide antiaddiction resources in the addict's recreational life.

In the next chapter, when we turn to social supports, we will examine CRA's approach to converting the addict's primary relationships into a support network for helping an individual progress out of addiction.

CRA's Job Club, Work, and You

CRA programs include job clubs run by a trained therapist, because unemployment is often a key to alcoholism. CRA clients are taught to develop a résumé, get job leads, complete job applications, make phone inquiries and follow-ups, and go for job interviews. In situations where the subject already has a job, a CRA or other counselor may help patients to identify work situations that place them at risk to return to substance abuse. The therapist then counsels the patient about avoiding such trigger events or finding new ways to respond to them. For example, many addicts have a hard time when jobs take them away from home, creating dangerous loneliness. Counselors can then work with these individuals to cope with such travel, or even to find different work.

If you are employed already, it makes sense to deal with issues of work satisfaction, developing the skills to get ahead in your organization. Progress in your career is antiaddictive. Striving to accomplish professional goals—including furthering your training and education—can help you to resist addictive impulses.

With that said, since work stress is a significant contributor to addiction, you need also to reduce pressure by resolving the conflicts and difficulties that you face at work. You should not, for example, take on an overwhelming level of responsibility for which you are not prepared, and when your job consistently demands that you do, you should attempt to renegotiate your responsibilities, ask for more support, or else seek new work.

Most people encounter work problems at one time or another, and sometimes these difficulties translate into addictive problems. One patient of mine, Sue, was a highly trained technical worker in the computer software industry. She was widely recognized for her skills in technical support. However, Sue constantly found herself clashing with coworkers because she felt that they skipped necessary steps in developing projects, only to rely on her to bail them out in the end.

Sue never found that people's reliance on her technical expertise translated into social popularity. She was frequently distressed to learn that her coworkers had organized some function outside of work to which she had not been invited. Over time Sue found herself increasingly depressed, and she began to rely on food and pills to offset her bad feelings. Sue's goals in therapy were twofold. She worked to lower her high standards, or at least the unforgiving way in which she communicated them to coworkers, so that she could have better relations with her colleagues. At the same time, she developed alternative sources of emotional support—family, friends, and eventually a spouse—rather than expect that work was going to fulfill her need to be appreciated.

Popular mythology suggests that successful people are unhappy. In reality, people with better jobs have more control over their lives and thus have greater opportunities to do something about any unhappiness they experience. Sue, for instance, had a realistic opportunity to address her addictive behavior because she had professional skills, a work ethic, a long-term job, financial security, and a problem-solving mentality that she could apply to her feelings and personal situation. By developing your work and career skills, you are usually also developing skills that can be used to counteract addiction.

Leisure Planning

Although work stress often contributes to addiction, most people indulge in their addictive behavior during their leisure time. Some social groups may encourage your addiction, leading you to settings and activities in which your addictive behavior is most likely to occur. Other social settings can reliably provide a healthy, supportive environment. Selecting, even creating, such positive groups for yourself is a topic in the following chapter.

CRA programs provide hospitalized and homeless addicts with a social club. These clubs offer social activities during weekend nights, times when patients are most likely to turn to alcohol or drugs or to get together with people and in places where these substances are consumed. If you are not in a CRA progam, you will not have a social club organized for you. But you probably have more options of your own than CRA alcoholics for finding social activities with people not involved in your addictions—for example, by attending church, joining clubs with people who share similar interests, even going to a pub (if the company is pleasant and drinking is not your problem). You are led to companionship by your interests, positive things you like to do and which contribute to your life and to others.

In addition to such support, you can anticipate leisure activities and locales likely to trigger your addiction. For example, a husband's basement den may be where he typically engages in excessive drinking. Puttering around the kitchen while preparing dinner may lead a woman to overeat. Other recreational triggers are linked to certain times of the year. For example, holidays may make you feel lonely, depressed, or left out of the festivities, thus driving you toward your addictive behavior. Robert Downey Jr.'s highly publicized relapse while he was working on the television series *Ally McBeal* occurred when the divorced actor was separated from his son and spent Thanksgiving by himself in glitzy Palm Springs.

Even when your addictive episodes fall considerably short of Downey's all-out binges, a similar type of social and recreational planning will help you fight your addiction. Start out by reviewing your typical day, both during and after work. Identify the situations in which you are most likely to resort to your problem behavior. Then devise alternative ways of filling this time. For example, if late in the afternoon you feel a letdown that you typically fill with something you regret—a smoke, a snack, perhaps a drink—you can simply accept that you are not going to be productive at that time. With this acceptance, you can then program something that is not self-destructive in the time slot. For larger periods of recreational time, explore resources in your community and among your repertoire of interests to fill voids.

Life's Long Journey

The recommendations and cases in this chapter (and throughout the book) often make it seem as though people power through their self-cure or therapy for addiction. This is rarely the case. A footnote in the introduction informed you that placebo was as good as nicotine patches in therapy for smoking cessation, but that each resulted in conclusive abstinence in only about 5 percent of cases. Yet half or more of people who have ever been addicted to tobacco have now ceased smoking. The fact is that, on any given occasion, most people fail to quit, even when they deeply want to. Addiction, and its reversal, is a lifetime process.

More typical than Ozzie's case of momentous and instant cure is the story of Paula, a musician who led a peripatetic professional and personal existence for much of her early life. It took Paula years to build up her smoking addiction, hanging around with fellow musicians. At one point, after smoking for several years, she visited a friend on a farm and stopped smoking without difficulty for two months. At the time she thought, "This shows I'm not really addicted!" After several more years of smoking, she realized she was in fact addicted, but she did not want to quit. Cigarettes were a reassuring companion accompanying her through the trials of establishing herself as a musician.

Prompted by a friend's death from lung cancer, however, Paula began attempting to quit in her forties. By this time, so few of the professional people she knew smoked that it no longer was any benefit to her work relationships. Now she had to sneak her cigarettes, or seek out one of her few remaining fellow tobacco addicts to smoke with. Paula finally achieved a position in a reputable orchestra and was able to set up a stable existence; she now felt she was in a position to quit.

Paula considered entering a smoking cessation program but found she wasn't able to commit herself to participating in such a group. It just wasn't her. Finally, when she developed bronchitis one winter, Paula stopped out of necessity (although others certainly continue to smoke when ill). She managed to extend this period of abstinence after she recovered from her illness.

Facing life without cigarettes, Paula realized that smoking had served a number of functions. For one thing, it compensated for stresses or failures in her career. She also realized that she smoked as a way to avoid working through conflicts with people, including the man she was living with at the time. One day after an argument she walked outside, realized she wanted to smoke, and was depressed that she couldn't. Paula was already abstaining from cigarettes, but thinking of the negative function it served in her personal life affirmed Paula's decision to quit permanently. It also made her work on her ability to express her needs directly to others.

Only at this point did she seek the help of a behavior modification therapist. Paula attended only two sessions with this therapist, but he gave her what Paula felt was the best tool she had in maintaining her abstinence when he said, "People know when they're ready to stop." Paula felt she knew that now. The therapist also suggested running as a replacement activity, which Paula took up. She realized that when you make one decision to change your life, you find you're able to make others as well.

After the death of a friend, considering quitting for a long time, and actually ceasing smoking, Paula was able to make not smoking a pillar of her existence, along with the running, which she initiated partly to replace smoking. What enabled her to do so was the natural evolution of her resources in life, including career success, a secure life structure and personal calm, and her development of critical relationship skills.

Paula had matured, and smoking cessation went hand in hand with her "being kind to myself." Although she felt she was still developing musically, Paula also no longer felt like a novice trying to prove herself. She had not completed her life's journey—far from it. But she had arrived at the point where she could—almost had to—quit. These additional considerations— dealing with others in your life, achieving maturity and psychological security, creating a new self-image and a nonaddict identity, and pursuing and achieving career and other larger life goals—are the topics of the remaining chapters in this book.

5

Support: Getting Help from Those Nearest You

Human beings are social animals. Our peers and intimates have an enormous impact on our perspectives and our behavior. We learn much from our parents and the groups we grow up among; we act consistently with the people we associate with; we respond—in both positive and negative ways—to those we are intimate and live with. This is true about drugs and alcohol, eating and fitness, and other addictive behaviors as much as it is in any other area of our lives.

Parental and peer group attitudes extend to what people expect from alcohol, drugs, and food and how they learn to rely on these substances. If you learn to invest these substances with an exaggerated power to affect how you feel about yourself, and to control you and your behavior, you are on the path to wrestling with this substance perhaps for as long as you live. If, on the other hand, you learn to look at the experience as one that you can manage, then you are more likely to internalize the mechanisms to control it.

The process of learning from others is called "social learning," or "social influence." Its critical importance is one of the fundamental realities that contradict the disease view of addiction. That is, accepting the social sources of control and excess means that people's biological reactions are *not* the root of addiction to alcohol, drugs, or food. And if social influence is the most powerful determinant of reactions to drugs and other addictive sensations or experiences, then it can also be the most powerful tool for preventing or recovering from these addictions. Social learning can also be used to teach your children how to avoid addictive behavior from the start.

There are many ways in which people can help you to change addictive behavior. One well-known technique for harnessing the power of groups against an addiction is to join a support group, such as AA, Moderation Management, or SMART Recovery, or a support group for partners of alcoholics, such as Al-Anon.

But even without joining such a group, you can enlist others to help motivate and support change. You may choose to associate with people who don't engage in the activity or who do so in a moderate way. You can internalize the urgings of people close to you who wish the best for you and want you to change. You can also use techniques for getting others to internalize your desire that *they* change. And you can find ways to work together with your partner so that you both can change.

How You Learn Addiction

People often learn very early in life strong predispositions toward use of substances such as alcohol. One area of psychological research concerns people's expectations about the effects of drinking, called "alcohol expectancies." Quite young children, even before they drink, have very clear expectations about what alcohol does. And these alcohol expectancies subsequently influence how they experience the actual effects of drinking and the style of drinking they adopt. When people believe alcohol to have a large, powerful impact, both positive and negative, they are far more likely to be susceptible to problematic and alcoholic drinking.[1]

Alcoholics, many of whom come from homes where drinking has been a problem, often talk about the first great rush they got when they drank. For example, Cathleen Brooks, who was president of the National Association for Children of Alcoholics, described her first drink (at age eleven) in euphoric terms: "I remember the warmth, I remember the well-being."[2] But this more likely reflects what she had seen or been taught than what her body inherited.

Where do alcohol expectancies come from? Among the influences are the cultural groups to which people belong, the people with whom they associate (peer groups), and their parents. A quick summary of this phenomenon is that if the people you know—including parents, extended family and community, and friends and peers—view and use a substance in a certain way, you are likely to view and use it the same way.

This is true of alcohol, of food, and even more so of drugs. This is because there is no legitimate education into drug use—you pick it up from those who show you how to use a drug. A classic work of sociology, Howard Becker's *The Outsiders*, studied groups of marijuana users in the 1950s, before use of the drug became widespread. Since the sensations produced by the drug were so novel, users looked to the smokers who initiated them to know they were high, to find out how to act when they were stoned, and even to learn why the experience was enjoyable!

We have all witnessed the effect of social interaction and influence on substance use, intoxication, and addiction. You know, for instance, that when you are with certain friends you are more likely to do things you regret, like overeating, smoking, or drinking too much. You know that you behave differently when you are with other friends who either don't indulge in these behaviors at all or do so moderately.

Social Influences, Children, and Addiction

The social nature of substance use and abuse is demonstrated by the social groups that affect children. When people think about social groups, they often focus on peers. These are important influences, and children who end up in high-risk groups isolated from the mainstream of their peers are primed for a range of high-risk and self-defeating behavior.

But children and adolescents are also influenced by their cultural groups of origin in ways that sometimes surprise us.[3] As we noted in Chapter 1, drinking is part of early family experiences in some cultures. In many Jewish, Italian, and Chinese families, drinking is shared by family members of all ages, and respectful, controlled drinking is an inviolable rule. In these environments, young people learn that alcohol is neither a magical potion that can suddenly transform them and their behavior nor an excuse or signal to lose control and misbehave toward others.

Other cultural groups are not favored by such traditional advantages in dealing with alcohol. For example, Harvard psychiatrist George Vaillant continued a study of Boston teens that tracked them for fifty years.[4] These youths, who grew to middle and old age under the eyes of researchers, included many from two ethnic groups—one of which Vaillant termed Mediterranean (primarily Italians, but also Greeks and Jews), the other being Irish Americans.

There were remarkable differences in how these groups drank. Over the five decades they were studied, seven times as many Irish as Mediterranean Americans became alcohol-dependent (alcoholic). Yet a higher percentage of Vaillant's Mediterranean subjects drank alcohol, and they drank more regularly than the Irish American subjects. Even if they developed a drinking problem, Italian Americans were more likely than Irish Americans to simply cut back, rather than quit altogether. As Vaillant explained these remarkable ethnic differences:

It is consistent with Irish culture to see the use of alcohol in terms of black or white, good or evil, drunkenness or complete abstinence, while in Italian culture it is the distinction between moderate drinking and drunkenness that is most important.[5]

The Skills of Moderation

All human beings must learn somehow the skills of moderate consumption. If you don't learn moderation in eating, you will surely pay for it over your lifetime. Everyone must deal with this issue. And most Americans will also need to learn moderation with alcohol. Finally, many groups of youths will also need to develop and demonstrate this ability with illicit drugs.

In some groups, the same negative cultural associations that occur around alcohol in other groups appear in regard to food or drugs. For example, some cultural groups invest food with intense emotional meaning. Children in these groups can learn to view food as an emotional reward and use it to buoy their own emotions under stress or when they are depressed. Social learning extends beyond the use of substances altogether. Your social group also affects your attitudes about sex and relationships, gambling, and shopping habits.

If we can generalize about types of social learning that predispose people to excess, then we can also use these factors to develop moderation and self-control. No one is doomed to live out any cultural template. For one thing, many people have several cultural models to choose from within the same family. And nothing stops people from adopting a new pattern, one they choose to be consistent with values they hold or a new social world they are entering.

An old friend of mine, psychologist Ron Johnson, who worked as both an academic and a laborer throughout the western United States and the South Pacific, told me about his own surprise when he socialized with a fellow Alaskan heavy machine operator who was an Inupiat (Eskimo). Ron knew about the great alcohol problems among the Inupiat. But when Ron went to his friend's house, he was struck—even surprised—by how he and his friend typically drank a few beers together and then stopped without getting drunk.

Ron is anything but a bigot. But sometimes we become so impressed with group characteristics that we forget that human beings are individuals. However, we *can* be aware of and borrow from cultural recipes for moderation to employ in our homes and when teaching our children about drinking or other areas of consumption.

Cultural and Family Recipes for Moderation or Control

The social learning of addictive behaviors involves factors that make an individual more or less likely to be overwhelmed by negative behavior. Some of the social learning factors that lead to unhealthy and addictive substance use include:

Recipe for Excess
1. The individual is not part of a responsible social group and a stable social setting.
2. The individual uses a substance either in isolation or with people who don't or can't care for him or her.
3. The user is introduced to the substance by people whose own use is uncontrolled or harmful.
4. The substance is seen as having magical properties to transform the user, and also as being impossible to control.
5. Use of the substance is seen as an excuse for or signal to engage in antisocial, irresponsible, or uncontrolled behavior.

On the flip side, there are important social learning factors that facilitate moderate and sensible habits:

Recipe for Sensible Use
1. The activity or substance use takes place in a larger social

context and does not produce negative experiences or danger for other people.

2. The decision to partake of the activity or substance is made freely, not as a result of social pressure, in the belief that it will be a positive experience.

3. The activity or substance is never an excuse for antisocial or irresponsible behavior.

4. Participants in the activity model and reinforce responsible behavior, particularly for new or youthful users or participants.

5. The activity or substance is part of positive social interactions, taking place in the family, involving people of a range of ages, or taking place in celebratory or pleasantly ritualistic (but not orgiastic) settings.

The Absence of Social Templates Is Itself Negative

Social groups are such powerful forces that activities that are learned or take place in isolation, or outside of a supportive social system, are much more prone to be unhealthy and addictive.

For example, young people brought up in a drunken and abusive household obviously find controlled drinking difficult to attain, and may even decide there is no such thing. On one hand, people from such backgrounds are more likely to imitate the excessive drinking of the adults in their family. On the other hand, such young people may attempt to avoid alcohol while at the same time imbuing it with tremendous power. Neither is a healthy outcome.

Children in a family where drinking is altogether absent can face similar difficulties. Here, no social learning about alcohol takes place, or else there is a covert message that alcohol is dangerous and unmanageable. The danger here is the same as for individuals who refuse to drink because they were raised in a family where alcohol is abused: that the social setting in which they eventually learn drinking may not facilitate moderation.

When young people have not been exposed at all to alcohol at home, they often learn their drinking habits from peers. This means they learn to drink with other high school (or even junior high) students. Alternately, they may learn about drinking from fellow college students or in the military, when they are among other young men and women living away from home for the first time, without a support network of moderate drinkers.

Periodically we read about a college student who dies of alcohol poisoning, often during a fraternity hazing. One highly publicized example was the death in 1997 of Massachusetts Institute of Technology freshman Scott Krueger from alcohol poisoning at his fraternity.[6] His blood alcohol level was .41 when he arrived at the hospital—four to five times the legally defined limit for drunk driving.

This tragedy provoked calls to prosecute fellow fraternity members, and for MIT (and other universities) to enforce bans on alcohol or underage drinking on their campuses. Both peer pressure and a lack of supervision were blamed for Scott Krueger's death, but one avenue that was never explored was Scott's preparation for drinking before college. In interviews following his death, Scott's parents reported that they did not drink at home and that, as far as they knew, Scott had not drunk alcohol before coming to MIT. In a sense, this young man's abstemious background and his sudden exposure to an alcohol-soaked fraternity were a lethal combination.

In the same way that attitudes about alcohol are passed along to children by families, cultures, and peer groups, children also learn about eating patterns. When parents emphasize healthy foods over junk foods, encourage their kids to eat primarily at mealtimes rather than snacking constantly, and to eat for nutrition rather than for solace, their children tend to have healthy eating patterns. On the flip side, female adolescents are particularly susceptible to the influence of their peer group when it comes to eating disorders. For example, many college students share strategies for attempting to be thin (like using purgatives or self-inducing vomiting, often combined with junk food binges) with dormitory neighbors or sorority sisters.

What to Do When There Is No Template: Drugs

We have already seen that reactions to and patterns of drug use are learned, like other powerful habits. Actually, this social learning is even more intense with drugs than with alcohol, since the learning experience takes place out of the home, often under secretive and otherwise emotionally volatile conditions. This is the way it is in a society where drug use is illegal and yet not uncommon.

There may be precious little you can do about this as a parent—you are not going to teach your child how to smoke marijuana. At the same time, it pays not to panic in case you find out that your child has done so. That is, unless you have demonstrable information that your child's life is being harmed by this behavior, you should be careful before taking drastic steps such as sending him or her to a drug treatment program.

Nor, of course, are you yourself doomed to excessive drug use by the fact that you learned about drugs from your peer group. For one thing, many people in youth peer groups are clearly able to distinguish between excessive and controlled drug use. You could learn to do the same from them. Even if you do not learn moderation from peers, you may be able to identify its value for yourself without having to undergo too much trial-and-error learning.

As we have seen, many more people experiment with drugs than ultimately are harmed by them, let alone become lifelong addicts. The danger (as we shall see in the next chapter) is that children, or you yourself, may adopt an identity as a lifelong addict without any basis in reality for doing so, and in a way that can be as harmful and limiting to one's life as actual drug use.

Society Makes You Fat

Although Americans are preoccupied with drugs and alcohol, the substance that most worry about in their daily lives is food. And they should worry: Obesity is the number one preventable health problem in the United States. Sixty million Americans are obese; a majority of us are overweight.

How is it that we are so concerned about our weight, and yet we fail so miserably in controlling it? The answers lie with the larger culture. The superabundance of prepared foods, commercial advertising, and sedentary lifestyles creates social currents that the average person simply cannot overcome. In particular, obesity is epidemic and growing among children, along with atherosclerosis (fatty deposits in the arteries that lead to heart disease) and diabetes. Fifteen percent of children (and more than 20 percent of black and Hispanic children) were found to be obese in 2000, an increase of 150 percent from 1980.[7]

Thus when we consider our collective weight problems we need to think creatively about how to modify our social experiences. That is, following the dominant cultural templates in the case of food often *causes* excess.

Harnessing Social Forces to Aid Recovery

In order to fight food addictions as well as alcohol, drug, shopping, or gambling addictions, we have to find ways to reverse the very forces that create these addictions. Social factors are the most potent determinants of addiction, but they can also be harnessed as a tool for recovery. The ways to do this include (1) finding people and groups to support your recovery, (2) working with the significant others in your life so that they become a supportive force to reduce the pressures that lead you to succumb to your addiction and thus enhance your chances for recovery, and (3) playing the same positive role for others as a friend, spouse, or participant in a group.

Using Twelve-Step Groups for Sobriety

Among the most straightforward things you can do to lick an addiction is to shift social groups. AA is a group of former drinkers, and AA spin-offs such as NA, Gamblers Anonymous, Sex Addicts Anonymous, Shoppers Anonymous, Overeaters Anonymous, and so on provide ready-made groups of former addicts in many other areas of behavior. Although these networks are often referred to as "self-help groups," they are really groups that individuals join to find support from others, rather than go it alone.

Support groups like AA are easy to find, are time-proven, and do work for some. A few non-twelve-step alternative groups, such as SMART Recovery and Moderation Management (MM), have also appeared over the last decade or so.* Alternative groups are as yet relatively hard to find, and it is often easiest to participate in such groups through Internet lists.†

When AA succeeds, it does so in good part because it creates a nondrinking social network for the alcoholic.[8] But there are downsides to such social support networks as well. The problem may occur when, in joining AA or a similar program, you isolate yourself from others outside the group. Some AA members or groups may actually insist that you should now associate mainly with your fellow twelve-step group members. As part of this focus on the group, you learn a way of thinking and expressing yourself that often leaves others out in the cold. For example, you use code words and concepts—"friend of Bill's"

---

* I serve on advisory boards for both SMART and MM. SMART espouses an abstinence goal, while MM aims for moderate drinking.
† See www.smartrecovery.org and www.moderation.org.

(referring to one of the founders of AA), "one day at a time," "serenity prayer," and "dry drunk"—that non-AA members don't understand or respond to.

Perhaps your spouse will be motivated to join an Al-Anon group, or your children will join Alateen. These programs teach family members the same things you learn in AA. A treatment program should likewise allow family members to participate in the process. But sometimes this does not occur. Sometimes, in fact, family members experience the recovery process as actively hostile toward them. Jane was eager when her husband began treatment. She thought that it could only help her life. But although the treatment center invited spouses in for some group sessions, Jane felt more and more alienated from her husband: "I got the feeling that he was learning to blame me for his problems. I was so glad when he entered the program—but I found that I was the odd woman out."

Jane and her husband were eventually divorced, and she remains tremendously bitter. Her story seems extreme, but in one form or another I hear it often. Thus you can become alienated from your spouse, family members, and close friends in seeking recovery—just as you once were alienated from them due to your drinking or other addiction. In finding support in AA and similar groups, your goal should be to continue to work with those close to you to avoid simultaneously losing other primary supportive relationships in your life.

Finding Support Networks

Closing off your life to nonaddicts is a steep price to pay for quitting your addiction. Whether or not you join AA or another support group, you need to continue to balance your life with other social supports for sobriety and change.

There are people and places to turn to for support in quitting your addiction other than those in addiction support groups. One option is to surround yourself with people who are not addicted and never have been. These nonaddicts may simply be people who don't drink (or who drink moderately), don't smoke, don't gamble, and so on, and who are fully involved in life, work, and other positive activities. In doing so, you replace the unhealthy and excessive groups with which you have been associating with people who will model moderate and constructive behavior.

This can be a long process, as it was for Lana, who initially enjoyed AA and another twelve-step group, Overeaters Anonymous (OA): "For the first time in my life, I was eating properly and felt alive and clear." She joined AA partly because of a man there.

> At that point in my life I was really winging it on my own, with little to no emotional support from my family. I began a sexual relationship with that guy, and became involved in AA. Once my fear began to subside, I felt I had found the missing link in my life. I was an alcoholic with a disease, and this program was my cure and key to finding happiness.

Lana found that "the AA community gave me endless support. I was constantly going to meetings. I had a group of friends I loved, and learned to socialize and enjoy many experiences in life without partying. My core group and the AA literature were my complete identity."

However, "in my third year my core group of AA friends fell apart—some relapsed, some paired off and went their separate ways within the community." The worst blow was that the man she was dating relapsed and died of an overdose. Even though their relationship had been "chaotic," Lana was obviously devastated by her lover's death. "I felt lonely and unsatisfied. It wasn't the literature that allowed my good feelings for life to evolve—it was the bond and relationships I had with my friends."

Lana began to see a therapist, who encouraged her to develop a life outside of AA, including returning to her art, which had been an important part of her life. She continued with AA, but she found that some members were intolerant of her movement away from the group. "Many of the people who had supported me in the past turned their backs on me. Some said I was going to die." Of course, her problems in associating with a severely addicted lover and others who relapsed could not be blamed on AA. Nonetheless, Lana finally left AA, embarking on a search for social roots.

I chose to leave but continued to stay sober. I didn't know what I believed—I felt continual fear and doubt for the rest of that year.

It was a slow process integrating into the outside world. I was so used to relating to people with the AA language, I often felt awkward. But I branched out. I got involved with a martial arts group, reconnected with a relative with whom I had a loving relationship as a kid, began working with other artists and reconnecting with that community. In therapy, I learned to tolerate all of my feelings, and then go out and live my life as I choose.

My life is full now, but it took a while. It was a long, bumpy road to find the strength and awareness to be independent. For me, the support from my therapist and my art teacher was crucial to leaving AA. Because of it, I flourished. This fall I'm going back to college to earn a degree in a field that feels meaningful. And because I branched out, there are so many things that bring me pleasure, fulfillment, and challenge that going out and drinking in excess doesn't interest me.

Lana continues to view AA positively: "I feel AA is a valuable part of our society, even though I now disagree with its perspective. There are many people who are suffering with a physical and/or an emotional connection with alcohol who have no other resources except the twelve steps. Not everyone can afford or is willing to make the sacrifices to pay for therapy or to find other kinds of support."

Lana may have found that AA ceased working for her because of her own seriously dysfunctional relationship with a lover. AA seemingly reinforced this relationship, rather than allowing her to outgrow it. Nor did AA adequately fill the gap when her personal life collapsed. Despite her difficulties with AA, Lana did not succumb to despair. She systematically and inclusively reached out to people she had known (including relatives) and new friends and mentors to find support for a positive lifestyle, one she was now motivated to pursue.

Should you be in a similarly dysfunctional relationship or peer group, and should AA not be a satisfactory solution for you, you can still pursue associations and groups of nonaddicts in the course of your normal life. For example, when Vietnam vets returned to the United States after serving in the military, they became involved once again with their families and other non-drug-using friends. This support network of nonaddicts helped them to overcome the powerful draw of heroin addiction. Similarly, as you mature and develop new interests and life possibilities, you will usually find yourself moving away from drug-using friends. This should be part of your conscious creation of a new social network of people who will support you in living a positive life. Just as Lana did, you can search your life and the people you know and review your interests to find such people.

Creating Support Networks

The Community Reinforcement Approach, as we have seen, actually organizes social clubs to engage alcoholics in leisure activities with nondrinking friends. Although you might not have a therapist to walk you through this process, you might easily find a church or club whose members are good role models for you. Think of things you want to do, and associate with people who do these things.

Another option for locating the support you need to change your behavior is to form your own group among people you know with needs similar to yours. For example, many people exercise with friends. Groups of like-minded people bicycle and run together on weekends or walk with neighbors during the day. In this approach, while changing your behavior you associate with people you already know and like to spend time with—people whose goals and expectations are similar to your own.

With the advent of the Internet, many people find their support groups far and wide, as like-minded people or those with similar problems, no matter how rare, can be brought together over broad distances. For some common problems, such groups are ready-made. For cigarette smokers, for example, New Jersey QuitNet on the Web, organized by New Jersey's Department of Health and Senior Services, features the banner "Don't Quit Alone." The site provides "support from the QuitNet community," people to turn to when you have the urge to smoke.

One television ad created as part of this program depicts a man lying in bed who reaches over to his nightstand to grab a cigarette. As he does so, a diverse group of people gather around his bed, and one of them stops him from grabbing the pack. It is very reassuring to conceive of a large group of supportive people out there, even if you never actually meet them.

If you have difficulty finding the kind of group you need, you may organize one yourself, recruiting others who are looking for the same kind of support, perhaps via the Internet. It may only involve a handful of people with similar interests or problems, but you should be able to find some other people who want to become involved.

While the idea of quitting addiction on your own typically meets with skepticism in the United States, the QuitNet Web site indicates that people can quit smoking without formal treatment. You should, of course, maintain a relationship with your physician in quitting smoking or any other critical health matter, as QuitNet states. But the QuitNet site is a good model for an alternative support network for people who don't want to enter treatment, who don't have an immediate support group, and who may eschew the groupthink mentality of traditional support programs.

Family as a Support Group

In most cases you don't want to stop associating with your friends or family in order to change your behavior. You do not want to get divorced in order to quit smoking, lose weight, or cut back your shopping. Nor do you need the stress of family separation while struggling to recover from drug or alcohol abuse. The fact is that your family, friends, and business associates are often a big part of the reason why you were moved to quit your addiction in the first place. Having those nearest to you disapprove of your behavior can cause difficulties in a relationship, but this opposition is also a hugely motivating force, one that can be harnessed for change.

In the previous chapter we looked at David, who quit smoking rather than endure seeing his young daughter in tears every day when he returned home. This is a common story among the sixty million ex-smokers in America. One man I worked with told me with a smile that he gave up cigarettes after his wife refused to have sex with him until he quit. People who have people are the luckiest people in the world in terms of quitting addictions. And your loved ones are always around to remind you why you quit in the first place. Marriage and intimate relationships are so critical to the recovery process that the Community Reinforcement Approach creates a buddy system for those who don't have a spouse or other intimate.

Since people often share problems with those close to them, a logical step may be to attempt to change together. For example, spouses often quit smoking, lose weight, reduce alcohol consumption, or work together to eliminate other addictions. Sometimes an entire family can make life changes as a team. When I met Mike, he had just run two marathons with his brother. His entire family, including his parents, were a close-knit, active—and trim—group.

So when Mike told me he had been overweight as a young man, I took notice. He told me that he hadn't thought much about his overeating then because his parents and brother were all also overweight. Mike's parents were second-generation Americans. In their immigrant families, a hefty build was a sign of wealth and health, and eating together was a family tradition.

When Mike graduated from college, he got a job on Wall Street, but he continued to live with his parents. Every morning he would eat breakfast at home. Then he would have ham, eggs, toast, and potatoes when he got off the subway at work. But it wasn't long before Mike realized that his eating habits were isolating him from his fashionably lean coworkers.

When Mike discussed this problem with his family, he found that they also felt the need to change their eating style—including his brother, who was in medical school. As a group, they concluded that they would stop eating their traditionally starchy, fatty meals, followed by desserts. Mike and his brother began a program of running, while their parents walked together. The results of the changes were quickly evident. Not only did everyone become fitter and look better, but their new confidence spilled over to other areas of their lives. Within several years, Mike and his brother both got married. Thirty years later, Mike's entire extended family remains trim.

Those Closest to You Are Your Biggest Help, and Your Greatest Burden

As Mike's experiences illustrate, your family can be one of your best support networks. After all, they are available to you twenty-four hours a day, they know you intimately, and they have an interest in your well-being. However, the same people who can help you kick your addiction can also keep you on your addictive course. That's why a successful treatment program such as CRA focuses so much on marital communication and negotiation.

Sometimes a person's dissatisfaction with a spouse is the immediate stimulus to return to smoking, a night of drinking, or a shopping orgy. In this case, your rationale may be "My spouse is annoying and attacking me again—I'll get even." Even your spouse's complaints about the addiction can act as an irritant that contributes to the addictive motivation. Therefore, a necessary step toward resolving your addiction is to work with your spouse to turn his or her concern into a positive motivation. Instead of him or her badgering you or bitching constantly (at least as you see it), you and your spouse need to work out a method for harnessing your mutual desire for change.

Maintaining a healthy relationship overall requires that you know how to negotiate with your partner. You need to be able to express your needs reasonably and to be forthcoming in fulfilling the other person's needs. If you give too much or too little, or feel perpetually used or ignored, you cannot comfortably relate to other people. This truism is especially evident in the area of addiction.

Because the Community Reinforcement Approach—which, as we have seen, is among the most successful addiction treatments—addresses all the critical functional areas of a person's life, it includes relationship therapy as one of its central elements. Other alcoholism therapies likewise focus on marital or couple relationships as being key to sobriety.[9] These approaches have many elements in common, which can also be generalized to other addictions. All work to have a spouse discourage the addictive behavior and to reward change. CRA relationship therapy emphasizes the couple's working together to achieve the goals identified by the client on the Happiness Scale, described in Chapter 4, and both partners fill out a Relationship Happiness Scale.

CRA emphasizes skill in offering and taking in critical information, as discussed in the last chapter, so that you and your spouse can bring about the changes you want from each other. CRA relationship counseling also aims at removing fights with your spouse—specifically about the behavior of concern—as a trigger for the addiction. Instead, the marriage or relationship can be made into an antiaddictive resource in which you and your partner work together in the cooperative pursuit of shared goals. Then your interactions with your partner can be turned around so that they are no longer suffused with negatives, complaints, demands, and recriminations. CRA encourages you and your partner to pick out the positives in each behavior and praise them. It encourages you to offer to do things that your spouse wants along with requesting that your partner change his or her addictive behavior.

In CRA a therapist specifically trains a couple in communication techniques. But there are other ways of learning how to practice better give-and-take as spouses, including practicing on your own. In fact, whether or not you have such counseling, even after therapy it is up to the participants to continue practicing its principles.

RELATIONSHIP COUNSELING FOR ADDICTIONS

1. Clarify each partner's satisfaction with/expectations of the relationship using the Relationship Happiness Scale:
   a. *Household responsibilities*
   b. *Parenting*
   c. *Social activities*
   d. *Money management*
   e. *Communication*
   f. *Sex and affection*
   g. *Job/school*
   h. *Emotional support*
   i. *Partner's independence*
   j. *General happiness*

2. Express positives about the relationship:
   a. *What drew you together*
   b. *What you admire in your partner*
3. List positive behaviors to increase together:
   a. *Compliments*
   b. *Showing appreciation*
   c. *Pleasant surprises*
   d. *Open affection*
   e. *Pleasant conversation*
   f. *Helping*
4. Change partner's behavior toward addicted partner:
   a. *Reward behavior change*
   b. *Allow addicted partner to suffer negative consequences of addiction*
   c. *Actively discuss addiction-related situations*
   d. *Help partner avoid addictive behavior*
5. Develop communication techniques for requesting change:
   a. *Be specific*
   b. *Do not generalize to a whole list of "wrongs"*
   c. *Express request as positively as possible (e.g., start with a compliment)*
   d. *Take partial responsibility (e.g., "I realize I contribute to your actions")*
   e. *Imagine how partner will feel about the request*
   f. *Note and compliment when partner does the requested actions*
6. Practice responding to requests:
   a. *Do not reject request out of hand*
   b. *If you feel you cannot fulfill request, suggest a specific alternative*
   c. *Express your alternative as positively as possible*
   d. *Take some responsibility*
   e. *Imagine how partner is feeling*
   f. *When you fulfill request (or alternative), mention it and ask if it is okay*

Larry's wife, Alice, had gained weight, and Larry didn't like it. What's more, he communicated to her about her eating habits and lack of exercise mainly in negatives. When Larry harped on Alice's unhealthy habits, she retaliated by reminding Larry of all that she had done to help him—in his career, in his own good health (since Alice prepared the family's meals), in her household responsibilities (Alice returned to work after their two children entered school full-time, but she still maintained the home). "Why should Larry be so high and mighty?" she'd ask herself angrily.

Therapy for this couple began with acknowledging the positives that had brought them together and that helped them to maintain a functioning—and basically positive—household. Larry in fact did have good insights into why and when Alice overate or missed opportunities to exercise. While his insights could have been very helpful for her, he had to learn how to communicate these so that Alice did not experience his words as attacks on her worth as a person. For her part, Alice needed to learn to see Larry as a resource and an ally in achieving a goal that they both wanted. Larry loved and depended on Alice, and even with her weight gain he found her attractive. As Alice made positive changes in fighting her weight problem, Larry could respond to her successes with genuine appreciation. Not only did she become even more attractive to Larry, but Alice's improved health made it likely that she would be around longer as a companion.

Fighting Against *Change*

At the other extreme from focusing together on a shared goal of change are cases where an intimate relationship is based on one partner's addiction. The less obviously addicted spouse, in what could accurately be called codependence, feels needed by the more obviously addicted spouse and thus more valuable as a person. In these instances, an addict's partner may actually sabotage attempts to change an addictive habit. Insecure about her own attractiveness or her role in her partner's life, this spouse may feel that the less attractive the addicted partner is to the outside world, the more dependent he will be on her. Who else would be able to put up with his addiction? This is a common dynamic with an alcoholic's or drug addict's partner.

Gail was an example of a woman who resisted any efforts to get her husband, John, into therapy, though his anxiety attacks and depression made it almost impossible for him to leave their home. Gail turned frequently for help, financial and emotional, to her extended family. Yet when they tried to secure treatment for John, she always resisted, claming John would never accept it. In this case, Gail required therapy as much as John. Her behavior not only permitted John's problems to grow worse, but was harming her own life.

The worst example of a toxic spouse may occur when both members of the couple share the addiction. If one spouse refuses to change, often he or she cannot tolerate the efforts that the partner is making to recover. In the classic 1962 movie *Days of Wine and Roses*, Lee Remick induces her husband (played by Jack Lemmon) to break his abstinence vow and to drink again. Ultimately, he must walk away from his alcoholic wife in order to stay sober.

There's an old joke about a spoiled wife who accompanies her husband to the hospital. The doctor asks to meet with the woman separately and tells her, "The only way your husband can live is if you prepare a hot meal for him every night when he comes home." On the ride home, unable to contain his curiosity, the man turns to his wife and asks, "What did the doctor tell you?" His wife, looking up slowly from her mirror, replies, "Darling, you're going to die." This joke actually reflects a real and commonplace attitude that isn't funny.

I observed a remarkable example of this phenomenon in an ordinary middle-class home. Elaine was apparently happily married to Phil, a man approaching late middle age. With their children out of the home, Phil began gaining a considerable amount of weight. When Phil had a severe coronary, his near-death experience shocked him into dropping thirty pounds. Yet his wife, who was herself thin, continued to prepare meals exactly as she had before her husband's coronary. Slowly he put weight back on. Within two years, Phil suffered a fatal heart attack.

An outsider might ruefully guess that Elaine must on some level have wanted Phil to die. Why else wouldn't she modify her meal preparation habits? But the truth was that Elaine was totally dependent on her husband. Shortly after his death, she suffered a nervous breakdown, and she was never free of mental illness until she died a few years later. Yet it was her dependence on him that drove her to keep Phil as the familiar, overweight person she knew who loved her cooking. By resisting the lifestyle changes he needed to make, however, she contributed to Phil's death. Is this an example of the cynical adage "Love kills"? The answer is that only unhealthy relationships foster an addiction. If you find yourself in one of these situations, then fighting your addiction may mean you need to reevaluate or even end your relationship. Certainly you need to change the way you deal with your partner and the lifestyle you're accustomed to together.

Failing to Respect the Other Person

Sometimes there is a debate over the exact nature and severity of a problem. There are cases where the problem is in the eye of the beholder and represents a failure on the partner's part to respect honest choices by the other person that are not actually unhealthy. For example, there is no potentially addictive activity on which men and women more frequently disagree than drinking. In every culture in the world, men drink more than women. More women than men react to a drinking problem by abstaining—and by forcefully encouraging their husbands to do the same.

I once met a well-known psychologist who had had two

heart operations. When I asked him what his cardiologist had advised him about drinking, the man said, "He told me a glass or two of wine a day could be beneficial." But the psychologist did not follow this prescription because his wife forbade him to drink. I thought, "She would rather that he died pure!"

In my therapy practice, I often encounter people (both women and men) who want to reduce their drinking but whose spouses disapprove of their drinking entirely. The drinkers often resort to secret drinking in less-frequented parts of their house, such as basements, kitchens, and laundry closets. As well as contributing to their bad feelings about their drinking problem, drinking in secret causes them to drink more and more rapidly in their hideaways. (The wife of one of the characters in the TV series *The Sopranos* likewise had a secret cache of chocolates that she gorged on in her laundry room.)

One of these "closet drinkers," a woman named Laura, often had several quick glasses of wine while making dinner so that she could sit down to a wineless meal in front of her husband. In cases like this, I invite the abstemious spouse to come into therapy and if possible to agree to work toward a goal of reduced drinking with his or her spouse, rather than insisting he or she give up alcohol altogether. My goal is not to get the abstainer to drink. Rather, it is to gain acceptance of a habit that can and should be practiced openly within the family context, rather than as a guilty pleasure.

In this instance, Laura found that when she was able to sit down at the table and relax while she drank, she tended to drink just a glass or two of wine, as opposed to sneaking off to drink the better part of a bottle.

Helping Others Change Without Hurting Yourself

Really, all of the information in this chapter about gaining support from others points not only to how you can rely on others to help you, but also to how you can serve as a helper to others, particularly those near and dear to you. The communication techniques described above apply to both the helper and the helped, and the point is, of course, that both parties benefit. Many people suffer badly due to the addictions of others. In such cases, you may not even realize how much your partner's addiction is damaging your own life.

The most common message I get at my Web site is from partners—most often women—who find themselves with a mate who is heavily addicted to Internet porn, drugs, or alcohol. These individuals write of the many depredations they (and often their children) have suffered due to their partner's addiction. They experience very little satisfaction—emotional, financial, or sexual—from the relationship. One trick I use is to extract from their own messages (often very long ones) the litany of broken promises, ignored feelings, selfish acts, and personal and family suffering, and send it back to them, in effect holding a mirror up to them in which to view their situation.

These experiences have led me to the following realizations, which I share with people in this position:[10]

• Fundamentally, you can't help another person by violating your own safety and happiness, the safety of other family members, and your own moral standards.

• You must take care of yourself. A relationship that is destroying you must be changed or terminated. Your being a victim will not bring benefits to anyone else.

• You cannot sustain a relationship that requires you to lie to others, to treat people badly, or to violate your own moral precepts. You'll always lose out because your self-esteem and dealings with others will suffer.

• You are obligated to protect helpless family members, especially children. Think, as a negative role model, of Hedda Nussbaum, a victim herself who placated her lover, Joel Steinberg, while allowing him to kill their adopted daughter.

Getting the Person into Treatment When Needed

As readers of this book by now well realize, I don't think that the goal of turning people over to professional helpers is inevitably the right one. But there are certainly cases where it is—where the problem is so severe that it exceeds the partner's or other concerned parties' personal and emotional resources. Gail—the woman whose husband was tortured by anxiety, but who resisted all efforts by her family to get her spouse into therapy—is a person who needs to find professional help for her husband, and who herself could benefit from professional help.

If you are struggling with an addiction and feel that your spouse or partner is part of your problem, suggest that you attend treatment together. If you are concerned about an addicted partner and worry that you cannot give that person the help he or she needs, then you may have to find a way to get your partner to agree to enter treatment. Once again, the Community Reinforcement Approach has unusually helpful techniques. Based on the principles of reinforcing change throughout the person's environment, Community Reinforcement and Family Training (CRAFT) was developed to improve both the concerned party's and the drug user's situations, along with getting the addicted person into treatment.[11]

COMMUNITY REINFORCEMENT AND FAMILY TRAINING

1. Increasing the concerned person's motivation to change—e.g., questioning the person about how his or her life has changed for the worse due to the addict's drug use
2. Communication skills—training on providing nonantagonistic feedback and encouragement to the drug user
3. Increasing positive interactions
4. Nonreinforcement of drug use—ignoring the addict when he or she is using

5. Initiating activities that interfere and compete with addict's drug use
6. Developing outside activities and reinforcement for the concerned person
7. Planning to escape dangerous situations—such as those with the possibility of violence
8. Planning to introduce the idea of treatment at the right moment

Researchers at the University of New Mexico tested the impact of CRAFT on both concerned others and the targeted drug abusers.[12] Not only did three-quarters of the targeted drug-abusing individuals enter treatment, but the concerned others showed significant improvements on eight measures of well-being, including much-reduced levels of depression and anxiety. This is because CRAFT allows concerned others to take steps to gain control over the situation, even aside from having the other party get treatment. Through a combination of the efficacy of knowing they were taking steps to improve their own and the targeted person's lives and actual improvements in the other person's behavior, the concerned parties' emotional situations improved markedly.

Miller and colleagues tested CRAFT with alcohol abusers in comparison to two other well-known techniques.[13] One was the popular style of intervention developed by Vernon Johnson, where concerned others are prepared to surround and confront the alcoholic with a nonnegotiable demand that he or she enter treatment right away. The other comparison group was Al-Anon, which does not actually encourage partners to change the alcoholic; rather, Al-Anon's message is that partners must recognize that the alcoholic has a disease, accept the alcoholic's helplessness, and practice "loving detachment." CRAFT subjects were more than twice as successful (64 percent) in getting the alcohol abuser to enter treatment as the Johnson interventions (30 percent; after their intervention training, more than two-thirds of concerned partners declined to go through with the actual intervention). Al-Anon subjects got problem drinkers into treatment in 13 percent of cases. Of course, to be thoroughly satisfied with this result, we need to know more about the appropriateness and efficacy of the treatment the alcoholics actually entered.

Changing the Group

When problems with people's substance use or more general health behavior are widespread throughout a social group, community, or business organization, rather than tackling each individual one at a time, the group or organization may be the best target for change. In fact, the group change model has spawned an entirely new industry: the corporate wellness program. Johnson & Johnson, a major pharmaceutical manufacturer located in New Jersey, was a pioneer with its "Live for Life" program, which has since spun off into an entirely new business that consults with other corporations to develop their own wellness programs.

A company program typically involves introducing healthy portions and foods at lunch, installing walking paths near the lunchroom, making therapy and medical referrals when necessary, and arranging meetings of weight loss groups. Together, these changes contribute to a shift in corporate culture, signaling that a healthier diet, more exercise, and overcoming harmful addictions are shared goals. When you can exercise with people you see every day, as a part of your work routine, the average person is going to be much more successful in practicing this or any other healthy behavior.

A successful corporate wellness program will include many of the following elements:

Diet
Healthy, low-fat foods in lunchroom
Healthy snacks at meetings

Corporate programs and goals for weight, blood pressure, and cholesterol

Employee Assistance Programs
Screening for risk factors, unhealthy habits, addictive behaviors
Making available weight loss and smoking cessation groups
Encouraging appropriate treatment for behavioral and other problems and providing referrals
Obtaining appropriate medical care (e.g., medication for cholesterol)

Exercise
Walking paths
Corporate gym or discount memberships at local fitness centers
Exercise classes at lunch, after work

Stress
Minimize overwork
Time permitted for family matters
Relaxation techniques, opportunities offered

Psychological Well-being
Opportunities for individuals and groups to discuss problems
Confidential outside therapy offered
Work respects people's relationships inside and outside company

Johnson & Johnson's program incorporated many aspects of this list, including linking the program to employee health care and providing financial incentives for employees to join the program. In the first long-term, systematic analysis of this corporate program, Johnson & Johnson reported significantly lower medical expenses for over eighteen thousand of its employees who participated in the program from 1995 to 1999. A separate component of the program screened a smaller group of about forty-five hundred employees for thirteen specific health risk factors. A year later, a second screening found reductions in eight of these risk factors (including an increase in employees' physical activity levels, lower blood pressure, lower cholesterol, cessation of smoking, higher dietary fiber intake, and safer driving practices).[14]

Of course, the people most likely to sign up for such a program are going to be those most highly motivated to change (like those who are reading this book). Finding support among fellow employees and concentrating on changing your health behaviors in your daily work environment is a great strategy for making these changes. It can provide the last push that many people need to initiate and maintain healthy behavior changes.

You Create Your Own World

We began this chapter by discussing how critical, almost overwhelming, group pressures are in eating, drug use, and attitudes toward alcohol. This has the slightly pessimistic impact of suggesting that you are doomed to suffer from whatever problems afflict your own social group. In other words, if American attitudes toward drugs and alcohol are screwed up, how can you do any better on your own?

Likewise, if the entire country is getting fat, is your only solution to wait until your employer decides to create a comprehensive corporate wellness program? Of course not. The best strategy is to create your own small culture of health and responsibility—at work, at home, or elsewhere. Every human being can succeed in modifying his or her own thinking, behavior, social reality, and life course. In order to succeed, you must select from and reshape your social environment to support the positive changes you want to make. These changes are in keeping with who you believe you are and who you want to be.

■■■■■
Exercise: Emulate Successful Friends

Think of five people you know whose behavior in the area of
your addiction you most admire or want to emulate. How can
you spend time with them, especially engaging in the behavior you want to change? Can you ask them directly for suggestions for how they manage in this area (this is often called
coaching)? They will be flattered and will know that you are
interested in improving. They thus become part of your
change support group.

■■■■■
Exercise: Inspect Your Relationships

List your five closest relationships. How does each one support
your bad habit or addiction? How does each offer leverage
against your negative habit?

Which of these relationships would you be better off leaving behind to overcome your addiction?

Which of these relationships can be modified to support
changing your addiction?

What needs to take place in these relationships to shift
their balance from possibly supporting your addiction to
helping you to quit and stay off your addiction?

Think of one thing to do about each of these relationships,
and do it, telling the person in each case what you are doing
and why. Involve that person, where possible, in the discussion.

■■■■■
Exercise: Join or Create a Support Group

Join a group whose members do not share your problem or
addiction and which is not organized specifically to tackle
your problem. For example, if you are a substance abuser, join
an exercise group or an outdoors group whose participants
will be in good shape and pursue other healthy behaviors.
Members of a church group are also unlikely to be drug or

alcohol abusers. Nor will those in a study group usually be looking for a party.

If you aren't a joiner, but an independent person who is perhaps a leader, form a group of your own. Even one other person counts as a group, but try for at least two others. Walk every morning or evening with this group as an exercise program. If you are facing an emotional problem or stressful situation (say, you are divorcing or newly divorced), meet regularly with one or more people sharing this experience. If you communicate with one or more people by e-mail about a topic or problem of special concern to each of you, think about this as a group, and consider specifically identifying the group as such to other participants.

Finally, use an existing group to find fellow participants in a behavior you want to change or adopt. For example, create a Jazzercise group among your coworkers. Join them at the lunch table, where you all agree to eat healthily and reduce your calorie consumption.

Remember: there is power—emotional power—in groups, so long as they reflect who you are and don't require more sacrifice than what you gain from them.

■■■■■

6

A Mature Identity: Growing into Self-respect and Responsibility

Addiction is a search for immature gratifications—it is self-seeking behavior resembling that of a dependent child. As a result, overcoming addiction requires growing up and assuming adult roles. In this process you learn to take responsibility not only for yourself and your own behavior but for other people in your life. One natural outgrowth of this mature outlook is that you may no longer see yourself as a powerless addict. You may no longer feel any need for the addiction, so it ceases to have any presence in your life.

The addiction field has an evocative term for this phenomenon—*maturing out*. Heroin addicts themselves sometimes use this term. The typical reason heroin addicts give for outgrowing their addiction is that they are tired of the lifestyle—being on the outside, being cut off from normal life, the constant hustling and evading the law, the absence of anything new or better stretching out before them.

Of course, maturing out is not limited to heroin; it happens with all addictions. As you mature, you become dissatisfied with your limitations. You develop more connections to life, through marriage, parenthood, or career accomplishments. While undergoing these external developments, you simultaneously experience critical internal emotional changes. At the same time, your self-image and identity change.

Gaining a Positive Identity

To mature, you need to do more than simply get older—you also need to experience life and learn its lessons. And one of the most difficult lessons is that you can become more than the addicted individual you once were. The new behavior that you display means that you deserve a new self-image, or identity.

At some point—actually, at various points—in your life, you decide who you are, that is, what your identity is. We have seen these shifts occur in cases throughout this book, when people decided they were no longer going to be addicted. For many, this evolves into a longer-term, larger shift, where the person ceases to think of himself or herself as a recovering or even former addict.

One woman, for example, labored throughout her life to conceal the fact that as a young woman she had been hospitalized for her drug use. She was no longer that person, and she rejected it as a part of who she was now. She didn't see herself as a former addict and did not want others to see her that way.

However, many in addiction treatment feel that people must accept that they are lifelong addicts—that no changes they undergo or create for themselves will ever allow them to escape this identity. In this view, it is dangerous—a matter of tempting fate—to say that you are fully recovered.

This book takes a different tack. I want you to know that there is no reason you can't change who you are, including your addict identity. It may be tough, but adding the baggage that you must always think of yourself as an addict will only weigh down your recovery effort.

Addiction as Immaturity

As I noted in my 1975 book, *Love and Addiction*: "Addiction is a childlike search for constant security and gratification—infantile desires that maturity tells us are impossible to fulfill." One interesting memoir from a former heroin addict is *How to Stop Time*, by Ann Marlowe. According to Marlowe, heroin is an excuse for "not getting on with your life."[1] Marlowe notes that heroin "isn't that wonderful: it's a substance some of us agree to pursue as though it were wonderful, because it's easier to do that than to figure out what is worth pursuing."

Of course, Marlowe's book is a testament to the ability to outgrow this lethargy as a temporary (although perhaps prolonged) episode in life. She was assisted in her effort by her obvious insightfulness, as revealed in her book, and by maintaining an orderly life and identity even while taking heroin (she worked as a stockbroker). Despite her gifts and advantages, Marlowe is far from unique in her ability to overcome what most people think of as the most extreme drug addiction.

In the 1960s several New York psychologists explored the experiences of urban heroin addicts, who often began their habits as adolescents, when they had had few life experiences or responsibilities. Isidor Chein and his colleagues described these youthful substance abusers, who were enmeshed in lethargy and purposelessness, in their previously described book *The Road to H*. Based on his interviews with young inner-city addicts, Chein described the addicted individual this way in a later article:

> He could not find a vocation, a career, a meaningful, sustained activity around which he could, so to say, wrap his life. The addiction, however, offers an answer to even this problem of emptiness. The life of an addict constitutes a vocation—hustling, raising funds, assuring a connection and the maintenance of supply, outmaneuvering the police, performing the rituals of

preparing and of taking the drug—a vocation around which the addict can build a reasonably full life.[2]

Even if you have a more comfortable middle-class addiction—one that, unlike a heroin addiction, doesn't involve committing crimes and being isolated from ordinary people—Chein's description applies well to you. Your addiction is the safety net, the focus, the anchor of your existence. Even as other satisfactions that you might prefer pass you by, you continue to rely on your shopping, eating, or smoking for solace.

The first scientific analysis of maturing out was published in 1962 by psychologist Charles Winick.[3] Winick examined the roll of known addicts in New York City. He discovered that by the age of twenty-six, one-quarter of addicts had left the list, and by the age of thirty-six, three-quarters were no longer addicts. Some had been imprisoned or hospitalized or had died, but these were a minority. Winick described the process of maturing out for addicts who, he said, "began taking heroin in their late teens or early twenties as their method of coping with the challenges and problems of early adulthood. . . . The use of narcotics made it possible to evade, mask or postpone these decisions. . . . Becoming a narcotics addict in early adulthood thus enables the addict to avoid many decisions."[4] For those who didn't mature out, their life continued on to institutional dependence in jail or on social services.

However belatedly, even most of these cases of arrested development were able to face life on its own terms. After a time, the balance of reasons causing addicts to avoid adult decisions and responsibilities shifts. One factor is that as they get older, addicts begin to see what they are missing—a full life, a family, a job. According to researcher Dan Waldorf, self-curing addicts "felt that their addiction had run its course and it was time to do other things."[5] Another reason is that they recognize the costs of their continued addiction, including perpetual marginalization. As one such former addict interviewed by Patrick Biernacki put it, "I didn't want to be known as a tramp and I didn't want to feel like a nobody, a nothing."[6] Finally, they lose their fear of the requirements for living a straight life, of taking on adult responsibilities, and gain confidence in their ability to do so.

An Everyday Example of Maturing Out

Even if you are not a street drug user, you should be able to apply this phenomenon to your own life. Nicotine is a more commonplace drug than heroin, yet it is as potent and as harmful as any other drug addiction. People usually get addicted to cigarettes in their teens and twenties. At this age they are anxious about their identities, eager to fit in, and do not yet detect any signs of physical problems due to smoking.

As time proceeds and smokers take on families, jobs, and positions in the community, the forces fighting against the addiction add up and eventually outweigh the value and satisfaction of continuing the habit. Today, one of the primary reasons for quitting is that smokers face so much social pressure that they are in danger of becoming pariahs. Within corporate America especially, nonsmoking policies have become the norm.

Of course, as they get older, many smokers also become more aware of (and take more seriously) the medical information damning tobacco use. As they recognize their mortality and accumulate responsibilities that require them to stay healthy and to live, smokers become concerned about preserving their health.

There are comparable maturational processes at work all along the life span, not just in the emergence from adolescence or the assumption of adult responsibility. Studies of older people, including formerly heavy drinkers, show that they often modify their behaviors for the most prosaic and obvious reasons. They eat and drink less because their bodies can no longer tolerate excess. They also often don't have the disposable income to support expensive drug or alcohol habits.[7] On the other hand, one admitted alcoholic eliminated his problem drinking because he "felt that he and his wife could not continue drinking and expect to be able to take care of themselves in old age."[8]

Emotional Maturity

Maturing out would be a trivial thing to note if it were only about your changing physical and financial capacities, or even about your securing a stable job and family. It is also about developing emotional resources and stability. An addiction grows out of self-preoccupation and, often, self-pity. You feed your addiction because you feel constantly deprived: You are not getting what you deserve. Maturity means turning away from a preoccupation with your own needs and becoming aware of the needs of the people around you.

Along with abilities and assets that you gain with age, you also gain faith in yourself, patience with others, and self-awareness—a kind of overall equilibrium. This does not mean that you become perfect or that you shed the personal traits, both positive and negative, that distinguish you from others. But it often means that you are more forgiving of yourself as well as of others.

Maturity changes the way that we experience and react to different events in our lives. Think about the experience of young love and how it affects you differently than an adult relationship does. The first time you fall in love, you are unsure about what you are experiencing. What is the cause of this excitement, this desire? And when things go wrong in a youthful love affair, the young person is equally confused about the cause of the problem: "What did I do wrong? How am I failing? What's the matter with me?"

As a young adult, you are simply incapable of concluding that perhaps the match was not meant to be or that the other person has problems that are preventing the two of you from hooking up. Rather, you focus all your doubt on yourself. As you gain more experience, romantic and otherwise, your self-image becomes more stable. Your world does not depend on the approval of your lover. Your sense of worth is not entirely bound up in him or her.

Thus, the pain of the bad moments in the relationship and the anguish and withdrawal when it breaks up become less severe. At the same time, behaviors by your partner that earlier might have induced you to call a halt to the relationship no longer seem so intolerable. During the course of the relationship, your responses when some aspect of the relationship does not go as you wanted it to become more measured and less extreme.

Few of us cannot think of a way we once reacted to something or a way that we behaved that now seems ridiculous. A teenage athlete who threw tantrums after losing, a young lover who didn't want his girlfriend to see her old friends, the young wife who left the holiday dinner because of a chance comment by an in-law—many of us would deal with these situations differently as seasoned adults, rather than as passionate young people.

When you are able to control your reactions, or overreactions, you are less likely to need to resort to addictive remedies. In the first place, you experience fewer of the negative emotions, such as anxiety and depression, that impel addictions. In the second place, you feel more confident about being able to meet and overcome challenges. And third, even when you are not able to resolve an issue fully, you are more accepting of yourself and the situation. Age helps to clarify the fact that a lot of emotional turmoil, and the addiction that goes along with it, is unnecessary.

Responsibility

Growing into maturity means focusing less on your weaknesses and vulnerabilities and more on your responsibilities to yourself and to other people. Responsibility covers such a large territory that it needs to be broken down into separate categories.

TAKING RESPONSIBILITY FOR YOUR ADDICTION

You need to take responsibility for your addiction; it is yours and no one else's. This is hard because the bulk of conventional addiction theory attempts to shift responsibility for the habit away from the addict and onto the substance. But that is both nonsensical and counterproductive.

Recently, people have begun bringing lawsuits against fastfood chains and manufacturers of fattening foods for causing them to be obese and for the concomitant health and medical difficulties they experience. In 2003 Senator Mitch McConnell introduced a bill that would block people from suing restaurants and food manufacturers for making them fat. McConnell's rationale was: "I think it's important not to blame poor eating habits on someone else."[9]

McConnell might as well have said that it is important not to blame some*thing* else—that is, the foods we are tempted by. Of course, we regularly make this leap in absolving people of responsibility for using drugs, saying that either their bodies or the power of the drugs prevents them from desisting. This is based on the myth (discussed in Chapter 3) that drugs are irresistible, that once you have tried them you cannot stop. Once we recognize that this is not the case, that people can stop taking drugs just as they can stop eating potato chips, then McConnell's admonition that we need to accept responsibility for our habits extends well beyond overeating. It applies as well to drinking, drugs, gambling, shopping—whatever your habit.

In Chapter 2 of this book, we reviewed cases of "miraculous" cures, where a single incident reversed a seemingly irresolvable addiction. Don, for example, wrote me that after years of detox and rehab, it was reading my book that finally enabled him to change the way he looked at his drinking and finally quit. What happened for Don was that he suddenly realized that it was up to him to stop drinking—that no other agency or disease was responsible for his problem or could get him to stop. For Don, this realization of responsibility was liberating. He *had* to stop drinking, he *could* stop drinking, and *only he* had the power to do so.

Naturally, not everyone reacts to my books in the same way as Don. But at some level most people solve addictions by accepting that it is their responsibility to do so. It is painful and somewhat frightening to think that no one but you yourself can stop the madness. Yet this realization can also be exhilarating. You have gotten to the heart of the problem; at least you know what is required of you.

Believing that alcoholism is a disease, that no one escapes the grip of heroin or cigarettes, that withdrawal from either is too horrible to resist, or that you are born to be addicted imbues your addiction with power and irresistibility that it does not need to have. The more you believe any or all of these myths, the more likely you are to remain addicted. On the other hand, the belief that you have the power to attack the addiction—that is, a belief in your self-efficacy—helps you succeed at this challenge. This belief also contributes to your feeling that you can free yourself, not only now, but potentially forever, from the bugaboo of addiction.

TAKING RESPONSIBILITY FOR BEING AN ADULT

If you have ever watched any of the daytime court programs on TV, you may have been shocked and amused by the number of people who borrow a car, get into a wreck, and then say that it wasn't their fault and so they shouldn't have to pay to repair the damage. Judge Judy or whoever then typically asks, "Do you think the person who lent you the car should pay?" Children may be excused for defending themselves with the argument "It wasn't my fault." As an adult, however, you need to be able to fulfill your obligations, including that you show up on time, follow through on your commitments, and pay your debts. You must also accept the consequences when you do not.

Taking your everyday responsibilities and obligations seriously is a critical step toward beating an addiction. For example, Jerry had been a heroin addict since his teens. He had never attended school regularly. Instead, he spent his days hanging out with street gangs and leading a criminal life. But just when it looked like Jerry would never overcome his addiction—when he was already in his mid-thirties and fresh off a prison stint—Jerry decided to move to a new city. He went back to school, became a counselor, developed a new social group, and gave up illicit drugs.

Jerry described the strength and satisfaction that came from assuming a new identity as a moral, responsible person. He first realized the magnitude of the change he had made when

> I became genuinely concerned that there be money in my account to cover any check I wrote. Or when I made a point of honoring every commitment I made to be at a certain place at a certain time. By then I had found a way to feel good about myself by making my word, my presence mean something.

Assuming the mantle of a responsible person is often the first step toward making momentous life changes. If you identify yourself as a mature, responsible adult, then, like Jerry, you are reversing your addict identity.

TAKING RESPONSIBILITY FOR BAD BEHAVIOR

Of course, as an addict you explain that you can't pay your bills because you are spending your money on drugs, alcohol, bets, shopping, or whatever. And you can't show up on time for an appointment because you are hung over or because you are enslaved to another person who won't let you go. You commit crimes because you have to pay for your various habits . . . and so on.

Addicts tend to reverse the causal chain of their addiction. In truth, it's not that the addiction prevents you from paying bills, being on time, honoring your word, respecting the law, and taking care of your children; it is that the failure to assume responsibility for doing the right thing enables you to be addicted. Let us turn again to the former heroin addict and author of *How to Stop Time*, Ann Marlowe, for her interpretation of the claim that it is the nature of heroin addiction that the addict must do anything to avoid going without the drug:

> Not for a minute can I subscribe to the popular view, encouraged by William Burroughs, of addiction as uncontrollable need. Still less can I take addiction as the excuse for bad behavior. No one would condone a person who stole or neglected her children because he or she was feeling bad from the flu, and all but the severest dope-sickness is no more rigorous than a nasty flu. Unpleasant? Yes. Sufficient explanation for amoral selfishness? Scarcely.[10]

This idea was discussed by Lee Robins, the medical sociologist who studied returning Vietnam heroin addicts, when she noted:

> Beliefs about heroin based entirely on results in treated populations have created a self-fulfilling prophecy. Heroin is or was thought of, by law enforcement personnel and users alike, as the "worst" drug, virtually instantly and permanently addictive and creating craving so extreme that it overcomes all normal ability to resist temptations to theft and robbery to acquire it. Users who share this view show by their use that they are ready to commit themselves to their concept of an addictive life style.[11]

In other words, not only is addiction the antithesis of responsibility, but believing in the power of addiction actually makes it more likely that the addiction will lead you to behave in an irresponsible manner. Taking responsibility for avoiding bad behavior is thus both a characteristic of a mature identity and the antithesis of addiction.

ACKNOWLEDGING YOUR RESPONSIBILITY TO OTHER PEOPLE

Overcoming addiction also means shifting your focus from your own needs to the needs of other people. You do this by assuming responsibilities in work, marriage, and parenthood. Becoming a parent is not a solution for addiction, nor should remedying a parent's addiction ever be a child's obligation. But becoming ready to have and care for children signals a major step in moving from being dependent to being a provider, from weakness to strength, and from a taking role to a giving role. This is why parenthood eventually causes so many people to quit addictions, from smoking to drugs to gambling and so on.

AA recognizes this obligation to others when it states in Step 8: "Made a list of all persons we had harmed, and became willing to make amends to them." But thinking about your past sins is still a step away from recognizing that you are continually living your life in the context of others—that your actions impact those around you, particularly those close to you, such as family members, friends, and coworkers.

Take, for example, a couple I observed over many years, John and Terry. John was a talented man with a troubled background. His family had been disrupted by alcoholism, and he had been a periodic problem drinker. In his twenties, he sometimes showed an inability to control his consumption in a way that worried him.

Nonetheless, John was also a highly talented and sought-after engineer. In his thirties he met Terry. Like John, she was highly intelligent and successful. Unlike John, her family was stable and secure. John and Terry decided to get married.

At one point before meeting Terry, John had actually quit drinking altogether. But at the time they met, John had resumed drinking, although he limited his consumption to the occasional beer. However, at the bachelor party the night before his wedding, John got falling-down drunk, and he showed up for his wedding with a black eye! Although his bruise wasn't terribly noticeable, John labored under the impression that he had committed a terrible faux pas in front of Terry's family.

John vowed never to get drunk again. Five years later, he had not—with his busy career and new family, John could not even imagine getting drunk. He was far too committed to his wife and son, Will, to allow his drinking to get out of hand.

John's rejection of excessive drinking, like many people's maturing out, grew out of a desire to be a responsible parent and spouse. A mature sense of obligation is not one suffused with guilt. It is rather a readiness to accept that what you do matters to others and that your concern for those you love is key to who you now are.

How to Develop a Mature Perspective

Even if you agree with the basic argument of this chapter, that assuming a mature identity counteracts the negative pull of addiction, you may still be wondering how this is a help to you. Isn't maturity something that just happens to you? Not necessarily. By examining yourself and your life, you can mature out more quickly, more surely, and more completely. Understanding the nature of maturity and how it overcomes addiction can actually assist you in becoming more mature.

You can strive to develop the qualities that define maturity:

1. *Self-efficacy,* developing the expectation, tools, and experience that you can accomplish necessary and worthwhile things ("I am able")
2. *Self-acceptance,* as you both recognize the good you have done and also become more realistic and modest about

yourself and your accomplishments ("My life is worthwhile even if I am not a TV star, rich, or a great scientist")

3. *Tolerance* for others' limitations, paralleling your self-
acceptance ("People are who they are; you take the good
with the bad")

4. *Responsibility* for your actions ("I am the source of my addiction and other behavior and of what I do about them")

5. *Obligation* to others ("Other people are counting on me")

6. *Faith* in continued existence, since the world and you have
both endured and will continue to do so ("I will survive
this; life goes on")

What's the Latest I Can Mature Out?

Now that we understand the general phenomenon of maturing out, let's take a look at the statistics. Research has revealed
a remarkable drop-off in substance abuse problems after people reach their mid-twenties. The National Survey on Drug
Use and Health for 2002 found that 22 percent of Americans
in the eighteen-to-twenty-five age bracket—more than one in
five—were diagnosed with alcohol or illicit drug abuse or dependence. Yet a third fewer who were twenty-six or older met
these criteria.[12]

So if you are twenty-five or younger, the odds are good that
you will overcome your substance addiction within a relatively
few years. However, don't despair if you didn't beat addiction
while still in your twenties or even your thirties. The National
Survey found an immediate drop-off of about a third in drug
and alcohol abuse and dependence between those age eighteen to twenty-five and those twenty-six to twenty-nine. But
this figure continues to decline in virtually a straight line
through all later age groups, to about 3.5 percent of those fifty-
five to sixty-four and about 1 percent of those sixty-five and
older.

2002 National Survey, Drug or Alcohol Abuse or Dependence

Age	Percentage Abusing or Dependent on Substance
16–17	17
18–25	22
26–29	15
30–34	12
35–39	11
40–44	9
45–49	8
50–54	7
55–59	3
60–64	4
65+	1

This table shows us that young adults are the worst substance abusers. However, a serious drinking problem is not likely to continue into old age. Although we regularly read about the supposed susceptibility of the aged to alcohol and other addictions, they are actually doing better than the rest of us.*

---

* See the Internet alcoholism news service Buddy T's *What You Need to Know About Recovery* report "Seniors Drinking Is Mostly Unreported, Undiagnosed, or Ignored" (http://alcoholism.about.com/library/weekly/aa981118.htm). Some experts, at least in other countries, see things differently. A press release titled "Elderly Drinking May Be 'More of a Boon than a Burden'" was issued by the 2003 (UK) Annual Meeting of the Royal College of Psychiatrists: "Oliver James, Professor of Geriatric Medicine at Newcastle University, said that there are too many myths surrounding drinking in the elderly which end up emphasising the potential problems: 'Alcohol use in the elderly is associated in my view with more unsubstantiated assertions than the Loch Ness monster'" (www.rcpsych.ac.uk/press/preleases/pr/pr_452.htm).

Joe, for instance, drank heavily and alcoholically throughout his forties and into his fifties, while his kids were growing up. For Joe, the responsibilities of parenthood did not motivate him to change, but rather generated stress that drove his drinking. But in his late fifties he reduced his drinking dramatically. As with some empty nesters, the reduction in stress that came about partly due to his children growing up and leaving home actually permitted him to cap his drinking.

Divergent Paths in Old Age

DISAPPOINTMENT AND ADDICTION

The large majority of addicts overcome addiction with age. However, we should note that not everyone gets better as they get older. In fact, a small percentage of people actually develop addictions as they age.

The life and identity issues are different for older addicts than for younger ones. When people develop late-life addictions, their lives have usually been derailed by disappointments, discontents, or a loss of moorings. This can be due, of course, to genuine failures in life, such as unfulfilling marriages, poor relationships with children, career missteps, or a lack of connection to one's community. For some people, the gap between what they aspired to and what they actually accomplished grows worse with age.

Take the example of Morris, the father of a man I knew. Morris had a lovely family: a supportive wife and two talented, well-mannered children. He himself was an intelligent and motivated man. However, he also rubbed people the wrong way. His own perfectionism caused Morris to strike out at people verbally, and he had a tendency to criticize his family and coworkers whenever he felt a sense of disappointment with himself.

When he was in his mid-fifties, because of the problems he

had with people, Morris found himself unemployed and reliant on his wife's salary as a teacher. Both of his children got college scholarships and moved away from home. Neither was inclined to invite him to visit. Then, when his wife suddenly died of a heart attack in her early sixties, Morris was almost completely alienated from human contact.

Eventually Morris decided to move to Mexico, which had always held a romantic image for him. There he found a few other expatriates to whom he could rail about the failing United States government and economy. These discussions were usually held over drinks. Always prone to drink heavily on weekends, Morris became known as a chronic and obnoxious drunk.

For Morris, a series of life disappointments led to depression and an alcohol problem. This is not to say that all failures ultimately turn into addictions. Some people go to jail and are outwardly disgraced, yet they emerge from the experience to lead productive lives. Richard Nixon seemed to recover his emotional equilibrium after being dishonored in the eyes of history. Others never recover from such a misstep.

You do not have to suffer Morris's fate, no matter what befalls you in life. It is not just the severity of the disappointment that you experience that determines the depth of your despair. The manner in which you react to disappointment depends on several factors, including your general coping skills, your resources, and your support network. You can always develop these skills and networks so as to remain an involved and happy member of society.

At the same time, the fact that most people overcome addiction—or, on the other hand, that some people develop addiction only after decades—indicates that addiction is not something that is determined at birth. Rather, it results from how individuals react to their experience and their worlds. Choices you make determine how long and how severely addiction will affect your life.

RECOVERING FROM THE END OF STARDOM

Addiction is an occupational hazard for people who have had great success early in life and whose later lives do not match the excitement of their youthful success. Athletes and celebrities are particularly susceptible to this late-onset life disappointment. Don Newcombe, the Brooklyn Dodgers pitcher, was one such individual, and he and others have created counseling services for athletes to prepare them for life after professional sports.

Even if you are leading a less fabulous life than you once did, you don't have to play out a negative script. After all, you can be thankful that you have had your time in the sun, and use that past success for whatever additional advantages it offers you in the future. If people's past traumas can contribute to their current misery, then it is just as easy to imagine that past triumphs contribute to your current happiness. The key is to see yourself as a valuable person even though the world's spotlight no longer shines on you. Moreover, you can always continue to work to improve those things you still have control over, such as your family life.

Take the example of Ringo Starr. Ringo was part of one of the greatest entertainment and cultural phenomena in history—the Beatles. But he was a minor part. Few of his songs made it onto Beatles records. Worse, Paul McCartney occasionally belittled Ringo's drumming and replaced Ringo's drum tracks with his own on some Beatles recordings. Although Ringo seemed to shrug off these slights, his post-Beatles career was marred by a growing alcohol problem. At one point Ringo tried to halt the release of album tracks on which he played the drums because alcohol had been served during the recording sessions, and he felt he had been too inebriated to perform well.

But Ringo eventually developed the acceptance to appreciate what he had accomplished. As a part of coming to terms with the disappointments of his career, he quit drinking and was able to celebrate his successes. He now contentedly describes himself as having had a good run with a fabulous group and as a man with a fulfilling family life. In this way, Ringo experienced a normal pattern of maturation, but much later in his life than people normally do. It is most important to keep in mind that Ringo's success in overcoming his alcoholism is the norm; Morris's fate is the aberration.

Securing Your Nonaddict Identity

A mature identity is one that allows you to take responsibility. It does not labor under the idea that you are really an addict, one who is constantly fighting off impulses to relapse. In twelve-step programs, it is essential for people to believe, and publicly announce, that they are alcoholics or addicts. The approach I endorse instead asks you to address your problems with the resources at hand; calling yourself an addict offers no added benefit. In fact, it interferes with the steps you need to take to attack the addiction, and certainly to cast it aside from your life. How can you if it is always there, a part of you, as the disease model maintains?

WAS I BORN TO BE AN ADDICT?

We regularly read about genetic discoveries with implications for alcoholism and other addictions. Although I have dealt with these in professional journals and other books, the principal point to be derived from this research is far from the common wisdom.[13] *No gene exists to make you lose control of your drinking, or anything else.* There are genetically influenced reactions to alcohol (although such reactions also have large learned components). But a genetic predisposition toward feeling great when you drink does not explain why you continue to rely on alcohol to gratify yourself or excuse such behavior.

Some theorists suggest that an addiction gene might predispose people to any of a number of addictions in addition to alcoholism, such as addictions to food, sex, or gambling.[14] What if you were to accept the claim that you had a gene for addiction? Would you resolve never to have a drink or never to gamble? Even those most geared to genetic hypotheses surely recognize that a young person given such a message is being set up for a self-fulfilling prophecy when he or she finally does (as most will) have a drink or buy a lottery ticket. In any case, you certainly could not resolve never to have sex or eat. Actually, the most sensible course of action to follow if a gene reliably predicting a predisposition to addiction were ever identified and you knew someone with the gene would be to educate the person to be cautious about substance use or other dependencies—the same thing you should do with any child.

People regularly overcome alcoholic and addictive legacies. Contrary to popular belief, most people with an alcoholic parent (three-quarters of them) do not become alcoholics themselves. Indeed, for many (often daughters of alcoholic fathers) the parent's drinking problem drives them *away* from such problems, and they are *less* likely than the average person to become alcoholic.[15] What enables so many to avoid following in a parent's—even a same-sex parent's—alcoholic footsteps? There are several related factors: if the family maintains a stable household despite the alcoholism, if the child has models of moderate drinking to counter the bad example of the alcoholic parent, and if the child is able to make progress toward achieving success on his or her own.[16]

We have already seen the case of John, who had drinking problems as a young man but who, after quitting for a while, resumed drinking moderately in his own family. John grew up in a large family with an alcoholic father. His mother, who didn't have a drinking problem, was a buoyant personality and highly industrious. She finally divorced her drunken spouse, but not until John had spent his childhood with his father. John often stated: "I know I have to watch my drinking, and when I was younger, I got in a lot of trouble around alcohol." But, as we saw, by the time John had his own child, he had not been drunk in many years. As he matured, John was able to assimilate his knowledge of how his father's drinking had affected him and his mother, a cycle he was determined not to repeat in his own family.

John's story is really about how, under favorable circumstances, alcoholism is not inherited. Although he acquired the skill of moderate drinking slowly, his work, his wife, his kids, and his friends all combined to reinforce his moderate drinking. In fact, none of his siblings has a drinking problem, although one brother, like John, had to work to get his drinking under control, and now only drinks occasionally. John and his siblings, all with good jobs and their own families, illustrate how addiction occurs in a life context, as part of the individual's overall lived experience, values, and social world. This is the fundamental nature of addiction.

Moreover, John never learned to think of himself as an alcoholic. Thus he was able to assume his adult responsibilities with relative ease when these were presented to him. Furthermore, he would never tell his own children they had an alcoholic inheritance—information that would serve only to interfere with their natural development.

MUST I ADMIT I'M AN ADDICT TO GET BETTER?

If John had entered treatment, he would likely have been instructed that his father's alcoholism had been passed down to him. This, combined with his youthful drinking problems, would have been taken as clear evidence that he himself was an alcoholic. But this would not likely have assisted him to assume the mature identity as a parent and provider for his family that he did.

Yet in order to graduate as a patient from most substance abuse treatment programs in the United States, you must admit that you are addicted. This includes youthful drug users, along with many others, who might not be classified as dependent (or addicted) by any objective diagnostic tool.

According to the standard wisdom, it is this admission that enables people to improve. But this is simply one more unproved assertion. Research such as the NLAES study I reviewed in the introduction reveals that there are lots of people who overcome alcohol dependence and other addictions during the course of their lives without treatment.[17] And although they may at some point have qualified for the technical diagnosis of alcohol (or some other) dependence, they never saw themselves in such a light, and never labeled themselves "alcoholic" or "addicted."

Sometimes researchers attempt to contact these ex-addicts identified in general population surveys, in order to ask them how they managed to beat their addictions. For example, Canadian researchers contacted individuals whose responses to a survey indicated they had formerly been compulsive gamblers. But virtually all of the subjects contacted in this way denied ever having had such a problem![18] While it is customary to label such denial as dysfunctional, it seems that for many— indeed, for the typical alcohol-, gambling-, or sex-dependent individual—*not* acknowledging they were addicted actually made it *easier* for them to escape the addictive behavior.

Since, according to the NLAES national alcohol study, the most common response to alcohol dependence is self-cure and cutting back, why don't we hear as much from such people as we do from those who join AA or who go to treatment and want to tell us all about it? The modesty of self-curers is partly due to the fact that they often cure their addiction unselfconsciously. When National Public Radio did a program on alcoholism called *Thinking About Drinking*, Casey Kasem was interviewed. He described his heavy drinking when he was a band manager and spent much of his time at clubs. When he found he couldn't clear his throat while doing a commercial, "that's when I stopped, and that was the last time that I had anything that was heavier than wine."[19]

Many people lose weight, reduce their drinking, or make other alterations in their behavior simply because they change work and personal situations. These people never saw themselves as addicts, or even as having a problem. They may never even have intended to alter their behavior, but it happened nonetheless as the result of other changes in their lives, intentional and unintentional, such as a shift in location, in social group, or in daily routine. When they were ready and able to make a change, these people simply broke free and didn't need to unlearn the destructive labels that treatment sometimes imposes on people. Indeed, too much reflection on what it means to be an addict can impede the natural recovery process.

How to Change an Addict Self-Image: Identity Work

What about those people who do feel that they are addicted? How do they develop a nonaddict identity that leaves them free to express a mature, independent, and self-respecting outlook? A number of researchers have focused on the changes in self-concept that people need to make in order to overcome addictions. These changes are called identity work. For some people (such as illicit drug users who have devoted years, maybe decades, to an addiction that isolates and ostracizes them) this can be a big project. Patrick Biernacki, who studied former heroin addicts, was the first to address these addicts' essential work in developing nonaddict identities, which he described as their "becoming and being 'ordinary.' "[20]

I spoke earlier in the chapter about one such former addict, Jerry, who escaped his addiction by moving away from his home city, getting an education, and becoming a responsible person. Several years later, Jerry suffered a severe burn in a kitchen accident, for which he was hospitalized. In addition to the drugs he received in the hospital, Jerry's physician gave him a renewable prescription for a powerful narcotic. When Jerry saw this, he realized that his old self would have been thrilled to have such a prescription because it was a free ticket to take drugs!

At the end of a month, there was no more pain in his leg, so Jerry stopped taking the Percodan. He didn't say to himself, as he admitted he would formerly have, "Well, what the hell, I'll take another two and have myself a little high. It won't hurt anybody." The difference was in what was going on in his life. He had a different relationship with people, with work, with the things that had become important to him. Jerry is an example of someone whose mature identity evolved as he consciously associated with different people who had positive lifestyles and goals, a process described in the previous chapter.

As he mused on his former self and old, addict attitudes, Jerry realized what it would cost him to revert to his old lifestyle. His position of respect among his friends, his career, his own newfound self-respect—all would have to go out the window if he took this "opportunity." For Jerry, there was simply no choice. He wasn't even tempted to return to drug use. To do so would have meant sacrificing his new nonaddict identity and returning to the irresponsible patterns of his immature self.

Some former addicts use their addict identity to assist them in growing into a positive social role—for example, by lecturing others on drugs or becoming antidrug crusaders. Anja Koski-Jännes, a Finnish researcher who specializes in "identity projects," described the extraordinary efforts of Mikko.[21] Mikko was a drug dealer who was so ashamed when he was arrested that that he took the great risk of turning on his former associates. Rejecting drugs entirely, Mikko took advantage of every opportunity for education and other positive activities in jail. When he left prison, his wife had divorced him, yet he fought to regain custody of his children and became a public opponent of drug use and criminal activity. Thus Mikko continued to espouse his identity as an addict, albeit in order to transition into a positive lifestyle.

Mikko would require one further transition in order to leave his addict identity behind altogether. The danger of building a positive lifestyle out of being (or having been) an addict is that you will remain completely enmeshed in this identity. Thus, even after you stop taking drugs, quit drinking, or lose weight, you could be as enslaved by your identity as a former or recovering addict as you were enslaved by your addict identity. In either case, you do not permit yourself to mature further.

This is why some people reject AA, even if they want to quit drinking altogether. I often get letters on my Web site from people who once found AA to be helpful but who now believe it seriously limits who they may become. Their concept of themselves has expanded beyond the boundaries permitted by AA, and they are ready to go out and live life as nonaddicts, rather than as recovering ones. This reaction against being categorized as an alcoholic is often greatest for people who enter AA at an early age, without ever having tried on a mature identity other than as an AA member. One teenage addict presented the difficulty, almost trauma, in having accepted this identity at such a formative age:

I am a twenty-two-year-old who has been abstinent from drugs and alcohol for the past five years. I have been drug- and alcohol-free much longer than I used drugs.

I feel lost in life; I have become an adult with the twelve steps drilled into me, but I recently have been seeing holes in the lifestyle I am expected to live.

I have only had friends in this twelve-step program (NA) since I was seventeen. Although my boyfriend is normal, we have no alcohol in the house, and we live with two other twelve-steppers.

But I don't believe in the "Santa Claus" of Narcotics Anonymous anymore. NA worked at first to keep me from self-destructing, but I am dissatisfied with how my life is spent now. There is no goal for me in NA.

I honestly can say I don't know what will happen when I leave NA. I am scared that I have been overly socialized and will become a self-fulfilling prophecy. I would like to know what a glass of wine, alone, tastes like, too. (Being seventeen and drinking means you drink whatever is there, so I have never had a proper mixed drink or a single glass of decent wine.)

Can I escape the twelve-step world in which I'm trapped?

It is generally unwise to place people so young in AA or NA, while they are still growing up and deciding who they are. Older individuals, too, may decide they are ready to leave twelve-step groups behind. There are Web sites and books for people who feel they must be deprogrammed to fully get beyond AA. A number of books have related stories of how people fought free of AA identities—for example, Rebecca Fransway's *12-Step Horror Stories* and Marianne Gilliam's *How Alcoholics Anonymous Failed Me*.[22] These stories are of people who eagerly participated in AA but ultimately found it more degrading than uplifting. This occurs most often for women. Now, these individuals declare, they want to go out on their own to live as mature individuals without the addict label.

Of course, some people may have no other option for escaping their addictions (or at least they feel this way). Only the individual can say, and this book supports fully informed self-determination. As long as you choose freely and are an adult in a position to make this choice, AA and similar groups remain one viable route away from addiction, whether you choose a group as a way of transitioning from addiction or settle on group membership and your recovering identity as a permanent vision of who you are.

Developing a New Vision of Yourself

While the young woman who rejected NA was in her early twenties, some people log many more bad miles and incur many more visible scars due to their addictions. Yet they, too, seemingly finally achieve a mature resolution of their identities that enables them finally to leave addiction entirely behind. One historical case reveals just how far a person may go and how much he may have to do before this resolution occurs fully.

Sam Houston, the founding father of the state of Texas, was a raging alcoholic.[23] As a child, Houston lived with the Cherokee, who adopted him. He followed his stint living with

Native Americans by serving heroically as a soldier under Andrew Jackson. Houston was elected to Congress, then became the governor of Tennessee.

Houston got married while he was governor, but his wife quickly left him (possibly because of his drinking and other rough frontier ways). Devastated, he resigned the governorship and returned to the Cherokee Nation, where he impressed even his adopted people—known for their own drinking problems—with the magnitude of his alcohol addiction. Houston was given the Cherokee name "Big Drunk." During this period Houston was charged with contempt for a vicious verbal attack on a congressman, and defended himself by giving a drunken harangue on the floor of Congress.

From this low point, in his late thirties, Houston steadily improved his life. He moved to Texas (then part of Mexico), set up a law practice, and converted to Catholicism. When Texans rebelled against Mexico, Houston became commander of their forces, and after Texas gained its independence he was overwhelmingly elected the first president of the Republic of Texas. When Texas became a state, he became a U.S. senator and then governor. Houston was the only southern governor to fight (unsuccessfully) against secession from the Union.

As demonstrated by his political ascendance, Houston was no longer perceived as a "big drunk." Yet although he greatly reduced the frequency and amount of his alcohol consumption, he continued to drink and to become inebriated. While a senator, for example, Houston built on his reputation as a drinker, a womanizer, and a brawler. Finally, in his fifties, Houston married a strong, religious woman half his age, had eight children, became a Baptist, and swore off alcohol altogether.

What brought Houston's drinking under control? Apparently blinded by American myths about alcoholism, a reviewer discussing two books written on Houston's two hundredth birthday complained that "neither adequately explains the nature of his alcoholism or the means by which he overcame it."[24]

But no more explanation for Houston's success at reducing

and then eliminating his alcohol problem is needed than Houston's own life story. Through decades of success and recognition, marriage and family, religious conversion, and personal commitment, Houston continued to mature. Speaking to a local Rotary Club, I asked what had enabled Sam Houston to turn from a falling-down drunk to a Texas and national hero. One middle-aged man hit the nail on the head when he answered that "he developed a new vision of himself."

It might be harder to recover from some of Sam Houston's missteps today. But the world is always receptive to people who reclaim their dignity and who lead productive lives. In any case, it is always worth the effort and risk for you to bring your life to a point where you can see yourself in a new, positive light. In fact, another Texan was recently elected president of the United States despite having been arrested for a DUI and having engaged in other alcohol-inspired shenanigans, after which he underwent a religious conversion that helped him quit drinking. Only at that point could George W. Bush be seen as mature enough to be elected to state and then national office.

A New, Nonaddict Identity

As you already know, some views of addiction assert that people cannot change their addict identities. However, it is also important to note that changing one's self-image is difficult for all types of people, not just former drug or alcohol addicts. For example, people's body images are very constant. Thus people who have been fat since childhood tend to see themselves as they have always been—even after they have lost the weight.

You may feel that you are still on sensitive ground with your addiction. You may decide to abstain from alcohol, to avoid any possibility of casual sexual contact, or to consciously avoid buffets. However, you need no longer think of yourself as an addicted person.

Leading a whole life, not calling attention to your addiction, and not visualizing your addict self in every situation are all parts of developing your new identity. There are benefits to believing that you are not an addict, and to presenting yourself to others in this way. Their acceptance of your nonaddict self-image will bolster your new self-view, just as your conviction in your new identity will convince others of its veracity.

Louise's problems involve lifetime self-concept issues, without a drug addiction, but with a powerful addictive theme. Louise was a doormat in her relationships. When she dated a man, she turned herself over to him lock, stock, and barrel. Either because this tempted any man to mistreat her or because such behavior only attracted insecure males, Louise always found herself in relationships where love meant sacrificing every aspect of her life to her lover.

After numerous relationships like this, it seemed only logical for Louise to marry a man whose interests and predilections determined everything for the two of them. Yet it was he who seemed to tire of the relationship and who initiated the divorce.

After her divorce, Louise simply concentrated on making a life for herself. She felt a sense of urgency, since she was to receive alimony for only seven years. To her great satisfaction, she created a catering business that enabled her to support herself and to keep the small home she had retained from the marriage.

Into this busy life came Larry, a man with his own divorce and baggage. When he asked her out, Louise agreed, but indicated that she wanted to keep things strictly casual. In Louise's mind, an intimate relationship with a man could go only one way—and that way meant hell for her. So Louise was shocked by her own behavior after she started to date Larry. She called off some dates because of late job assignments or employees who got sick, and it was Larry who seemed to wait for her calls and to cautiously but insistently ask when she would be free.

"This is *wonderful*," Louise thought. "I didn't know that I could get to play this role in a relationship!" She decided that men, love, and sex *could* now be part of a self-respecting life, something that her life up until then had never offered her. This experience cemented Louise's maturing conception of herself as an independent, self-confident woman—something her employees and customers had always seen in her.

Integrity

Along with their belated maturity, Sam Houston, Jerry, and Louise finally achieved integrity in their lives. That is, when they grew to a point where they could leave behind their addictions, they came to lead lives that were consistent with their basic values, which others admired, and of which they themselves could be proud.

The themes of maturity, responsibility, and integrity—and how these both impact and result from your changing identity—lead to the themes explored in the next chapter. If you have become secure enough to look outward to other people and to expand the scope of your life—to be a more productive, healthier person, a better friend and parent, a better community member—then you are prepared to define larger goals for yourself. You are also growing to become someone who works to create a better world for yourself and others. These larger goals are the subject of our next chapter.

■■■■■

Exercise: Pick a Maturity Role Model

Think of a person you've known, observed, or heard about (maybe a family member) who went through a process of maturation, including outgrowing addiction. Now review the details of the life changes and maturation that enabled this person to quit his or her addiction. What guidelines does this example offer for achieving maturity in your own life? Keep this model before you as you strive to make similar changes, including escaping addiction.

Exercise: Ask How You're Doing

Have you quit an addiction in any area: smoking, overeating, relationship addictions, drinking? Perhaps your image in your own eyes does not adequately reflect the changes you have made. Ask someone you met since you quit this addiction how he or she views your self-control, particularly in the area of your addiction. Ask if the person sees any ways in which he or she acts differently than you do in that same area. You may reveal that you were formerly addicted, or you may simply say, "You seem to have good self-control; I just wanted your opinion." Take the person's feedback seriously. You may now be as normal as that person is.

Exercise: Whom Do You Admire?

Name a person whom you enjoy seeing or interacting with. What is it that defines this person's appeal? Think about yourself in these terms—do you have any of the qualities you admire in this person?

Now visualize yourself as though you had all of this admired person's qualities, conducting your life with his or her grace and command. Can you imagine yourself living your ideal self? Step outside and try it now, or else practice living this ideal at the very next opportunity.

Exercise: Bridge the Gap Between Your Self-Image and Reality

Where do you feel your self-image most lags behind your actual self? That is, in what area do you constantly find that you underestimate yourself, your ability, or your image in the outside world? Explain this discrepancy. What can you do about it?

7

Higher Goals: Pursuing and Accomplishing Things of Value

Your goals in life are the directions you are pursuing. These goals are important advantages for overcoming addictions. You will not usually be sufficiently motivated to give up an addiction or habit simply because it is bad for you or because others want you to stop. But when a habit or addiction interferes with accomplishing a goal you want to attain, or something larger you are committed to, you are more inclined to quit. Thus instead of focusing on what you need to quit or escape from, it is critical to focus on what you want to achieve. Giving up your addiction then becomes a necessary step on the road to getting where you wish to go.

Of course, your goals have to mean something. After all, scoring drugs is a kind of goal, as is winning the lottery or driving a large car. But these are self-centered goals that simply feed your appetites. The goals I mean are those that have larger value in the world and for the world—goals that represent accomplishments, benefits to others, and contributions to your community. When you enhance and improve your contributions to others, or your output, you will find it easier to curtail excessive intake.

This chapter focuses on becoming fully involved in life. Among the most important things that you should do in order to overcome your addiction are to take active steps to improve your life in itself, but also your relations to other people and the world. In an ideally nonaddicted kind of life, you interact with people seriously and care about them. This begins with your family and extends to your community and the world at large. When your perspective is focused on other people and such larger goals, you are not inclined to be tripped up by destructive, self-focused addictions.

A Moral Approach to Life

We began this book with a discussion about values and the many ways in which they help people find their path out of addiction. We identified a variety of values—health, independence, self-control, religious faith—that strengthen people's resolve to escape destructive behavior. In this chapter, I am calling on you to function on a higher moral level by living according to values that have a positive impact on other people's lives.

AA recognizes the importance of reaching out to other people as a part of the recovery process. The twelve steps encourage former addicts to "carry the message" of AA on to alcoholics. The message AA participants are expected to spread is the "spiritual awakening [they have had] as a result of these steps." But AA advocates that its members help people only insofar as this involves sharing the AA message.

There is more to becoming involved with others, however, than rescuing alcoholics. If the essential problem of addiction is that addicts are preoccupied with their own lives, then it follows that the real problem is that addicts are insufficiently connected to those around them. Furthermore, if our society's addiction problem is the result of damaged communities, then effective solutions must involve repairing those communities. Activities directed toward improving the fabric of society take the form of prosocial actions by the individual.

Revisiting the Sources of Addiction

The disease theory of addiction has two essential flaws in considering people's need for prosocial action. First of all, if you really believe addiction is a disease, then it is something that *happens* to you. Second, if addiction is a disease, then people will be equally likely to suffer from it regardless of their environment or where they stand in society.

Let's examine the second disease assumption first. If addiction is a biological reaction to drugs or alcohol, then settings such as inner-city ghettos or Native American reservations should not impact addiction. Likewise, we could see our communities destroyed, but young people would not become more susceptible to drug and alcohol abuse, overeating, or desperate love affairs if they live in frightened and barren communities. And yet, as we have seen, deprived communities encourage excess and addiction, from obesity to drug abuse.

Addiction does not stand alone. It is not an isolated biological fact of your life. Who you are, where you are situated, what you believe, and what company you keep are fundamental factors in the addictive equation. Trying to understand the eating disorders of college women without accounting for their anxious, encapsulated environments is a pointless exercise, just as it impossible to comprehend drug addiction without understanding people's lack of opportunity and hopelessness.

To make this crystal clear, think back to the Vietnam veterans we discussed in the introduction to this book, and how so many quit substantial heroin habits. In that case, when young men were taken out of a frightening, boring, and hostile environment and returned to a rich and engaged home life, most readily overcame their addictions. As for the veterans who remained engrossed in drugs, they showed the same inability to become meaningfully involved with their lives at home that many of their cohorts had in Vietnam.

Obviously environment is critical in addiction. But, returning to the first point, what is wrong with assuming that addiction is a disease that simply happens to people? What's wrong with viewing addicts as hapless victims? For one thing, even in cases of severe addiction, it just isn't true. Furthermore, throughout this book, we have seen that there are costs to thinking of yourself as powerless against your addiction. The most successful strategy for tackling addiction is to see yourself as an active participant in the addiction and its solution. Your selection and pursuit of goals is among the best ways to make sure you overcome and avoid addiction.

Personal Goals

Worthwhile personal goals are those you pursue to make yourself a better person, to improve and advance your life. In Chapter 4, we reviewed the Community Reinforcement Approach and its Happiness Scale and Goals of Counseling. These are forms addicted clients complete to identify where they stand in all the major areas of life, and how they want to change each. These include, in addition to substance abuse or another addictive behavior, money management, social life, family relationships, and others. At a personal, individual level, examples of such self-bettering goals and the steps necessary to achieve them include exercising, pursuing your education or other training, advancing your career, maintaining and improving relations in your family, confronting personal issues in therapy, and eating properly—all things that contribute to a constructive and happy life.

You can chart your progress in all of these areas of your life like a grid, where your progress in one area contributes to success in the others. Of course, one category you would include in the grid, interrelated with all the others, would be any addictions you are addressing. You'll see as you fill in the grid that pursuing the other goals naturally leads to improvement in the addictive behavior.

Personal Life Goals Grid

Family	Work	Addiction(s)	Project(s)	Health
GOALS				
Enjoy home life	Get promotion	Stop excessive drinking/eating	Build patio	Lose weight/improve health
STEPS				
Spend time with kids	Impress boss	Come home right after work	Spend time on project	Jog/walk four days per week
Come home	Do good work	Feel good about work/family	Take masonry course	Skip snacks at work
Create positive home climate	Concentrate on work	Think better of myself	Ask brother-in-law for help	Eat meals with family

These goals are good and necessary as a part of fighting addictions. They contribute to and create the resources that counteract addiction. They make you feel better about yourself and help you learn that you have control over the things that matter in your life. In and of themselves they enhance your power over an addiction.

But the goals listed in the grid are also limited to your own immediate life framework (although this will usually include other family members). They do not describe how you will relate to the larger world, outside of those people and activities that are essential to your own functioning. They are focused solely on you and your success. This is good, but not sufficient, for a full and nonaddicted life.

Addiction Is Self-Centered

Addiction is a style of consuming food, drink, drugs, bets, shopping binges, or lovers in excess. Why is it that addicts so avariciously seek these things? One answer is that they are focused exclusively on their own needs, or supposed needs, and are insufficiently connected emotionally with the larger world and the lives of the people around them. William Bennett, Ronald Reagan's secretary of education and George H.W. Bush's drug czar, is a moral philosopher who wrote *The Book of Virtues*. He was also a gambling addict who lost $8 million.[1] As he defended himself against charges of hypocrisy and immorality, Bennett could not grasp the way his actions impacted his loved ones or the larger community. Where was his family all those nights he was sitting in high-roller rooms in casinos incessantly pulling slot machine levers? Why didn't he contribute his excess wealth to his church or to education funds for underprivileged kids, rather than to casinos?

Substance abusers, compulsive gamblers, shoppers, and lovers are often notable for their superficial, neglectful, and manipulative relationships with relatives and friends. They may steal from them or leech off them as an irresponsible child does with an indulgent parent. This lack of concern for others, the absence of moorings in the community, permits people to pursue addiction without compunction. As you probably realize by now, you are behaving selfishly while you pursue your addiction; this is a powerful reason for you to quit.

Stories of compulsive gamblers are often narratives about people who have floated through life on the backs of others. Greg was a good-looking man who had a series of attractive lovers. He intentionally never lived with one, however, because then the women would see how much of his time he spent placing bets, reviewing racing forms, and going to gambling casinos. Instead, he made up a series of imaginative fictions to explain his life and extract money from the women; when a woman grew tired of this treatment, he moved on to a new one. Greg and many others like him never really connected to their own nuclear families, either because the family was not intact (this was true for Greg), or because of abuse, turmoil, and alienation within the home.

Oddly, this lack of commitment to others characterizes even cases where one person is addicted to another. A person's ability to ignore everyone besides the person he or she is obsessed with (and him- or herself) makes this destructive addiction possible. Monique had a consuming relationship with a man who was in and out of prison. One time she had her sister over for dinner. While Monique was preparing dinner, her boyfriend called to say he had just been arrested. Monique flew out the door, shouting to her sister, "I have to bail Tom out. Take the chicken out of the oven, eat what you want, and let yourself out." Of course, Monique's family and friends were reluctant to have anything to do with her when they realized that at any moment she could be called on to assist Tom and they would be shown the door.

For her part, Monique considered herself selflessly devoted to her lover; she was willing to give up everything in her life to help him. But she was really gaining satisfaction from feeling that Tom needed her. This satisfaction came at the expense of disregarding everyone else who cared about her. Her behavior demonstrated the lack of self-respect of a person who would allow her plans and her life to be disrupted at a moment's notice by a needy lover. Monique felt so bereft of love, nurturance, and emotional resources that it seemed natural to her to sacrifice so much of herself and others to this one unworthy dependent.

Addiction Is Antisocial

It's no coincidence that many smokers don't hesitate to throw their filthy cigarette butts in the street. This disregard for the well-being of other people is common to addicts. When people point out the social costs of addiction, they often point to crime, lost productivity, and health care costs entailed by substance abusers. But many of the social costs of addiction-related behavior are much more immediate. Here are some of the side products of addiction that are irritating or harmful to other people:

- Noisy intoxication
- Irresponsibility
- Litter (e.g., cigarette butts)
- Theft
- Assault and violence
- Modeling poor behavior for children
- Cost to society (e.g., health care)
- Inability to contribute to others or to society

Working Within the Family

In looking beyond your selfish concerns and negative social impact, your family is the first place to examine. In Chapter 5 we saw the critical role of the family in addiction treatment for the individual. Taking this back one step, your dealings with your family influence the likelihood of addiction for you, your partner, and your children—or your and their resistance to addiction. Thus your family is the first group beyond yourself with which you must be concerned in combating addiction. It is also the first point of attack for drug or other addiction problems.

Once they use or develop a problem with drugs, adolescents are often targeted for substance abuse and mental health therapy. In three-quarters of cases, they are ordered to undergo such treatment by a court or by their school system.[2] For example, when teenagers are caught with marijuana in a school locker or have a positive drug test, they are likely to be ordered into counseling as a condition of remaining in school. This, in turn, often leads to formal drug treatment. Between 1993 and 1999, the number of teens admitted for substance treatment rose almost 50 percent, from 95,000 to 135,000.

Will this treatment really work to reduce adolescent substance abuse? Why do families need so much assistance from, or turn so readily to, professionals? For one thing, they are encouraged by educators to look for outside help at the first sign of trouble. But the family must remain the child's greatest resource. It cannot be replaced by outside expertise, and it is a sign of impending trouble for the individual family, and for our society at large, that the family is so frequently bypassed.

This is especially true given the particular problems of applying traditional treatments to teenage addicts. We have seen that it is harmful to children to be told they are lifetime addicts and that they are powerless over their addictions. When children with relatively less severe substance abuse problems are lumped in with more severe abusers instead of being seen as slightly troubled members of otherwise healthy families, their severely addicted fellow group members become the children's primary role models. One consequence is that the children may become demoralized by thinking they are as badly off as these seasoned addicts. Most important, they—and their parents—don't learn the skills necessary for managing themselves and the family after therapy.

The film *Traffic* dramatically depicted this dysfunctional aspect of traditional treatment. In the film, a young girl, the daughter of the new drug czar, played by Michael Douglas, is shown spiraling out of control with drugs. At one point, she attends a group session with older drug addicts and alcoholics. She is shown arguing with other group members who dispute her claim that she never had a drinking problem in addition to her drug use, as indeed she had not. The movie shows her quickly relapsing. Because she rightly rejected the message of the group and didn't feel she belonged with the other members, she was as far adrift as before she attended.

Later in the movie, the young woman is shown participating together with her parents in another program. This dramatization pointed viewers in the right direction. Successful therapy does not convey disease mantras or label adolescents. Instead, it focuses on developing skills such as communication, self-control, and problem solving, particularly within the family. Effective treatment programs for teens are those that encourage them to take an active role in shaping their environments—focusing outward, as well as inward, to improve the conditions of their lives.

One such program is a multifaceted family approach called Multidimensional Family Therapy (MDFT).[3] This therapy includes sessions with the child, sessions with the parents, and sessions with the child and the parents together. The therapist works with the adolescent and parents in family-building tasks, focusing on relationships, communication, and problem solving within the family and in the larger world.

Children's coping and life-building skills are at the center of MDFT treatment, with the family serving as a supportive network. Once the family has learned to examine their own interactions, they and the child can apply the same insights and skills to the child's life outside the family. Agreement and cooperation are sought in addressing important areas of the child's life, such as how the child is relating to peers and authority figures, and the child's school participation or vocational training.

The strength of MDFT training is that it recognizes the need to address both individual and family problems, rather than treating the child's behavior as an isolated pathology or assuming that the family is automatically able to deal with such behavior without learning techniques to address family interactions. The importance of combining personal work with work within the family and helping children is illustrated by

Marie, who came to me because she needed help with her drinking—and with her dysfunctional family.

Marie felt that her marriage was the source of her alcoholism. She had basic value conflicts with her husband about how they should live and how they should interact with their children, who were now out of the home. Marie had to stand up for her values: to insist that they visit the children more often, that they spend more time traveling (they had the money to do so), and that they engage in healthier activities (compared with the social scene they were involved in, where heavy drinking was the rule). Marie was also struggling to deal with the fact that her daughter was also a heavy drinker—worse off, in fact, than Marie.

As Marie mastered the communication techniques she needed to express herself in her marriage, she became much more helpful to her daughter. Her daughter began to recognize and admire her mother's efforts, and to begin to stand up for herself in her relationships—for example, the daughter refused to relocate and change jobs when her current lover demanded that she move with him. This in turn reinforced Marie's confidence in asserting herself in her own marriage. Thus the two women's sense of self-efficacy increased in tandem: As Marie gained control over her drinking problem, her daughter also began to see an avenue to escape her alcoholism.

What If the Family Is Deficient and Irremediable?

Marie's and her family's problems were not so severe that they were insurmountable. However, some families are so crippled that it will be difficult for children ever to succeed solely within the four walls of their homes. Popular movies and TV shows don't focus on the kinds of families with the highest risk for drug and alcohol addiction—they are simply not photogenic. These are families that are deeply deprived and include many truly disturbed homes.

A group of psychologists led by David Hawkins at the University of Washington reviewed all the available research conducted on adolescent substance abuse in order to identify children's risk factors.[4] These involve deep-seated individual and family problems:

- Physiological factors (e.g., genetically transmitted traits that predispose kids to use or rely on alcohol or drugs)
- Family alcohol- and drug-related behavior and attitudes (e.g., heavy alcohol or drug use by other family members)
- Poor and inconsistent family management practices (e.g., insufficient parental involvement, unclear or unrealistic expectations of children, inadequate or inconsistent discipline)
- Intense family conflict
- Poor bonding (attachment or connection) to family
- Early and persistent problem behaviors by the child
- Academic failure
- Low degree of commitment to school
- Peer rejection in elementary grades
- Association with drug-using peers
- Alienation and rebelliousness
- Attitudes favorable to drug use (e.g., believing drug use is acceptable or "cool")
- Early onset of drug use

In addition to these family and individual problems, Hawkins and his colleagues identified four larger environmental or contextual factors:

- Laws and norms favorable toward behavior (i.e., community acceptance of heavy drinking or of drug use)
- Availability of drugs and alcohol
- Extreme economic deprivation
- Neighborhood disorganization

Thus beyond the family are broader social contexts, including the neighborhood the child lives in and the community of which the child is a member. The disintegration of community is more notable in some communities than others. But it is something relevant to us all.

Building Communities for Children

In 2003 the National Institutes of Health (along with other federal agencies) released the report on *America's Children*. It further solidified the realization (expressed by the U.S. surgeon general, among others) that the number one public health crisis for American youth is not drugs or alcohol. It is adolescent obesity. In the twenty years from 1980 to 2000, the rate of obesity among children rose two and a half times, from 6 percent to 15 percent. The figures were even higher for Hispanic (25 percent) and African-American (22 percent) children.[5]

The health consequences of this leap in obesity are tremendous. In the first place, substantial numbers of children now display atherosclerosis (fat deposits in their arteries), which leads to the single greatest cause of death in the U.S., coronary artery disease. Large numbers of children are also developing type 2 diabetes—known formerly as adult-onset diabetes because it is triggered by lifestyle factors. Type 2 diabetes has increased tenfold among the young in the past five years, and now accounts for almost half of childhood diabetes.

An article in the *Journal of the American Medical Association* identified the culprits in the fattening of America's children: fast foods, soda, and other junk foods in schools, and the absence of activity in the lives of children, who spend most of their recreational time sitting in front of electronic entertainments.[6] Thus childhood weight problems arise from behaviors deeply rooted in our social customs and daily lives.

One recommendation for reducing childhood obesity is to remove soda and candy machines from schools.[7] Michael

Jacobson, executive director of the Center for Science in the Public Interest (CSPI), recommends that the federal government support school gym programs and mass media campaigns about the problem. Another way to fight obesity at home is to reduce the amount of fatty and sugary snacks and to set limits on television, video games, listening to CDs, talking on the phone, and home movie viewing. Of course, the same result would be achieved with far less stress if children became involved in engaging outdoor activities.

In fact, many parents welcome passive electronic entertainments for their children as a safe alternative to what they perceive as a dangerous world. Because their local communities are eroding, parents no longer feel safe sending children outside to play with other children. Today's kids simply don't view physical activity as part of their daily routines. While many play organized sports like soccer, they never think to venture outside on their own to kick a ball around. As they enter their later teen years and most drop out of organized competition, this generation does not have the means on its own to engage in physical exercise or exertion.

In order to buck the childhood obesity trend, we need to create new outlets for children to interact with their peers. But no recreation program can replace what was once the most effective form of weight control ever discovered, one that is unfortunately disappearing from our world—the natural exuberance of childhood. Nonetheless, there are ways to support these experiences of childhood friendship and fun. Following are steps to help foster a safe and joyful community for your children:

1. Expose your children early on to close contact with relatives and friends.
2. Play outside with your children and invite other children to join.
3. Encourage your children to spend time with other children in different settings.

4. As they age, encourage your children to play with other children on their own.
5. Emphasize that your children take their commitments to peers seriously.
6. Do not engender fear in your children by venting exaggerated fears of your own.

In addition to providing your children with a supportive and enriching community, it is important to teach them to deal with their peers responsibly and with respect. From the earliest moment, you can teach children that it is important to take others seriously. Are they taught to welcome other children, in their own home and on the playground? Must they share their toys? Must they treat other children's toys and property with respect? Are they punished for harming other children or destroying their property? In teaching your children to respect others, you set a pattern for the rest of their lives.

That being outdoors and involved with others prevents childhood obesity actually suggests steps for you to take if you are an overweight or obese adult. Obviously, getting outdoors and exercising, and finding companions who will join you, are positive steps. Of course, you need to be involved with and respect other people to have these opportunities to be drawn into and to have company in your outdoor forays.

Your actions, whether you are combating a weight problem or not, have critical implications for your children's attitudes toward themselves and others. As you take responsibility for yourself, you also teach your children to take responsibility. It is another step beyond this to teach children to be kind, to respond to the needs of others, and to be concerned about their well-being. In the same way, following through on your own commitments teaches children that they need to keep their word, and beyond this to extend themselves in their dealings with others.

Quality Time with Children and Time on Their Own

Parents are frequently lectured that the key to producing healthy offspring is paying attention to their children. Yet constant attention does not produce successful kids. Strong values and engagement with your children are what is required. Rebecca is one example of an incredibly active and involved parent whose children have reproduced their mother's energetic commitment to life and to others.

Rebecca and her husband had three children. When her children were still young, Rebecca became active in, and was soon the director of, an influential environmental defense and education group. Rebecca was known as an extremely effective manager and also as a political infighter. Many of her projects involved organizing outdoor educational activities. Others required tracking and combating environmentally unfriendly building projects. Although she preferred working cooperatively, Rebecca was not afraid to do battle when that was required.

Rebecca's job was not nine to five. Educational programs, which frequently occurred outdoors, were often held on evenings and weekends. Rebecca also regularly attended municipal board meetings concerning development projects. Her husband also worked long, irregular hours. Thus the children were often required to prepare their own dinners, to see to their homework, and to perform household tasks. Nonetheless, Rebecca and her husband made sure to be with the children during critical performances and whenever they required real assistance.

Although frequently left to their own devices, Rebecca's kids excelled both academically and in a variety of extracurricular activities. When people marveled at the children's multi-talented success, particularly given that they had two busy parents who were often out of the home, Rebecca replied, "We didn't think you had to watch them every minute in order to provide them with good values, direction, and support. We never demanded A's. But we did insist that they do the best they can possibly do at whatever they turn their hand to."

Not only did these children excel at school and at a wide range of activities, but they were nice kids. Some wanted to commit themselves, like their mother, to public service. Rebecca explained: "We have always emphasized to our children that they have to take responsibility for their actions; that commitments to others are real and important; and to be kind and caring toward others."

It is reassuring to note that neither Rebecca nor her husband was brought up in an ideal home. However, they rose above their own upbringings to improve the setting in which their children were reared. This is not to say that Rebecca's family lived a trouble-free life—in fact, their family had just as many day-to-day conflicts and struggles as most—but they demonstrate how instilling a sense of responsibility and community contributes to children who are successful in all kinds of ways. Of course, you do not have to head a government agency or environmental defense group to create this kind of spirit in your family.

Contributing to Communities

Community involvement was once a ticket for human existence—if you were not part of a community, you could not survive, let alone function. The beauty and the failure of modern life is that this is no longer true. We can function almost exclusively alone, at least with electronic and paid help. So being involved in your community now requires you to make an active choice. But we cannot defeat excess and addiction in a society of isolated individuals.

The value of community effort is reciprocal. It is therapeutic for you as an individual, strengthening your sense of responsibility, your interactions and interdependence with other human beings, and your satisfaction with life. Additionally, we've discussed how strong communities support (and discipline) their members and aid in preventing addiction. But the maintenance of a strong community requires the efforts of many individuals. Thus, when you contribute to your community, you not only reduce your own susceptibility to addiction, but also help others avoid or overcome addictions.

In these efforts, you need to look for people to connect with. Community is not an abstract concept. Start out by strengthening some of the connections you already have. For example, you might try to engage more with family members, neighbors who need help, or friends and business associates who are already part of your life. In Chapter 5, Lana turned to a nurturing relative with whom she had been out of touch, to fellow artists, and to several mentors for a new sense of self and of her possibilities. She then entered a group—a university community—where she felt welcome and where she was ready to participate fully.

You may already engage in group and community activities, especially if you have children—for example, helping out at school or church or assisting in your kids' soccer and baseball leagues. You can contribute to the well-being of your community in even small, anonymous ways—by participating in a local fund-raiser, being cautious to reduce your speed when driving through residential areas or school zones, or avoiding littering.

It is my bias, of course, but clients I treat for addiction invariably lack sufficient connections with others. This void is demonstrated in virtually every case in this book—recall David or Monique, who fell for destructive lovers when they were unable to connect with their families or anyone outside their dysfunctional affairs. My therapeutic inputs always include encouraging the person to reach out to others and make contact with broader communities.

After you connect with the people who are closest to you, you can then broaden your scope to address your relationships with others—people in your neighborhood, your city, your country, and across the world. Of course, you probably already spend time with, or thinking about, all of these people and groups. But you can always make these involvements deeper and more satisfying.

There are many ways to do this—by working with people who are physically or psychologically injured; by striving to reduce poverty, injustice, and suffering; by protecting the future of the planet and the health and welfare of future generations. These efforts sometimes involve influencing public policy, either directly or through the election of those who make policy. Not everyone is comfortable engaging in political activity. But you can strive to create personal truth, morality, and beauty. You can accomplish this through artistic and scientific contributions, working to improve the ethics of your profession, or even participating in a community garden. The important thing is to decide to expand your contributions to the world. Once you make that decision, the right opportunity will present itself.

Community Involvement as Personal Sustenance

Being a part of something larger than yourself—making contributions to other people's lives—provides you with the life purpose and meaning that will sustain you through times of trouble. The role of community effort in personal sustenance was critical for Jim and Ruth. A couple in their thirties, Jim and Ruth had lived in their neighborhood for several years. A neighbor invited them to join their local neighborhood association, and they began picking up trash and planting trees in a neglected local park. After many years, the town recognized the efforts of Jim and Ruth's group and its contributions to the well-being of the community, and began to upgrade and maintain the park with town funds.

Around this time, a private developer announced that he wanted to build condominiums in another area of the neighborhood that contained important wetlands. Jim and Ruth began a fight against this development that was to take more than a decade. They and other community leaders got substantial numbers of people to attend municipal meetings, and the town was forced to pay attention to their concerns.

Over the years, as the neighborhood group succeeded in holding up the development, the town came to see the property as valuable to the health and vitality of the community, and thus to the town. As times changed, voters set aside public funds for buying some of the little remaining open space within the town's borders. The town finally purchased the contested property, preserving it forever as open space for the enjoyment of residents.

As they attended municipal meetings, Jim and Ruth became very aware of how their town functioned, of environmental regulations the town needed, and of other groups working on similar concerns throughout their state. They played a large role in modernizing their town's environmental ordinances, and became known to others concerned about preserving the environment.

At one point, Ruth—who had an MBA—decided she no longer wished to continue working for a Fortune 500 company. Although she and Jim had children and college expenses, she was willing to take a cut in salary in order to do something more meaningful. The job she chose was an extension of the volunteering she had been doing for years. It built on the knowledge she had acquired, the connections she had made, and the skills she had developed. Jim supported her in this career change.

Some years later, Jim and Ruth met someone who had made a great deal of money as a private entrepreneur. This woman now wanted to retire from her business to devote her time to worthwhile causes. But when Jim asked her what she planned to do, she said she didn't know, never having volunteered or having any civic interests. Instead, she powered on, making money and shouldering stress, but with no goal in sight.

By contrast, as Ruth and Jim reflected on their lives, they took pleasure in having contributed to the community and world around them. It had brought them satisfaction, respect from neighbors, and even, for Ruth, an alternative career. They had taught their children (who often helped out in the park and other projects) the value of contributing to their communities.

However, the couple encountered significant financial and emotional reversals, and Ruth and Jim divorced as they approached their sixties. Still, both left the marriage with great feelings of accomplishment and mutual respect. They felt that they had led worthwhile lives and that they would continue to do so. They were able to avoid the worst consequences of what otherwise might have been a devastating blow to the family, one that might have caused one or more members to slide into emotional problems or addictive or self-destructive behavior.

Not everyone is as willing or able to become involved in community affairs as Ruth and Jim. However, you don't have to be a model citizen or a self-sacrificing idealist to take a step in the right direction. For example, take a look at the experiences of Bill, a highly successful insurance company attorney who felt his life was lacking something important.

Bill was an intelligent man, as indicated by the success of his legal career. He had had a horrible marriage until his wife died, leaving him a single parent. Although his marriage had not been good, his wife's death left Bill very depressed. One day Bill picked up the paper and read about a church group that trained laypeople to counsel couples with marital problems. Bill called, and after a few training sessions he was accepted as a lay marriage counselor. Over a period of several years of counseling, many couples reported to the church that Bill had helped them tremendously.

Bill was struck by how much his involvement in helping strangers changed his outlook and improved his own life. He became much better at dealing with his kids, and their lives benefited. He felt his relationship with the new woman in his life was likewise vastly improved. Finally, Bill developed a whole new view of the world and his relationship to it. He experienced so many benefits from this part-time role that he decided to make a midlife career change to become a counselor.

Small Steps to a Positive Life

You may not be ready to change careers or to make broad positive choices. This may especially be true if you have been wrapped up in a serious addiction. But you can still take positive steps and be a contributing citizen. Think about what values matter to you most—protecting the environment, honesty in politics, spiritual or religious faith, peaceful conflict resolution, and so on—and make your life consistent with these values. Find ways to drive less; conserve resources; recycle even when you can get away with not doing so. Join the Sierra Club, a peer counseling group, or any other organization that does good. Start writing poetry, pick up that instrument you dropped, or join a choral group.

Even if you don't want to join a church, you can still follow the precepts of your chosen religion or ethical philosophy; even if you don't belong to a political party, you can still fulfill the responsibilities of citizenship by voting thoughtfully. Inform yourself about public issues and discuss them with others, or pick a municipal or town meeting to attend. You may simply pick something going on around you and take the plunge. Volunteer. For example, join a cleanup effort. As well as elevating your vision of your life, you will also meet some great people.

Even small exercises of public responsibility can make you feel better about yourself and give you a sense of purpose and of being connected. AA speaks about resisting the urge to drink "one day at a time." I am talking here about taking one step at a time in ever-expanding positive directions. Perhaps the first step will lead you to take more steps and to become more deeply involved.

Helping others and contributing to your community reduce the impulse to be addicted by making it harder for you to be consumed by your own needs. Many successful treatment programs have been founded on teaching addicts to get out of their own heads. For example, therapeutic communities have traditionally taught participants that their obligations to the group trump their personal needs. As a new resident begins to undergo withdrawal, for instance, Daytop Village throws the person a mop: "It's your turn to clean up." The message inherent in this gesture—"Stop feeling sorry for yourself and do something worthwhile"—is part of a larger message the community is trying to convey: that people need to find better things to do with their lives than to take drugs.

Not only can a sense of commitment and responsibility help you overcome your addiction, but it is such a powerful force that it can save lives. Many suicidal people are prevented from acting on their self-destructive impulses by their sense of responsibility to the survivors who would be wounded by their action. At their worst moments, they are rescued from utter despair by their sense of connection and obligation to those they love.

Just as it often takes many small steps to lick an addiction, living a worthwhile, positive life takes a progressive approach. This is especially true if you are depressed and if you feel your life isn't worth much. Think of the very basic things that Jerry (the former heroin addict in Chapter 6) had to begin doing in order to become a regular citizen. In addition to leaving his criminal lifestyle, he had to learn such mundane lessons as to pay his bills and to show up on time. A person who is both depressed and addicted can build self-respect with these small steps. Like Jerry, you will begin to develop a positive view of yourself and your place in the world. Over time, you will come to realize that your life does make a difference.

You and the World

We are human beings in a human world, and none of us leaves without making an impact, and without being deeply influenced by the world around us. This book has addressed your personal needs, the needs of your family and your loved ones, and your concerns for addicted people you may know or deal with. As such, it has armed you with tools to fight addiction successfully. These tools are both time- and research-tested. But they work only to the extent that you employ them. Indeed, your commitment is the essential ingredient to activating any and all of these tools—values, motivation, rewards, resources, support, a mature identity, and higher goals. You can succeed with these, and even with other tools you develop for yourself. Count on it.

People turn to addictions when they find themselves in environments where it is difficult to thrive. As I have said throughout this chapter, your contributing to your community will help us all survive and flourish. In the meantime, if you live in an unsupportive, ailing environment, you can take steps to insulate your own life and home from the problems faced by your community. You can turn to other communities and groups for support and healthy opportunities. You can take steps to avoid the pitfalls of your environment by fostering a sense of personal community in your own life and among those you deal with. This is right and it is good. It's one more step to take to fight addiction.

■■■■■

Exercise: Pursuing Goals
- What changes in your life would be most beneficial, including personal, work/professional, health, family, and any other changes?
- What steps have you ever taken in each area? What steps within the last year? What steps currently? What steps are you now planning?

- Create a goal grid for each area, identifying specific steps you wish to take in each, and plan to do so.

Personal Life Goals Grid

	Personal	Health	Family	Work
GOALS				
STEPS 1.				
2.				
3.				

Exercise: Addiction and Social Well-being

- Consider your worst moments of addictive behavior. How were you impacting other people and the world at the time?
- Now imagine yourself in your most positive role with other people or with your community. Are your addictive behavior and your contributing self compatible?

Exercise: Calculate Your Contributions

- What good things do you do for yourself during a typical day? How do these activities make you feel?
- What good things do you do for your family? How do these make you feel?
- What good do you do for others? How do these things make you feel?
- What major good things have you ever done for other people? How did these things make you feel?
- List your daily activities, and consider how you can conduct these in a way that's more positive to those around you. How would that make you feel?

- What contributions have you made to society? How did these make you feel?
- Which of these activities can you plan to repeat and to build into your life? What other such activities can you envision adding to your life? How would conducting your life this way make you feel?

■■■■■

Exercise: Belonging and Joining

- List your existing group, public, civic, church, political, and community activities.
- What are you most concerned about in the world? What worries you or do you think most needs improvement? How are you best equipped or situated to improve people's lives?
- List five group, public, civic, church, political, or community activities that entail these concerns and skills. Call local church, civic, or charity organizations for suggestions.
- To which of these groups can you most comfortably contribute your time or effort—effort that helps the group and that is within your capability?

■■■■■

Afterword: Society's Tools for Fighting Addiction

We have now developed a set of tools to fight addiction. In the course of doing so, we have discovered surprising truths about addiction's nature and its causes. This knowledge will help you to free yourself from addiction in your own life. However, as we have also learned, as long as our society continues to approach addiction in an irrational way, then the overall incidence of addiction will increase.

Conventional treatment programs in the United States steamroll all research and reason; their efforts serve merely to reaffirm easy and familiar beliefs and treatment methods. The understanding of addiction we have reached leads us instead to scrutinize how we treat alcoholism and other addictions, including our failure to provide alternatives to treatments based on the twelve-step philosophy. The approach to addiction outlined in this book also casts new light on U.S. drug policies, including overseas drug interdiction, efforts to reduce drug supplies, court-assigned drug and alcohol treatment, and the incarceration of drug users.

Particular kinds of drugs do not cause addiction, nor does being an addict mean that you must be an illicit drug user. Therefore, any attempt to curtail addiction as a whole by outlawing the use of any one substance is doomed to failure. Even if the United States managed to succeed in some area of its drug control policy, such as preventing heroin or cocaine from entering the country, then people would immediately replace the suppressed drug with another substance. People inclined toward addictive behavior will pursue other unhealthy compulsions aside from currently popular illegal drugs. These compulsions can take the form of new illicit substances, currently legal ones such as alcohol or prescribed drugs, or even unhealthy involvements with sex or food.

Given this reality, we must revise the way we teach children about drugs and alcohol, as well as what we teach them about the meaning of addiction. The goal and practice of moderation and self-control in all areas of life must somehow be conveyed. At the other extreme, a new approach must also address how we treat the worst drug abusers, who are rarely reached by current programs. Hope for such a change has arrived in the form of a new perspective on drug use and drug treatment called "harm reduction," which accepts that there will be persistent substance abusers who nonetheless can benefit from help.

In general, we need to recognize the larger goals implicated in the fight against addiction. There is no substitute for teaching people to become engaged, competent, and responsible. Waking up to a world worth living in, living in real communities—these are the factors that actually prevent addictive behavior across the society. If these issues are not addressed, then U.S. treatment programs, domestic and international drug policies, and medical research will have no impact on basic addiction rates.

American Attempts to Curb Drug Importation Always Fail

In the United States, the fight against addiction is seen as a fight against illicit drugs (although American ambivalence toward and bias against alcohol also run deep). Neither prescription drugs nor nondrug compulsions are part of the thinking about combating addiction. But our concern over illicit drugs is unending and ever-expanding. Combined federal, state, and local budgets in the war against drugs and their effects reached $40 billion in 2003 (calculating for inflation, this is about twenty-five times as large as Richard Nixon's original 1973 drug war budget of $430 million). But for all the attention paid and the enormous and ever-increasing budget dedicated to the war against drugs, the level of illicit drug use far exceeds levels in the 1960s and early 1970s.[1]

A cornerstone of the U.S. antidrug crusade is our effort to reduce drug production in other parts of the world. However, limiting the amount of heroin or cocaine imported from one area of the world generally just means that some other region will provide the drug. For decades, the United States has tried to reduce or eliminate heroin production in Asia and Mexico. American agencies have also tried to suppress the sources of cocaine in Latin America, particularly in Colombia. But this has not affected the quantity of imports to the United States. For example, in 2000 the Taliban effectively suppressed Afghan poppy crops used to produce heroin. After the Taliban was removed by the United States, however, poppy production quickly returned to record levels in Afghanistan.[2] At the same time, opium production in Colombia and Mexico had quickly risen to replace Afghan and other Asian suppliers—and Colombia and Mexico are now the largest sources for American heroin.[3]

Colombia's status as the primary source for American heroin is doubly ironic since so much of American drug policy in recent years has been directed toward eliminating coca crops in Colombia. Thus attacks on Colombia's cocaine production have had a twofold effect. First, much drug production in Colombia shifted from cocaine to heroin. Meanwhile, while cocaine production remains high (although it is diminishing) in Colombia, more cocaine is being produced in neighboring Peru and Bolivia.[4] The United States has yet to show that it can sustain long-term reductions in overseas supplies of drugs to this country.

This interchangeable substitution of sources for heroin and other drugs is a long-standing pattern. Richard Nixon attacked the Turkish opiate trade in 1973. After the administration announced that the corner had been turned on heroin, however, Mexico developed into a major source for the drug. Attacks on Mexican heroin production in turn led to its being replaced by Asian sources, until Mexico resumed its leadership status in this area after Asian supplies of the drug were disrupted.

The failure of successive administrations to stanch the flow of drugs is well documented by U.S. government agencies. In December 2002 the Congressional Research Service issued a report entitled *Drug Control: International Policy and Approaches*. The report summarized the situation this way:

> Efforts to significantly reduce the flow of illicit drugs from abroad into the United States have so far not succeeded. Moreover, over the past decade, worldwide production of illicit drugs has risen dramatically: opium and marijuana production has roughly doubled and coca production tripled. Street prices of cocaine and heroin have fallen significantly in the past 20 years, reflecting increased availability.[5]

Despite previous failures, each administration feels obligated to take up the cudgel and to accelerate the fight. The Bush administration continues this tradition. In 2003 the Justice Department implemented the $17.4 million program called "Operation Containment" to once again disrupt heroin trafficking in Afghanistan.[6] The United States likewise is escalating its efforts to curb cocaine crops in Colombia and neighboring Latin American countries, including growing use of a devastating chemical, Agent Green, a pervasive herbicide whose use violates international agreements. In Colombia, this was part of the Bush administration's three-year $2.5 billion effort to stem drug production.[7]

U.S. policy toward the developing world is based on our perception that we are deluged by drugs that originate in these countries. For their part, many in these countries feel that it is in their best interest to continue to grow drug crops, both because drugs are profitable to produce and because the crops have other local uses.[8] To their way of thinking, it is up to the United States to deal with drug use within its own borders. Leaders throughout Latin America grumble about the United States' preoccupation with drug crops in their countries. In Bolivia, which like Colombia produces coca paste, Evo Morales almost won the presidency in 2002, based in good part on his support for the right of the Indian population to grow coca.[9] The victorious candidate, Gonzalo Sanchez de Lozada, who supported U.S. drug policy, was deposed by a popular uprising in 2003.

One consequence of American attempts to stifle the drug trade is the massive corruption it has spawned, corruption that exists even at the highest levels of government, as it does, for example, in Mexico. Carlos Salinas, Mexico's former president, diverted large amounts of drug money to his own pockets. In 2003 the Mexican military raided and closed the offices of the country's own drug policing agency due to persuasive corruption there.[10] Charles Bowden, in his book *Down by the River: Drugs, Money, Murder, and Family*, calculates that the illicit drug trade accounts for 63 percent of Mexico's economy.[11] Illicit drugs also create a multibillion-dollar underground economy in the United States. Wherever illicit drugs generate so much money, corruption will be an inevitable presence, as it is in American as well as Mexican police forces.

American Attempts to Curb Drug Traffic Within U.S. Borders Always Fail

The domestic policy parallel to our war on overseas drug supplies is to use police, courts, prisons, and other internal security efforts to prevent the sale, trade, and use of drugs within the country. Punitive domestic policies not only have failed, but also have taken a tremendous toll. The United States imprisons its citizens at a higher rate than any other country in the world (having passed Russia). According to Justice Department statistics, more than 2.1 million Americans were in prison in 2002. This burden is especially felt among the African-American community, where one in eight African-American men between the ages of twenty and thirty-four was in prison in 2002.[12]

This mass of imprisoned Americans is being fueled by the war on drugs. The rate of Americans imprisoned for drug offenses increased tenfold between 1980 and 1997. About 60 percent of current inmates in federal prisons are incarcerated due to drug offenses. African-Americans do not take drugs more frequently than white Americans; they are only imprisoned more often and with longer terms for doing so. This is because blacks participate more in street-level drug trades, which are easier for police to identify and bust. Blacks constitute 13 percent of all drug users but 59 percent of people convicted for drug offenses.[13] This imprisonment rate further endangers black communities. As University of Wisconsin sociologist Pam Oliver observed: "You can't lock up that high a percentage of the young black male population without devastating black communities."[14]

Our Efforts to Reduce Domestic Drug Use Are Equally Unsuccessful

The effort to curtail importation and sale of drugs is called "supply reduction." At the same time as U.S. policies have failed in this area, so, too, have efforts at "demand reduction," or getting Americans to cease wanting to use drugs.

Each administration has claimed that its team has made progress in cutting back drug use in the United States. For example, William Bennett (who served as the U.S. drug czar for the first two years of George H. W. Bush's administration) continued to claim after he left office that he and the first Bush administration made great progress in this area, advances that the Clinton administration failed to maintain. Bennett cited the drop from peak illegal drug use in the late 1970s and early 1980s to slightly less drug use in the late 1980s and early 1990s as evidence that conservative Republican drug policies worked.

However, the data don't fit very neatly into the picture that Bennett paints. According to the National Survey on Drug Use and Health, the annual number of new marijuana users peaked in the period from 1973 to 1978.[15] It began to drop *before* Ronald Reagan became president in 1981, and certainly before Bennett became drug czar in 1989. Moreover, it began to rise again in 1990, right after Bennett took office. While Bennett can blame the Clinton administration's lack of follow-through on Republican policies for the shift, what we are actually observing are larger patterns of fluctuating drug use that have little or nothing to do with government policy.

The truth is that no American administration since the 1970s has managed to reverse trends in drug use for very long. Every president since Richard Nixon has promised unrealizable drug use reduction targets and then claimed success even when the data don't support this claim. They do so by crowing whenever drug use rates temporarily dip. For example, when drug czar John P. Walters, George W. Bush's White House director of the Office of National Drug Control Policy, announced the administration's drug control policy for 2003, he boasted that youthful drug use had begun to decline for the first time in ten years.[16]

In fact, the percentage of twelfth graders using any illicit substance in 2002 dropped a minuscule half a percentage point, to 41.4 percent in 2002 from 41.0 percent in 2001, according to the Monitoring the Future high school drug survey.[17] What Walters failed to mention was that during George W. Bush's (and Walters's) first year in office, 2001, dangerous drug use surged significantly, according to the National Survey. There was a small overall increase in drug use in 2001 over 2000. More significant, however, was the increase in drug use among young adults ages eighteen to twenty-five, which grew from 16 to 19 percent between 2000 and 2001. Moreover, the worst forms of drug use—those qualifying for a diagnosis of drug dependence or abuse—increased from 1.9 to 2.5 percent.[18]

More bad news greeted the administration. Along with the Monitoring the Future study, the government also funds PRIDE, the privately run Parents' Resource Institute for Drug Education survey. The PRIDE 2002–2003 results showed that the number of teens (including all those ages eleven to eighteen) using illicit drugs rose from 22 to 24 percent over the previous year. Obviously, no one in the Bush administration crowed about these data.[19]

Impressed by the microscopic improvement shown in the Monitoring the Future survey of high school seniors' drug use in 2002, Walters reiterated the Office of National Drug Control Policy (ONDCP) and White House goals of reducing drug use by 10 percent over the next two years and 25 percent over five years, by 2008. However, when Congress passed funding for the PRIDE and Monitoring the Future surveys in 1998, it specified a five-year goal (ending in 2003) of 3 percent of teens using drugs over the prior month.[20] The actual figure was five times as great. This goal, of course, has conveniently been forgotten.

We need to realize that drug use rises and falls within a small range every year. While figures for some types of drug use go down, others often simultaneously rise. These peaks and valleys then tend to reverse themselves every few years. Indeed, forgetting Congress's ambitious 1998 goal for cutting drug use, Thomas Gleaton, the chief PRIDE investigator, noted that over the last decade, "We are locked in somewhere around one-quarter of our 11- to 18-year-old kids using drugs."[21] Trends over the last decades indicate that we will never return to the smaller number of drug users in the United States prior to the 1970s, before we began our incessant drug wars.

Addiction Is Not Limited to Overseas or Illicit Drugs

NEW AND SYNTHETIC DRUGS

What if the percentage of Americans using illicit drugs actually did dip back to pre-1970s numbers? At the same time, what if the United States' simultaneous goal of substantially reducing (or even eliminating) coca, poppy, and marijuana crops and trade all over the world was actually achieved? Let's pretend for a moment that the U.S. government achieved one or both of these impossible antidrug goals. Would we then find ourselves in an addiction-free paradise?

The eradication of all natural drug crops would have little impact on the prevalence of illicit drug use and abuse. Synthetic recreational drugs are already a major part of the illicit drug landscape. Roughly every decade a new drug enters the arena of popular use and abuse. In the 1990s Ecstasy burst upon the scene, and methamphetamine (which had been popular in the late 1960s) rejoined the list of major drugs of concern in the illicit American market, as well as worldwide. The UN now warns that these drugs are replacing cocaine and heroin as the major global drug scourges.[22] Since these drugs are synthetic and are produced domestically (although substantial amounts are also produced in Mexico and overseas), they cannot be eliminated through overseas interdiction. These and other new drugs are *always* ready to replace any foreign drug blocked from the pipeline.

Moreover, there are many legal domestic substitutes for illicit drugs. Alcohol is legal and easy for youths as well as adults to obtain, and it can ruin lives as well as any illegal drug. But alcohol is only the most obvious example of a legal, domestic substance to which some Americans become dangerously attached. For example, the United States instituted its Drug Abuse Warning Network (DAWN) emergency room data system in the 1970s; in 1980 it identified Valium as the most frequent cause of hospital emergency admissions. Yet since Valium is prescribed as a pharmaceutical, its abuse is ignored in government statistics and by government policy.

THE ADDICTIVE EFFECTS OF PHARMACEUTICALS

Illicit drugs and alcohol are not the only drugs that can lead to addiction and other negative health results. The sale of psychotropic (mind-altering) drugs is a major legal industry. Modern medicine is quick to prescribe these drugs, and there are major commercial interests and marketing dollars dedicated to making sure that they are widely prescribed and used. Americans of all ages, in large and growing numbers, are turning to tranquilizers, sedatives, painkillers, and antidepressants for emotional relief. When use of these drugs is under medical supervision, prescription drug use is usually, but not always, better monitored than illicit drug use. There is also a large illegal market of diverted prescription drugs. In any case, many people suffer negative effects from them, including dependence (Rush Limbaugh being a notable example).[23]

In 2001, the DAWN report on major drugs of abuse listed cocaine, marijuana, and heroin as the most frequently reported drugs in emergency room visits.[24] The largest category of illicit drug admissions in 2001 was for cocaine (193,000). However, the numbers of admissions for other illicit drug categories were surprisingly small—fewer than 15,000 methamphetamine admissions, 5,500 Ecstasy admissions, 500 inhalant admissions, and not enough certified admissions for Rohypnol (the date rape drug) to list.

But the government report failed to discuss the enormous number of emergency visit admissions due to the use of prescription drugs revealed in DAWN: more than 175,000 admissions for painkillers, 135,000 for sedatives and hypnotics, and 60,000 for antidepressants.[25] Overall, there were about half a million emergency room admissions in 2001 for prescription drugs.

To consider some comparisons, there were about twice the number of admissions for prescription painkillers as for heroin, twice as many for antidepressants as for LSD, PCP, and methamphetamine combined, and more admissions for tranquilizers and sedatives than for marijuana. Government agencies that fight illicit drugs do not want to publicize the frequency with which these legal drugs cause hospitalization. This might, in their view, cast an onus on many leading drugs prescribed by doctors, diverting attention from the "bad" drugs whose dangers officials want to highlight.

Dependence (addiction) is the most common motive listed in DAWN for drug use that resulted in an emergency room visit—and pharmaceutical use can lead to dependence. Indeed, sometimes the media become fixated on legal drug dependence, perhaps even exaggerating its frequency or inevitability. In 2001 *Newsweek*, *Time*, and the *New York Times Magazine* featured articles on the abuse of prescription painkillers Vicodin and OxyContin. The problem of addiction to painkillers is a long-standing one; the search for a nonaddictive analgesic has been a holy grail for pharmacologists for more than a century. But many claim that instead of achieving this goal, the latest painkillers are the most addictive. The *New York Times Magazine* article, entitled "The Alchemy of OxyContin," reported, "It takes about five seconds to effect the transformation [due to using the drug]—and not much longer to create an addict."[26]

How addictive is OxyContin? In 2001, about a billion dollars' worth of the drug was sold legally.[27] Granted, the large majority of these users did not become addicted. Of course, according to the National Survey on Drug Use and Health data that we reviewed in Chapter 2, a large majority of heroin users are not addicted, either. OxyContin and Vicodin do seem to produce irresistibly welcome effects for some people, however, and affect people who would never try a street drug but who feel that it is okay to rely on prescription medications. Some of these claim to be ordinary individuals who became dependent on these drugs unwittingly, after receiving a prescription for a standard medical or psychological condition (as did Limbaugh).

THE SPREAD OF LEGAL DRUG ADDICTION

Increasingly, people report being addicted to antidepressants. In 2001 the World Health Organization (WHO) warned of an addiction risk for Prozac, the largest-selling antidepressant in the world. The head of the World Health Organization's unit for monitoring drug side effects declared that although Prozac has been "billed for years as a harmless wonder drug," it often "creates more problems than the depression it is supposed to be treating."[28] Groups have formed to support members in overcoming Prozac dependence and withdrawal.

Antidepressants such as Prozac have revolutionized the practice of psychiatry. Their growth seems never-ending—antidepressants were the top-selling category of drug in the United States once again in 2001, with sales of $12.5 billion, up 20 percent from 2000.[29] And antidepressants are being prescribed more for children, as are other psychotherapeutic drugs (such an antipsychotic drugs and medications for anxiety, obsessive-compulsive disorder, and attention deficit hyperactivity disorder). A study published in 2003 found that the use of psychiatric drugs among children was increasing more rapidly than the use of these drugs in the population at large, with more and more pediatricians and child psychiatrists relying on drugs to treat children's emotional problems.[30]

Yet these drugs have rarely been tested on those under the age of nineteen, which worries some researchers. As Dr. James Leckman, professor of child psychiatry at the Yale School of Medicine, put it: "We're doing these experiments more or less with our own children."[31] There was considerable alarm when British drug authorities and the U.S. Food and Drug Administration (FDA) announced in mid-2003 that new data revealed that Paxil (which is in the same class of antidepressants as Prozac) caused substantial risk that teenagers and children would consider (and attempt) suicide. At the same time, the drugs were not found to be more effective than placebo in treating depression in the young.[32]

Despite these findings by the FDA, which regulates prescription drugs in the U.S., the *New York Times* reported several months later that "so far, there is little evidence that the warnings have affected doctors' prescribing practices."[33] How could they, considering the revenues that drug manufacturers receive from these drugs, and how reliant physicians have become on them for treating difficult emotional problems?

People find that these legal drugs eliminate unpleasant, perhaps intolerable, feelings they normally experience. And the range of recommended uses for some of the most popular drugs is remarkable. Paxil, for instance, is (according to its Web site) prescribed in the treatment of depression, generalized anxiety disorder, social anxiety disorder, panic disorder, obsessive-compulsive disorder, and post-traumatic stress disorder. Paxil and other antidepressants are used for a litany of other conditions (including weight loss and alcoholism) for which in some cases they have not been officially approved. As people use these legal drugs for such a wide variety of key emotional and behavioral concerns, they come to rely on this chemical method for relieving their distress, and they become less capable of relieving it on their own. They may then become just as dependent on the medically prescribed drugs as other people are to street drugs to feel an essential (but illusive) sense of well-being.

Thus the emphasis on the dangers of illegal drugs in American public health downplays the serious and growing danger of legal drug addiction—and this is without having touched on addiction to alcohol, nicotine, or caffeine, the three most widely used psychoactive substances in the United States. All of these commonplace substances can lead to addiction, especially nicotine.[34] U.S. society has, of course, come to recognize this danger in the case of alcohol and smoking, if not so much with caffeine. Nonetheless, these substances continue to be omnipresent in our lives, and we are certainly not prepared to outlaw them (having tried to do so, with dismal results, in the case of alcohol).

Since caffeine, nicotine, alcohol, and popular prescription

drugs are all capable of producing addiction under the right set of circumstances, attacking one category of drug—whether painkiller, antidepressant, alcohol, cocaine, or heroin—will not eliminate widespread drug addiction. Psychotropic substances have existed throughout recorded history. At the same time that we fail to overcome addictions to these age-old substances, we are expanding our addictive pharmacopoeia virtually daily. Drugs will never be eliminated, and we need some better way to deal with addiction other than campaigning to eliminate the illicit drugs we most fear.

Addiction Isn't Limited to Drugs

Even if, improbably, all illicit drugs—or all drugs—were eliminated from the face of the earth, the motivation toward addiction would not itself be erased. Any powerful experience can be the object of addiction. Excessive shopping, gambling, use of the Internet and other media, and sex can lead to addictions that are fully as powerful, debilitating, and harmful as drug addictions. The pain and compulsivity displayed by people in these areas remind us that addiction is not a harmless phenomenon, whatever its object. Moreover, such nondrug addictions are far more pervasive, affecting an enormous percentage of the American population.

What Are We Teaching Our Children?

Unhealthy dependencies begin early in the lives of American children, including constant reliance on television, the Internet, and video games. Aside from their own debilitating effects on children's lives, these early dependencies bespeak the possibility of additional addictions later on in the child's life. Few children, even those who use alcohol and drugs regularly, show the clinical symptoms of addiction. Yet many of them have experienced addictive involvements that they could subsequently transfer to drugs, alcohol, gambling, or the other dependencies that we fear most.

Learning about the psychological force of dependency and how to avoid it is not the goal of addiction prevention in schools. Instead, contemporary American education focuses all antiaddiction efforts on drug and alcohol prevention programs that have typically been revealed to be ineffective and sometimes even counterproductive.

Fundamental to these programs' approach to drugs and alcohol is a zero-tolerance message. Students are taught that all illegal substance use, including underage drinking, must be avoided. Although schools have been driving home this message for the past twenty years, government measures of alcohol and drug use by high school students reveal that it is not getting across. In 2002, the annual study tracking U.S. high school alcohol and drug use, Monitoring the Future, revealed that 53 percent of twelfth graders had tried an illicit drug, while 78 percent had tried alcohol and 62 percent had been drunk.[35] More than a quarter of high school seniors had used an illicit drug in the past month, 49 percent had consumed alcohol in that time, and 30 percent had recently been drunk.[36]

How do we interpret the fact that by the end of their high school careers, the large majority of American youth have disregarded the antidrug and antialcohol messages that have been so fervently fed to them? It means that they don't believe what they hear. Fewer than a third of sophomores in the Monitoring the Future survey believed that the risk of occasional marijuana use was great.[37] And this belief decreases through their high school careers: Fewer than a quarter of seniors perceived occasional marijuana use as a great risk.[38] Ten years earlier, almost half of sophomores and almost twice as many seniors as today (41 percent) felt that occasional marijuana use was a great risk.

What accounts for this rejection of antidrug and antialcohol messages? Apparently most children's observations and actual experiences contradict the information they receive in school. As a result, they learn to discount such messages. If kids regularly drink and/or take marijuana without experiencing bad outcomes, they may well eventually disregard all the warnings that they hear. The trouble is that there are actually a number of negative consequences that they might suffer and which they should be warned against and guard against.

The most immediate of these consequences is that they might harm themselves through a car or other accident, through unprotected sexual activity, or through alcohol poisoning or other overdose (or, more often, through mixing different drugs or drugs and alcohol). Obviously, schools, parents, and others want to prevent these outcomes in any possible way. However, there is little room left for attention to the real dangers of substance abuse when so much indiscriminate effort goes into telling kids to "just say no" to any substance all of the time.

The good news is that is while few tenth graders felt that occasional marijuana use was a great risk, a solid majority (61 percent) understood that regular use is dangerous.[39] Unfortunately, the percentage of seniors who believed that regular marijuana use was dangerous was lower (53 percent).[40] The fact that a large minority of students do not see the risks of such use and that their numbers increase over their school careers is disheartening.

This difficulty in distinguishing between the consequences of moderate and excessive substance use is also apparent with regard to alcohol. Most high school seniors accept that it is not a great risk to "take one or two drinks nearly every day." But while a majority of tenth graders (52 percent) believe there is great risk in having five or more drinks at a time on weekends, this figure declines to 42 percent for seniors. In addition, only a relatively small majority of seniors (59 percent) think there is great risk to "four or five drinks nearly every day."[41] All the antialcohol lectures these young people have heard have not convinced many of them that regular heavy drinking is dangerous.

The most prevalent substance abuse educational program in the United States (used in about three-quarters of school systems nationwide) is D.A.R.E., which stands for Drug Abuse Resistance Education. D.A.R.E. was started by Los Angeles police chief Darryl Gates in 1983 as a program to send police officers into schools to discourage children from using drugs. Although it is ubiquitous, D.A.R.E. has never demonstrated that it is effective. Virtually every impartial, well-designed evaluation has found D.A.R.E. to have little or no impact on drug and alcohol use—and some studies have even found that kids who have gone through the program are more likely to use these substances. Yet municipal officials across the country continue to swear by it.

D.A.R.E. has always been more of a social phenomenon than an educational package. Its main hook is that it brings police officers into the classroom. There is no reason to think that the police are effective educators, but once they are involved in a project, it becomes a badge of loyalty to approve of their efforts. Bumper stickers, T-shirts, and banners announce people's commitment to D.A.R.E.—which is to say, their opposition to drugs.

The first sign of trouble for D.A.R.E. came in 1994 when a study by the Research Triangle Institute found little short-term effectiveness to the program. The study noted that D.A.R.E. was *less* effective than other programs that emphasize basic skills and that rely on interactions with students rather than on lectures.[42] A University of Illinois study found that six years later, D.A.R.E. students were *more* likely to use drugs than comparable kids not exposed to the program.[43] A ten-year study published in 1999 by a team of researchers at the University of Kentucky found that neither directly after the program nor ten years later, when students were twenty, did D.A.R.E. students show any less use of cigarettes, drugs, or alcohol than those who did not participate in D.A.R.E.[44]

By 2001, the backlash against D.A.R.E. had become so great that its director admitted that it had been ineffective. He announced that D.A.R.E. would devise a new program with a grant of $13.7 million from the Robert Wood Johnson Foundation. The foundation reasoned that it would be easier to change the content of D.A.R.E. than to try to sell new, effective programs with a different name around the country. The new curriculum was developed by Dr. Zili Sloboda, who was acting director of the National Institute on Drug Abuse. Dr. Sloboda pointed out, in faint defense of D.A.R.E., that "it is far from the only program that does not work—it has simply drawn the most criticism because it is the largest."[45]

From this point on, there will continue to be debate about whether the changes implemented by D.A.R.E. have made it more effective. Among the changes made were that the curriculum was shifted to later grades, that police officers would act more like coaches than lecturers, and that the students would participate in exercises in which they interact and practice targeted behaviors. The new D.A.R.E. will also focus on publicizing norms for drug and alcohol use, to show children that drug and alcohol use is not as common as they may believe.

Two investigators writing in the prestigious *Journal of Studies on Alcohol* found that negative outcomes from prevention programs—including *greater* substance use by some children in the programs—were not uncommon.[46] Will the changes in D.A.R.E. make it more effective? Let's hope that at least they don't make it even *less* effective.

A number of explanations have been proposed for the failure of the old D.A.R.E. program to show positive results. For example, when children had already begun using drugs and alcohol prior to receiving D.A.R.E. training, they reacted negatively to the program's antidrug and antialcohol messages. Yet one of the innovations in the revamped D.A.R.E. program is to use D.A.R.E. in later grades, when kids are more likely to have started using substances. Another potential problem is that the new D.A.R.E. focuses on social norms programs that tell children that there is less use going on around them than they believe. Such programs make sense in areas where general norms are in fact conservative toward drinking and drugs. But, as our review of high school data shows, drinking and marijuana use are in fact the norm in high schools around the country.

Indeed, a study by the group known for measuring the high degree of binge drinking on college campuses (the Harvard School of Public Health College Alcohol Study) found in 2003 that such social norms programs were ineffective at the university level. In fact, at some college campuses that used the social norms approach, drinking increased.[47] The Harvard study's chief investigator, Henry Wechsler, offered a possible explanation for these results: "One problem with this approach is that many students do not care about what the 'typical' student does," and "students are more likely to be influenced by their immediate circle of friends than by the drinking habits of a mythical average student, who is alluded to in social norms programs."[48]

D.A.R.E. is obligated to be negative and proscriptive toward *any* drug or alcohol use (all school-based drug education is required by federal law to be totally abstinence-oriented).[49] Whether this unyielding stance, a cornerstone of American drug education and national policy, can work in a world where drug and alcohol use is widespread remains unlikely.

An Alternate Approach: Recognizing and Learning About Moderation

Many kids are already drinking and using drugs. Rather than scold them and inform them that they either need to eliminate substance use from their lives or be damned to a life of depravity, educational programs need to provide for something in between. While they certainly do not want to accept or approve of underage drug or alcohol use, educational programs cannot afford to bury their heads in the sand and ignore that such use occurs.

It is important for adolescents to realize that regular drug use and heavy drinking are risky behaviors. Unfortunately, since their education fails to distinguish between what educators don't want them to do (sample substances at all) and what is really harmful to them (using large amounts of these substances) children sometimes fail to differentiate between moderate and excessive or compulsive substance use.

Americans almost inevitably engage in some use of psychoactive substances—certainly of alcohol. Furthermore, epidemiological research has even discovered that moderate alcohol consumption can actually be good for you. The critical message to convey to people is that they need to control their substance use, to avoid heavy or excessive use, and to protect themselves from immediate dangers when they do become intoxicated.

Children are far more able to understand these complexities than we might expect. That is, many already do perceive the difference between moderate and excessive use. More, particularly those children in high-risk categories, could be helped to learn this difference. Yet although most high school students are already drinking and will soon reach the legal drinking age, American education refuses (reinforced by federal law) to tell them that moderate alcohol consumption is preferable to heavy drinking and to explore moderation as a theme. One strange result of this situation is that while many kids realize that heavy drinking is risky (and even disapprove of it), they go ahead and get drunk, anyway. This "binge-or-bust," all-or-none approach toward substance use is not only dangerous in itself, it is a precursor to addiction further down the line.

Another Alternative Approach: Harm Reduction

Furthermore, children could use assistance in understanding and planning to avoid the worst consequences of substance use, like accidents and risky sexual practices. The failure to recognize the reality of substance use almost guarantees increased casualties from such use. To plan instead to counteract dangerous consequences is called "harm reduction." In fact, we all know of one such practice, promoted by Mothers Against Drunk Driving (MADD) and others: Safe Rides programs. Safe Rides means allowing children to signal that they are in no condition to drive, and providing alternative ways for them to get home. Parents don't want their children out getting drunk. But they most certainly don't want their kids getting behind the wheel of a motor vehicle when they do drink.

Harm reduction is an emerging conception for drug policy and even treatment. Harm reduction is based on three principles:

1. While absolute abstinence may be preferable for many substance abusers, very few will achieve it, particularly in the short run. Even those who eventually achieve abstinence will take time to do so and may relapse periodically.
2. Any kind of improvement in drug users' lives is to be encouraged and appreciated. This includes improvements in diet and health care, fewer risky behaviors, holding down a stable job, maintaining a stable social or family life, and the development of a crime-free lifestyle.
3. Any improvement is a potential stepping-stone to further improvements, including the eventual escape from addiction and the development of stable abstinence.

We know that people who remain with their families and who hold jobs will ultimately succeed better at reducing and eliminating their substance abuse than those who do not. Moreover, as with other kinds of health and medical care, even when people are abusing a substance, taking care with diet, disease prevention, and other health and social care means they can survive, preserve their health, and eventually succeed at licking their addictions. This effort to help imperfect human beings is evident in all areas of medicine—for example, when doctors provide insulin to people with diabetes even when they fail to follow fully their recommended diets.

In much of western Europe and the developed world, the concept of harm reduction is taken for granted. For example, every national government in the Western world endorses or provides needle exchange programs—except for the United States, where only some cities and states permit some forms of clean-needle programs. In the United States, harm reduction is considered too radical to be accepted by the public. Critics label it an acceptance of drug use and addiction. For example, New Jersey governor Christine Whitman rejected the recommendation of her state's Advisory Council on AIDS that the state allow addicts to have easier access to syringes. Providing clean needles to addicts is a primary example of harm reduction, since it prevents the worst outcome of drug use—HIV infection, AIDS, and death. When the council's chair, a conservative businessman and friend of Whitman's, persisted in recommending a clean-needle program, he was eventually allowed to resign and was replaced by a priest who could be counted on to expunge clean needles from the agenda. Whitman then supported a New Jersey sting policy of ferreting out and prosecuting needle exchange providers. "Doing drugs is wrong," Governor Whitman said. "And for government to start to engage in a policy of providing the wherewithal to engage in illegal activity, I think sends a very confusing message to young people."[50]

Every public health agency in the United States (including the government's own Centers for Disease Control and Prevention, National Institutes of Health, as well as the Institute of Medicine of the National Academy of Sciences and the American Medical Association) agrees with President Clinton's National Commission on AIDS that clean-needle programs reduce the rate of HIV and other bloodborne infection. Research has further shown that rather than encouraging increased drug use, these programs actually lead more addicts to enroll in treatment.[51] Thus it seems clear that the basis for the opposition to such programs is moralism, not medical effectiveness.

As a perhaps closer-to-home example of harm reduction, consider a man who regularly gets drunk in bars and often ends up in a fight, an accident, or incarcerated. A therapist who counsels this man that he should stay at home when he intends to drink could greatly improve the man's safety, protect the other people that he might injure, reduce his jail time, and otherwise improve the man's life. However, most American treatment programs would expel him from therapy if they found out that he continued to drink, even if he improved his welfare. Seeking to impose moral ideals, rather than caring for patients, creates serious consequences.

As for Governor Whitman, no one can accuse her of being soft on drugs. At the same time, New Jersey has one of the highest HIV infection rates in the country. As indicated by the state's Web site, most cases are due to intravenous drug use, and three-quarters of victims are minorities.[52]

Where Do We Go from Here?

Throughout this chapter, we have seen the many ways in which American drug, alcohol, and addiction policies ignore reason and research in favor of an unrealistic, ineffective, moralistic approach to substance use, abuse, and addiction. In the United States we throw money into useless interdiction campaigns, we ignore harmful addictions to legal drugs, we try to solve life problems by labeling them diseases and placing people in hospitals, we indoctrinate our children with impractical, counterproductive drug and alcohol education that fails to differentiate between substance use and substance abuse, and we ignore the need to give people the skills, motivation, and other life resources to avoid addiction. The law enforcement approach to drug use has led to hundreds of thousands of (mostly minority) men being incarcerated.

With all of this bad news and continuing misunderstanding of the nature and solutions for addiction, am I optimistic about the future of addiction in the United States? I began this book by saying that new ideas are slowly filtering into the field. But ineffective, moralizing, and nonscientific—along with overly medicalized—ideas still dominate most of what is done about drugs and alcohol.

Things can go in either direction, but it is necessary to encourage further movement of American policies along positive rather than negative paths in the following ways.

TREATMENT

We need to broaden and deepen our approaches to substance abuse treatment. This includes avoiding recommending, or certainly avoiding ordering through the court system, that people undergo treatment when they do not have diagnosable substance abuse problems. Even in cases where such programs are promoted as alternatives to incarceration and the targeted individuals have genuine problems with drugs or alcohol, we must reject a one-size-fits-all model. Aside from the ineffectiveness of forcing people into treatments that violate their values, mandated twelve-step participation has been found by a number of courts around the United States to violate constitutional protections.[53] Instead, we should offer as many different approaches to addiction treatment as people can respond to. We should especially make available treatments that provide needed skills and that enlist people's values and motivations without forcing users to identify themselves as lifelong addicts.

Furthermore, all addiction counselors should learn how to provide skills training, motivational enhancement, environmental molding (e.g., community reinforcement techniques), family relationship therapy, and other therapeutic practices that help addicts improve their lives. Counselors should not be true believers advocating for their personal route to recovery. Therapy for addiction should be coordinated with provision of other services, such as family support, housing, job training, medical care, psychotherapy for other emotional problems, and so on. Rather than denouncing independent recovery as unrealistic and a sign of denial, we should regard it as a viable alternative to treatment and incorporate and encourage self-initiated change as an adjunct to treatment—sometimes called guided (or directed) self-change.

THE SCIENCE OF ADDICTION

Government science programs may continue to churn out data from brain scans and neurochemical tests, arguing that addiction is a brain disease. They may continue to conclude that addiction and dependence are irreversible biochemical problems. But this approach provides no help for people struggling to cope with their environments, nor does it help to improve the condition of those environments, nor does it recognize and accept the regular occurrence of self-cure.

Instead, addiction science should focus on addicts as they live, experience, and react to the world in which they are addicted. This entails recognizing and incorporating that even severe addicts and alcoholics may change and improve their usage patterns and lives, and that many will completely escape their dependence diagnoses over time—in fact, they typically do so. How they accomplish this and how science, treatment, and policy may encourage them to do so are critical questions that must continue to be part of the research agenda.

When science is applied to inform policy, it should publicize rather than obfuscate the fact that addicts frequently get better without treatment. It should make clear that policies and programs that improve addicts' lives, including harm reduction and other positive steps such as learning job skills, holding a job, improving their health, stabilizing their family and home lives, reducing criminal activity, and so on, will lead to better outcomes for addicts. Research agencies such as the National Institute on Drug Abuse and National Institute on Alcohol Abuse and Alcoholism should likewise make clear that, as their own research shows, addicts and alcoholics can reduce or modify their consumption to produce healthier outcomes, even when they can't or won't abstain.

POLICY

American foreign policy cannot continue to be dominated by antidrug mania, as it is in Colombia, Bolivia, Mexico, Afghanistan, and elsewhere, so that we go on spending hundreds of millions of dollars to eradicate crops, support totalitarian regimes that promise to suppress the drug trade, and encourage the massive corruption that often dominates these developing societies. On the domestic front, the United States and local and state governments should not continue to escalate legal and police pressure to fight against the use of drugs. The criminal-justice approach will never impact the underlying problems of addiction. Instead, it will simply result in even more punitive actions against American citizens, many of whom, while they may use or abuse drugs, do not commit other crimes.

We need instead to accept (without encouraging or approving) that some drug use is inevitable, that the harms from this use can be reduced, and that improving the lives of the people at highest risk to abuse drugs is the only way to significantly reverse drug use and addiction levels. Harm reduction principles (including programs such as needle exchange and drug substitutes such as methadone for addicts in efforts to normalize their lives) should be made part of the policy package. Treatment policy should focus on assisting people by providing them with the resources and training needed to right their lives beyond the simple facts of their drug use.

EDUCATION GOALS

We cannot allow antialcohol and antidrug propaganda—predicated on the moralistic assumptions that no child should ever drink or use drugs, that there is no good to alcohol use, and that once people decide to use drugs and alcohol all possibility of self-control is lost—to continue to masquerade as education. Instead, education about drugs and particularly alcohol should distinguish between excessive and moderate consumption (including the information that moderate drinking prolongs life for many people by reducing coronary artery disease). In other words, education should recognize the reality and, for those who drink, the goal that drinking can be part of a fulfilling and healthy lifestyle.

Drugs, of course, are in a different category, since their use is illegal. Nonetheless, we need to attain some sense of balance such that we do not ruin people's lives either by making criminals of occasional drug users or by assuming that any drug use proves a person is addicted, must undergo treatment, and should be marked as a lifelong addict.

At a broader level, education and policy should recognize that substance use of all types occurs in a community context. Thus healthier communities produce less harmful drug use. Alcohol policy in particular should concentrate on encouraging beneficial, nonharmful patterns of drinking and identify how different cultures and communities use alcohol in more and less healthful and socially beneficial ways. *Sensible* drinking occurs in groups where drinking involves men and women and people of different ages, where it accompanies other activities such as meals or celebrations, and where it incorporates the norms of pleasant, respectful, and responsible behavior toward others.

THE WORLD OF THE FUTURE

Whatever problems exist around the concept of addiction today, future technologies hold out the possibility of even further intrusions into our lives in the name of addiction prevention and treatment. What if, for example, sensors could be implanted to detect when people—those suspected of using drugs, children, all people—used a drug or alcohol? In the name of preventing addiction and illegal drug use, would we use such an intrusive technology?

Currently, as we come to recognize that many compulsive activities that do not involve drugs are addictions, we may respond by applying many of the same wrongheaded ideas and treatments that we already utilize with drug and alcohol abuse and addiction. These include the misconceptions that the habits are inbred, that addicts can never again gamble, shop, or eat a sweet, and that only a higher power—or some yet-to-be-discovered medicine—can save them from themselves.

Since more and more areas of behavior—of even our inner selves—are being made a part of addiction treatment and theory, more medical justification may be claimed for labeling us as having a disease, for treating us (involuntarily if necessary) for these diseases, for labeling and monitoring us as though our problems were irremediable lifetime conditions, and for deciding that experts know what is best for us, including the only ways to stave off our addictions. Of course, these experts hope, eventually a true medical-chemical-genetic solution to addiction will be found.

In place of this growing intrusiveness into the very core of our beings, for illusory gains, we need to recognize that we will never find a single magical cure for addiction, as though it were located somewhere in the brain, like a tumor. Instead, addiction will be reduced only in a better world comprised of better-equipped people leading better lives.

A Final Word

When I entered the addiction field in 1975 with the publication of my first book, *Love and Addiction*, I knew that I was tackling a subject mined with prejudice and irrationality. There is still much to do; there will always be much to do. But I believe this is a fight worth fighting. Nothing else called a disease impacts so many people's core sense of who they are and what they are capable of doing or changing, or what they are trapped by.

I join this fight by writing professional and popular articles and books (including *Love and Addiction*, *The Meaning of Addiction*, *Diseasing of America*, and *The Truth About Addiction and Recovery*). My colleague and frequent coauthor Archie Brodsky has been a critical help in this writing. I also conduct workshops teaching the techniques and perspectives outlined in this book, and I am adjunct professor at the New York University School of Social Work. The professionals (and sometimes patients) I work with cover a wide range. Some are counselors in traditional treatment organizations that want to broaden their horizons, or at least the array of tools at their disposal. Some counsel Native Americans, for whom disease concepts of alcoholism and addiction have been an obvious irrelevance and a dismal flop. Some are professionals who are convinced that a harm reduction approach is best and who want to review techniques in order to best serve their clients (for example, youthful urban drug abusers). I also work with health professionals who seek to master emerging treatment techniques such as Brief Interventions and Motivational Interviewing, and I have helped to develop a Brief Intervention protocol that includes follow-up contacts with clients by e-mail and phone, in order to meet them "where they live."

I maintain an active Web site—www.peele.net—with the assistance of my Dutch colleague Arjan Sas. Along with posting my latest articles, book recommendations, and comments on timely developments, I field questions from people with addiction problems who want different answers from those they might get—or have already gotten—from conventional support groups or counselors. I often hear from individuals who are trying to break away from such groups or who have rejected or been rejected by them. I also hear from, and sometimes counsel, people coerced into twelve-step treatments by courts, employee assistance programs (EAPs), or medical boards or other professional bodies. For some individuals, I conduct focused, practical phone and Internet counseling (called coaching).

When someone writes a book pointing out fallacies in current beliefs and policy, he or she is part of a long line of people who have been questioning received opinion for some time. This is true in the case of this book, and I am indebted to a community of researchers and clinicians who have been talking sense about addiction for several decades, all of whom I cannot come close to citing here (see, in addition, the notes to the earlier chapters). I certainly rely on the work of the following and others.

In the area of natural recovery from drug addiction, I have found most useful Charles Winick's pioneering research on maturing out, the work of Dan Waldorf and his colleagues *(Cocaine Changes)*, that of Patricia Erickson and her colleagues *(The Steel Drug)*, the work of Patrick Biernacki *(Pathways from Heroin Addiction)*, Ronald Siegel's longitudinal study of cocaine users, and Lee Robins and her colleagues' study of returning Vietnam War heroin addicts.

In the area of natural recovery from alcoholism, key figures have been Barry Tuchfeld, Arnold Ludwig, George Vaillant *(The Natural History of Alcoholism Revisited)*, Harold Mulford, Don Cahalan, Robin Room, and Deborah Dawson and others involved in the National Longitudinal Alcohol Epidemiologic Survey. I also participated in a conference with the leading investigators of natural recovery, producing the book *Promoting Self-Change from Problem Substance Use* (edited by Harald Klingemann and others, including myself).

In terms of theoretical contributions to rethinking addiction, primary is Norman Zinberg and his work on controlled use *(Drug, Set, and Setting)*. Many other clinically oriented contributors have also advanced this field, including Alan Marlatt in the area of relapse prevention, James Prochaska and his colleagues' stages of change *(Changing for Good)*, Pat Demming and her colleagues' harm reduction treatment *(Over the Influence: The Harm Reduction Guide for Managing Drugs and Alcohol)*, Nathan Azrin's development of the Community Reinforcement Approach, and Peter Monti and his colleagues' skills training *(Treating Alcohol Dependence)*.

One investigator who has led the field in advancing new approaches to alcohol problems and other addictions is William Miller, of the University of New Mexico, who is coeditor of two monumental research/clinical books: *Motivational Interviewing* (with Stephen Rollnick) and *Handbook of Alcoholism Treatment*

Approaches: Effective Alternatives (with Reid Hester). These works are close to ideal in combining critical research, non-dogmatic thinking, and clinical skills. The Motivational Interviewing Web site, www.motivationalinterview.org, provides a good map to skills and training in this area. On a broader scale, the Drug Policy Alliance, headed by Ethan Nadelmann, is the single organization providing the most information (at its Web site, www.drugpolicy.org) and an organized effort to reform American policies toward drugs and drug users. (I am a senior fellow of the Alliance.)

We face critical choices about how we will view and attack addiction. Addiction is the symptomatic malady of our era. While my efforts and those of the people I respect are far from guaranteed to carry the day, I believe there are no more critical areas to be engaged in than drugs, alcohol, and the variety of addictive experience. I ended the preface to my book *The Meaning of Addiction* as follows:

> Our conventional view of addiction—aided and abetted by science—does nothing so much as convince people of their vulnerability. It is one more element in a pervasive sense of loss of control that is the major contributor to drug and alcohol abuse, along with a host of other maladies of our age. . . . [O]ur best hope is to convey these dangers realistically, by rationally pointing out the costs of excess and, more importantly, by convincing people of the benefits of health and of positive life experience. Otherwise, the idea of addiction can only become another burden to the psyche. Science cannot increase our understanding of ourselves and our world—nor can it show us the way to freedom—if it is held captive by our fears.

Thus I continue to struggle against what I see to be the dominant, but possibly changing, thinking that misleads America in this area today.

Notes

Introduction

1. By the 1980s, even before the current intense marketing of nicotine patches and other devices for quitting smoking, a large percentage of Americans were former smokers, and over 90 percent had quit on their own; see M.C. Fiore, T.E. Novotny, J.P. Pierce et al., "Methods Used to Quit Smoking in the United States," *Journal of the American Medical Association* 263 (May 23, 1990): 2760–5. This is true even though most people addicted to both cigarettes and other drugs or alcohol rate smoking as harder to quit; see L.T. Kozlowski, D.A. Wilkinson, W. Skinner et al., "Comparing Tobacco Cigarette Dependence with Other Drug Dependencies," *Journal of the American Medical Association* 261 (February 10, 1989): 898–901.

2. See A.I. Leshner, "Addiction Is a Brain Disease, and It Matters," *Science* 278 (1997): 45–7.

3. See N.D. Volkow, "Brain Imaging: Bringing Drug Abuse into Focus," *NIDA Notes* 18(2) (August 2003): 3–4; M. Duenwald, "A Conversation with Nora Volkow," *New York Times* (August 19, 2003): F5.

4. B. Vastag, "Talking with Alan I. Leshner, Ph.D., National Institute on Drug Abuse Director," *Journal of the American Medical Association* 285 (March 7, 2001): 1141–3.

5. H. Klingemann, L. Sobell, J. Barker et al., *Promoting Self-Change from Problem Substance Use: Practical Implications for Prevention, Policy and Treatment* (The Hague: Kluwer, 2001), 99–104.

6. J.H. Jaffe and T.G. Harris, "As Far as Heroin Is Concerned, the Worst Is Over," *Psychology Today* (August 1973): 68–79, 85.

7. L.N. Robins, "Vietnam Veterans' Rapid Recovery from Heroin Addiction: A Fluke or Normal Expectation?" *Addiction* 88 (1993): 1041–54.

8. Ibid., 1048.

9. Ibid., 1046.

10. Ibid., 1052.

11. CNN.com, "Joan Kennedy Arrested for Drunken Driving" (September 11, 2000), http://www.cnn.com/2000/US/09/11/joan.kennedy.arrest.ap.

12. CNSNEWS.com, "Roger Clinton Arrested" (February 18, 2001), http://www.cbsnews.com/stories/2001/02/18/national/main272924.shtml.

13. F.S. Stinson, H. Yi, B.F. Grant et al., *Drinking in the United States: Main Findings from the 1992 National Longitudinal Alcohol Epidemiologic Survey (NLAES)* (Bethesda, MD: National Institute on Alcohol Abuse and Alcoholism, 1998).

14. D.A. Dawson, "Correlates of Past-Year Status Among Treated and Untreated Persons with Former Alcohol Dependence: United States, 1992," *Alcoholism: Clinical and Experimental Research* 20 (1996): 771–9.

15. S. Peele, *Diseasing of America* (San Francisco: Jossey-Bass, 1995), 93–4.

16. "Klein and Fall," *Guardian Newspapers* (April 16, 2003).

17. Kozlowksi et al., "Comparing."

18. Fiore et al., "Methods."

19. J.H. Krystal, J.A. Cramer, W.F. Krol et al., "Naltrexone in the Treatment of Alcohol Dependence," *New England Journal of Medicine* 345 (December 13, 2001): 1734–9.

20. C. Holden, " 'Behavioral' Addictions: Do They Exist?" *Science* 294 (November 2, 2001): 980.

21. S. Peele and A. Brodsky, "Love Can Be an Addiction," *Psychology Today* (August 1974): 22.

1: Values

1. E.M. Dawson, "Understanding and Predicting College Students'

Alcohol Use: Influence of Attitudes and Subjective Norms," *Dissertation Abstracts International* 61(3) (2000):1320B.

2. M.L. Barnett, "Alcoholism in the Cantonese of New York City: An Anthropological Study," in O. Diethelm, ed., *Etiology of Chronic Alcoholism* (Springfield, IL: Charles C. Thomas, 1955), 179–227.

3. Ibid., 186–7.

4. B. Glassner and B. Berg, "How Jews Avoid Alcohol Problems," *American Sociological Review* 45 (August 1980): 647–64.

5. See N.E. Zinberg and W.M. Harding, eds., *Control over Intoxicant Use* (New Haven, CT: Yale University Press, 1982).

6. Glassner and Berg, "How Jews Avoid," 653–61.

7. K.K. Bucholz and L.N. Robins, "Recent Epidemiologic Alcohol Research," in P.E. Nathan et al., eds., *Annual Review of Addiction Research and Treatment* (New York: Pergamon, 1991), 7.

8. L. Saxe, C. Kadushin, A. Beveridge et al., "The Visibility of Illicit Drugs: Implications for Community-Based Drug Control Strategies," *American Journal of Public Health* 91 (December 2001): 1987–94.

9. Quoted in P. Kerr, "Rich vs. Poor: Drug Patterns Are Diverging," *New York Times* (August 30, 1987), 1.

10. S. Peele, A. Brodsky, and M. Arnold, *The Truth About Addiction and Recovery* (New York: Fireside, 1992), 100.

11. D. Yee, "Number of Black Men Who Smoke Is Dropping, CDC Says," Associated Press (October 10, 2003).

12. Centers for Disease Control and Prevention, "Cigarette Smoking Among Adults—United States, 2000," *MMWR Highlights* 51:29 (July 26, 2002).

13. *Alcoholics Anonymous* (New York: Alcoholics Anonymous World Service, 1980, originally published 1939), 46, 49.

14. W.R. Miller, V.S. Westerberg, R.J. Harris et al., "What Predicts Relapse? Prospective Testing of Antecedent Models," *Addiction* 91 (Supplement 1996): S155–71.

15. Ibid., S155.

16. Alcoholics Anonymous, *Comments on A.A.'s Triennial Surveys* (New York: Alcoholics Anonymous World Services, 1990).

17. B.S. Tuchfeld, "Spontaneous Remission in Alcoholics," *Journal of Studies on Alcohol* 42 (July 1981): 626–41.

18. Ibid., 631.

2: Motivation

1. Frank Keating, "Repealing Alcoholics Anonymous: The Courts Go Too Far—Again," *National Review Online* (December 13, 2000), www.nationalreview.com/comment/comment121300a. shtml.

2. J.O. Prochaska, C.C. DiClemente, and J.C. Norcross, "In Search of How People Change: Applications to Addictive Behaviors," *American Psychologist* 47 (1992): 1102–14.

3. B.S. Tuchfeld, "Spontaneous Remission in Alcoholics," *Journal of Studies on Alcohol* 42 (July 1981): 632.

4. Ibid., 633.

5. D. Premack, "Mechanisms of Self-Control," in W.A. Hunt, ed., *Learning Mechanisms in Smoking* (Chicago: Aldine, 1970), 115.

6. Substance Abuse and Mental Health Services Administration, *Results from the 2002 National Survey on Drug Use and Health* (Washington, D.C.: U.S. Department of Health and Human Services, 2003), Table 1.1B.

7. Ibid., Table 5.25B.

8. That addicted drug users likewise frequently quit was, of course, revealed by returning Vietnam veterans; see L.N. Robins, "Vietnam Veterans' Rapid Recovery from Heroin Addiction: A Fluke or Normal Expectation?" *Addiction* 88 (1993): 1041–54.

9. W.R. Miller, P.L. Wilbourne, and J.E. Hettema, "What Works? A Summary of Alcohol Treatment Outcome Research," in R.K. Hester and W.R. Miller, eds., *Handbook of Alcoholism Treatment Approaches: Effective Alternatives*, 3rd edition (Boston: Allyn and Bacon, 2003), 13–63.

10. For more detailed descriptions of Brief Interventions see N. Heather, "Brief Intervention Strategies," in R.K. Hester and W.R. Miller, eds., *Handbook of Alcoholism Treatment Approaches: Effective Alternatives*, 2nd edition (Boston: Allyn and Bacon, 1995), 105–22; A. Zweben, S.J. Rose, R.L. Stout et al., "Case Monitoring and Motivational Style Brief Interventions," in Hester and Miller, *Handbook*, 3rd edition, 113–30.

11. T.F. Babor and M. Grant, eds., *Project on Identification and Management of Alcohol-Related Problems* (Geneva: World Health Organization, 1992).

12. W.R. Miller and R.K. Hester, "Inpatient Alcoholism Treatment: Who Benefits?" *American Psychologist* 41 (1986): 794–805.

13. T.H. Bien, W.R. Miller, and J.S. Tonigan, "Brief Interventions for Alcohol Problems: A Review," *Addiction* 88 (1993): 315–36.

14. The research and theory in support of Motivational Interviewing, as well as detailed descriptions of its practice, are presented in W.R. Miller and S. Rollnick, *Motivational Interviewing: Preparing People for Change*, 2nd edition (New York: Guilford Press, 2002). One area in the addiction field that demonstrates the relationship between personal beliefs and change concerns problem drinkers' success at either reducing their drinking or abstaining depending on their beliefs about themselves and alcohol, and their own selection of a treatment goal. See P.G. Booth, B. Dale, P.D. Slade et al., "A Follow-Up Study of Problem Drinkers Offered a Goal Choice Option," *Journal of Studies on Alcohol* 53 (1992): 594–600; G. Elal-Lawrence, P.D. Slade, and M.E. Dewey, "Predictors of Outcome Type in Treated Problem Drinkers," *Journal of Studies on Alcohol* 47 (1986): 41–7; N. Heather, S. Rollnick, and M. Winton, "A Comparison of Objective and Subjective Measures of Alcohol Dependence as Predictors of Relapse Following Treatment," *British Journal of Clinical Psychology* 22 (1983): 11–7; J. Orford and A. Keddie, "Abstinence or Controlled Drinking: A Test of the Dependence and Persuasion Hypotheses," *British Journal of Addiction* 81 (1986): 495–504.

15. Modified from W.R. Miller, "Enhancing Motivation for Change," in Hester and Miller, *Handbook*, 3rd edition, 137–8.

3: Rewards

1. J. Orford, S. Dalton, E. Hartney et al., "How Is Excessive Drinking Maintained? Untreated Heavy Drinkers' Experiences of the Personal Benefits and Drawbacks of Their Drinking," *Addiction Research and Theory* 10 (August 2002): 347–72.

2. Ibid., 365.

3. Ibid.

4. Ibid., 366.

5. See S. Peele and A. Brodsky, "Exploring Psychological Benefits Associated with Moderate Alcohol Use," *Drug and Alcohol Dependence* 60 (2000): 221–47.

6. R.I. Lipton, "The Effect of Moderate Alcohol Use on the Relationship Between Stress and Depression," *American Journal of Public Health* 84 (1994): 1913–7.

7. W. Styron, "Darkness Visible (excerpt)," *Vanity Fair* (December 1989): 215.

8. J. Porter and H. Jick, "Addiction Rare in Patients Treated with Narcotics," *New England Journal of Medicine* 302 (January 10, 1980): 123; J. Morgan, "American Opiophobia: Customary Underutilization of Opioid Analgesics," *Advances in Alcohol and Substance Abuse* 5 (fall 1985): 163–73; D.E. Moulin, A. Iezzi, R. Amireh et al., "Randomised Trial of Oral Morphine for Chronic Non-Cancer Pain," *Lancet* 347 (January 20, 1996): 143–7.

9. I. Chein, D.L. Gerard, R.S. Lee et al., *The Road to H* (New York: Basic Books, 1964).

10. Ibid., 158.

11. C.E. Johanson and E.H. Uhlenhuth, "Drug Preference and Mood in Humans: Repeated Assessment of *d*-Amphetamine," *Pharmacology Biochemistry & Behavior* 14 (1981): 159–63.

12. Substance Abuse and Mental Health Services Administration, *Results from the 2002 National Survey on Drug Use and Health* (Washington, D.C.: U.S. Department of Health and Human Services, 2003), Table 4.2A.

13. P.G. Erickson, E.M. Adlaf, F. Murray et al., *The Steel Drug: Cocaine in Perspective* (Lexington, MA: Lexington Books, 1987).

14. Ibid., 80.

15. R.K. Siegel, "Changing Patterns of Cocaine Use: Longitudinal Observations, Consequences, and Treatment," in J. Grabowski, ed., *Cocaine: Pharmacology, Effects, and Treatment of Abuse* (Rockville, MD: National Institute on Drug Abuse, 1984), 92–110.

16. "Anti-Drug Law Backfires," *USA Today* (April 24, 2002).

17. A. Cox, "Yale Fights the War on Drugs," *San Francisco Chronicle* (May 3, 2002).

18. N.E. Zinberg, *Drug, Set, and Setting: The Basis for Controlled Intoxicant Use* (New Haven, CT: Yale University Press, 1984), vii.

19. D. Waldorf, C. Reinarman, and S. Murphy, *Cocaine Changes: The Experience of Using and Quitting* (Philadelphia: Temple University Press, 1992).

20. W.M. Harding, N.E. Zinberg, S.M. Stelmack et al., "Formerly-Addicted-Now Controlled Opiate Users," *International Journal of the Addictions* 15 (1980): 55.

21. I relied particularly on the scrupulously researched biography of Nora Joyce by B. Maddox, *Nora: The Real Life of Molly Bloom* (New York: Houghton Mifflin, 1988).

22. I.J. Goldberg, "To Drink or Not to Drink?" *New England Journal of Medicine* 348 (January 9, 2003): 163–4.

23. M. Cohen, I.A. Liebson, and L.A. Faillace, "A Technique for Establishing Controlled Drinking in Chronic Alcoholics," *Diseases of the Nervous System* 33 (1972): 46–9.

24. S.T. Higgins, A.J. Budney, W.K. Bickel et al., "Achieving Cocaine Abstinence with a Behavioral Approach," *American Journal of Psychiatry* 150 (1993): 763–9.

25. W. M. Cox, E. Klinger, and J.P. Blount, "Alcohol Use and Goal Hierarchies: Systematic Motivational Counseling for Alcoholics," in W.R. Miller and S. Rollnick, eds., *Motivational Interviewing: Preparing People to Change Addictive Behavior* (New York: Guilford Press, 1991), 260.

4: Resources

1. The relationship between the course of the crack epidemic and the resources of the populations affected by it is the subject of C. Reinarman and H. Levine, eds., *Crack in America: Demon Drugs and Social Justice* (Berkeley: University of California Press, 1997).

2. Quoted in P. Kerr, "Rich vs. Poor: Drug Patterns Are Diverging," *New York Times* (August 30, 1987): 1.

3. J.W. Finney, R.H. Moos, and C. Timko, "Course of Treated and Untreated Substance Abuse Disorders: Remission and Resolution, Relapse and Mortality," in B.S. McCrady and E.E. Epstein, eds., *Addictions: A Comprehensive Guidebook* (New York: Oxford University Press, 1999), 30–49.

4. J.W. Finney and S.C. Monahan, "The Cost-Effectiveness of Treatment for Alcoholism: A Second Approximation," *Journal of Studies on Alcohol* 57 (May 1996): 229–43. CRA was also rated in the top five by W.R. Miller, P.L. Wilbourne, and J.E. Hettema, "What Works? A Summary of Alcohol Treatment Outcome Research," in R.K. Hester and W.R. Miller, eds., *Handbook of Alcoholism Treatment Approaches: Effective Alternatives*, 3rd edition (Boston: Allyn and Bacon, 2003), 13–63.

5. CRA and its linked family training component, Community Reinforcement and Family Training (CRAFT—which is discussed in the next chapter), are described in J.E. Smith, R.J. Meyers, and J.L. Milford, "Community Reinforcement Approach and Community Reinforcement and Family Training," in Hester and Miller, *Handbook*, 3rd edition, 237–58.

6. J.E. Smith, R.J. Meyers, and H.D. Delaney, "The Community Reinforcement Approach with Homeless Alcohol-Dependent

Individuals," *Journal of Consulting and Clinical Psychology* 66 (1998): 541–8.

7. S.T. Higgins, S.C. Sigmon, C.J. Wong et al., "Community Reinforcement Therapy for Cocaine-Dependent Outpatients," *Archives of General Psychiatry* 60 (October 2003): 1043–52.

8. A manual for training skills in alcoholism and other addiction treatment is P.M. Monti, R.M. Kadden, D.J. Rohsenow et al., *Treating Alcohol Dependence: A Coping Skills Training Guide*, 2nd edition (New York: Guilford Press, 2002). See also P.M. Monti and D.J. Rohsenow, "Coping Skills Training and Cue Exposure Treatment," in Hester and Miller, *Handbook*, 3rd edition, 213–36.

9. Albert Ellis has pioneered this approach with his Rational Emotive Therapy; see A. Ellis, *Overcoming Destructive Beliefs, Feelings, and Behaviors: New Directions for Rational Emotive Behavior Therapy* (Amherst, NY: Prometheus Books, 2001); A. Ellis, *Feeling Better, Getting Better, Staying Better: Profound Self-Help Therapy for Your Emotions* (Atascadero, CA: Impact Publishers, 2001).

10. For a review of cognitive-behavioral therapy and its efficacy for depression and other disorders, see J.S. Beck, *Cognitive Therapy: Basics and Beyond* (New York: Guilford Press, 1995).

11. S. Shiffman, "Coping with Temptations to Smoke," in S. Shiffman and T.A. Wills, eds., *Coping and Substance Use* (Orlando, FL: Academic Press, 1985), 223–42.

12. Alan Marlatt pioneered in the development of relapse prevention. See G.A. Marlatt and J.R. Gordon, *Relapse Prevention* (New York: Guilford Press, 1985).

5: Support

1. M.S. Goldman, F.K. Del Boca, and J. Darkes, "Alcohol Expectancy Theory: The Application of Cognitive Neuroscience," in K.E. Leonard and H.T. Blane, eds., *Psychological Theories of Drinking and Alcoholism*, 2nd edition (New York: Guilford Press, 1999), Chapter 6.

2. Quoted in S. Peele, "Second Thoughts About a Gene for Alcoholism," *Atlantic Monthly* (August 1990): 58.

3. The various components in learning about drinking are dealt with comprehensively in E. Houghton and A.M. Roche, eds., *Learning About Drinking* (Philadelphia, PA: Brunner-Routledge, 2001).

4. G.E. Vaillant, *The Natural History of Alcoholism Revisited* (Cambridge, MA: Harvard University Press, 1995).

5. Ibid., 289.

6. ABC News Online, "Binge Drinking at Campuses: Death at MIT Resurrects Debate" (September 30, 1997), http://more.abc-news.go.com/sections/us/mit930.

7. Federal Interagency Forum on Child and Family Statistics, *America's Children: Key National Indicators of Well-Being, 2003* (Bethesda, MD: National Institutes of Health, 2003).

8. L.A. Kaskutas, J. Bond, and K. Humphreys, "Social Networks as Mediators of the Effect of Alcoholics Anonymous," *Addiction* 97 (2002): 891–900.

9. There are a number of variations of behavioral marital therapy used in alcoholism treatment, including CRA's relationship therapy and also general marital and family therapy (MFT). These approaches have many elements in common. See T.J. O'Farrell and W. Fals-Stewart, "Marital and Family Therapy," in R.K. Hester and W.R. Miller, eds., *Handbook of Alcoholism Treatment Approaches: Effective Alternatives*, 3rd edition (Boston: Allyn and Bacon, 2003), 188–212; J.E. Smith, R.J. Meyers, and J.L. Milford, "Community Reinforcement Approach and Community Reinforcement and Family Training," in Hester and Miller, *Handbook*, 3rd edition, 237–58.

10. See S. Peele, A. Brodsky, and M. Arnold, *The Truth About Addiction and Recovery* (New York: Fireside, 1992), 296.

11. W.R. Miller, R.J. Meyers, and J.S. Tonigan, "Engaging the Unmotivated in Treatment for Alcohol Problems: A Comparison of Three Strategies for Intervention Through Family Members," *Journal of Consulting and Clinical Psychology* 67 (1999): 688–97.

12. R.J. Meyers, W.R. Miller, D.E. Hill et al., "Community Reinforcement and Family Training (CRAFT): Engaging Unmotivated Drug Users in Treatment," *Journal of Substance Abuse* 10 (1999): 291–308.

13. Miller et al., "Engaging."

14. Johnson & Johnson, "First Long-Term Health and Wellness Program Evaluation Confirms Employee Benefit, Company Savings for Johnson and Johnson," press release (New Brunswick, NJ, January 24, 2002).

6: A Mature Identity

1. A. Marlowe, *How to Stop Time: Heroin from A to Z* (New York: Basic Books, 1999), 10.
2. I. Chein, "Psychological Functions of Drug Use," in H. Steinberg, ed., *Scientific Basis of Drug Dependence* (London: Churchill, 1969), 23–4.
3. C. Winick, "Maturing Out of Narcotic Addiction," *Bulletin on Narcotics* 14 (January–March 1962): 1–7.
4. Ibid., 5.
5. D. Waldorf, "Natural Recovery from Opiate Addiction: Some Social-Psychological Processes of Untreated Recovery," *Journal of Drug Issues* 13 (1983): 255–6.
6. P. Biernacki, *Pathways from Heroin Addiction: Recovery Without Treatment* (Philadelphia: Temple University Press, 1986), 51.
7. R. Stall, "Respondent-Independent Reasons for Change and Stability in Alcohol Consumption as a Concomitant of the Aging Process," in C.R. Janes, R. Stall, and S.M. Gifford, eds., *Anthropology and Epidemiology* (Dordecht, Netherlands: Kluwer, 1986), 257–301.
8. Ibid., 293.
9. ABC News Online, "US Senator in Bid to Fry Fast-Food Lawsuits" (July 18, 2003), http://www.abc.net.au/news/ newsitems/ s904857.htm.
10. Marlowe, *How to Stop Time*, 228.
11. L.N. Robins, "Vietnam Veterans' Rapid Recovery from Heroin Addiction: A Fluke or Normal Expectation?" *Addiction* 88 (1993): 1052.
12. Substance Abuse and Mental Health Services Administration, *Results from the 2002 National Survey on Drug Use and Health: National Findings* (Washington, D.C.: U.S. Department of Health and Human Services, 2003), Figures 8.3, 8.4.
13. S. Peele, "The Implications and Limitations of Genetic Models of Alcoholism and Other Addictions," *Journal of Studies on Alcohol* 47 (1986): 63–73; S. Peele, *Diseasing of America* (San Francisco: Jossey-Bass, 1995), 60–5; S. Peele, A. Brodsky, and M. Arnold, *The Truth About Addiction and Recovery* (New York: Fireside, 1992), Chapter 2.
14. K. Blum and J.E. Payne, *Alcohol and the Addictive Brain* (New York: Free Press, 1991).

15. N.S. Cotton, "Familial Incidence of Alcoholism: A Review," *Journal of Studies on Alcohol* 40 (1979): 89–116; E. Harburg, W. DiFranceisco, D.W. Webster et al. "Familial Transmission of Alcohol Use: II. Imitation of and Aversion to Parent Drinking (1960) by Adult Offspring (1977)—Tecumseh, Michigan," *Journal of Studies on Alcohol* 51 (1990): 245–56.

16. L.A. Bennett and S.J. Wolin, "Family Culture and Alcoholism Transmission," in R.L. Collins, K.E. Leonard, and J.S. Searless, eds., *Alcohol and the Family: Research and Clinical Perspectives* (New York: Guilford Press, 1990), 194–219.

17. D.A. Dawson, "Correlates of Past-Year Status Among Treated and Untreated Persons with Former Alcohol Dependence: United States, 1992," *Alcoholism: Clinical and Experimental Research* 20 (1996): 771–9.

18. Comments made by David Hodgins, in presenting paper "Natural and Treatment-Assisted Recovery from Gambling Problems: A Comparison of Resolved and Active Gamblers," at the International Conference on Natural History of Addictions, Les Diablerats, Switzerland, March 7–12, 1999. This paper was published by D.C. Hodgins and N. El-Guebaly in *Addiction* 95 (2000): 777–89.

19. National Public Radio (WGBH-FM, Boston), *Thinking About Drinking*, October 4, 1987.

20. Biernacki, *Pathways*, Chapter 5.

21. A. Koski-Jännes, "Social and Personal Identity Projects in Recovery from Addictive Behaviours," *Addiction Research and Theory* 10 (April 2002): 183–202.

22. R. Fransway, *12-Step Horror Stories: True Tales of Misery, Betrayal, and Abuse in AA, NA, and 12-Step Treatment* (Tucson, AZ: See Sharp Press, 2000); M.W. Gilliam, *How Alcoholics Anonymous Failed Me: My Personal Journey to Sobriety Through Self-Empowerment* (New York: William Morrow, 1998).

23. See J.H. Williams, *Sam Houston: A Biography of the Father of Texas* (New York: Simon & Schuster, 1993); M. De Bruhl, *Sword of San Jacinto: A Life of Sam Houston* (New York: Random House, 1993).

24. J.M. McPherson, "The Lone Star," *New Republic* (April 19, 1993): 41.

7: *Higher Goals*

1. J. Alter and J. Green, "Bennett: Virtue Is as Virtue Does," *Newsweek/MSNBC News Online* (May 2, 2002), http://www.msnbc.com/news/908430.asp?cp1=1#BODY.

2. M. Szalavitz, "Trick or Treatment: Teen Drug Programs Turn Curious Teens into Crackheads," *Slate* (January 3, 2003), http://slate.msn.com/id/2076329/.

3. H.A. Liddle and A. Hogue, "Multidimensional Family Therapy for Adolescent Substance Abuse," in E.F. Wagner and H.B. Waldron, eds., *Innovations in Adolescent Substance Abuse Interventions* (New York: Pergamon, 2001), 229–61.

4. J.D. Hawkins, R.F. Catalano, and J.Y. Miller, "Risk and Protective Factors for Alcohol and Other Drug Problems in Adolescence and Early Adulthood: Implications for Substance Abuse Prevention," *Psychological Bulletin* 112 (1992): 64–105.

5. Federal Interagency Forum on Child and Family Statistics, *America's Children: Key National Indicators of Well-Being, 2003* (Bethesda, MD: National Institutes of Health, 2003).

6. R.S. Strauss and H.A. Pollack, "Epidemic Increase in Childhood Overweight, 1986–1998," *Journal of the American Medical Association* 286 (December 12, 2001): 2845–8.

7. E.J. Fried and M. Nestle, "The Growing Political Movement Against Soft Drinks in Schools," *Journal of the American Medical Association* 288 (November 6, 2002): 2181.

Afterword

1. The percentage of twelve-to-seventeen-year-olds who had ever used marijuana went from 1.8 percent in 1965 to 7.4 percent in 1970 and stood at 20.6 percent in 2002. Substance Abuse and Mental Health Services Administration, *Results from the 2002 National Survey on Drug Use and Health: Detailed Tables* (Washington, D.C.: U.S. Department of Health and Human Services, 2003), Table 4.58B.

2. J. Seper, "Afghanistan Again Top Heroin Source," *Washington Times* (April 10, 2003).

3. J. Forero and T. Wiener, "Latin American Poppy Fields Undermine U.S. Drug Battle," *New York Times* (June 8, 2003): 1.

4. "South America: The Andean Drug Industry, the Balloon Goes Up," *Economist* (March 6, 2003).

5. R. Lee and R. Perl, *Drug Control: International Policy and Approaches* (Washington, D.C.: Congressional Research Service, December 11, 2002).

6. J. Seper, "Afghanistan: Afghan Drug Crops Up Despite Curbs," *Washington Times* (January 9, 2003).

7. "U.S. Restates Its Support of Colombia," *Miami Herald* (August 20, 2003).

8. L. Zurita-Vargas, "Coca Culture," *New York Times* (October 15, 2003): A19.

9. J. Forero, "U.S. Aid Foe Is in Runoff for President of Bolivia," *New York Times* (July 10, 2002): A5.

10. R. Johnson, "Crackdown in Mexico Points to New Policy," *Los Angeles Times* (January 18, 2003).

11. C. Bowden, *Down by the River: Drugs, Money, Murder, and Family* (New York: Simon & Schuster, 2002).

12. F. Butterfield, "Prison Rates Among Blacks Reach a Peak, Report Finds," *New York Times* (April 7, 2003): A12.

13. Drug Policy Alliance, "Race and the Drug War," Drug Policy Alliance Web Site, http://www.drugpolicy.org/race/.

14. D. Chapman, "State Ranks Highest in Incarceration Rate of African Americans," *Milwaukee Journal Sentinel* (April 10, 2002).

15. Substance Abuse and Mental Health Services Administration, *Results from the 2002 National Survey on Drug Use and Health: National Findings* (Washington, D.C.: U.S. Department of Health and Human Services, 2003), Figure 6.1.

16. National Institute on Drug Abuse, "2002 Monitoring the Future Survey Shows Decrease in Use of Marijuana, Club Drugs, Cigarettes and Tobacco," news release (December 16, 2002).

17. National Institute on Drug Abuse, *Monitoring the Future Study* (Ann Arbor: University of Michigan, 2002), Table 2.

18. Substance Abuse and Mental Health Services Administration, "Annual Household Survey Finds Millions of Americans in Denial About Drug Abuse," press release (U.S. Department of Health and Human Services, September 5, 2002).

19. PRIDE Surveys, *PRIDE Survey National Summary* (Bowling Green, KY: PRIDE Surveys, 2003).

20. M. Earleywine, "The Cannabis Crusades: Anti-Pot Ads Have Backfired," *San Francisco Chronicle* (September 26, 2003).

21. PRIDE Surveys, "Student Drug Use Consistent with 5- and 10-Year Averages," press release (PRIDE Surveys, September 3, 2003).

22. H. LaFranchi, "Global Scourge: Synthetic Drugs," *Christian Science Monitor* (August 7, 2003).

23. J. Barron, "Limbaugh, Telling of Pill Addiction, Plans to Be Treated," *New York Times* (October 11, 2003): 1, A10.

24. Drug Abuse Warning Network, "The DAWN Report: Major Drugs of Abuse in ED Visits, 2001 Update" (October 2002).

25. Substance Abuse and Mental Health Services Administration, *Emergency Department Trends from DAWN: 2001* (Washington, D.C.: U.S. Department of Health and Human Services, 2002), Table 2.1.0.

26. P. Tough, "The Alchemy of OxyContin," *New York Times Magazine* (July 29, 2001): 32–37, 52, 62–63.

27. C. Kalb, "Playing with Painkillers," *Newsweek* (April 9, 2001): 44; "Painkiller Crackdown," *Newsweek* (May 14, 2001): 38.

28. R. Mendick, "World Health Watchdog Warns of Addiction Risk for Prozac Users," *Independent* (April 29, 2001), http://news.independent.co.uk/uk/health/story.jsp?story=69366.

29. National Institute for Health Care Management Foundation, *Prescription Drug Expenditures in 2001: Another Year of Escalating Costs* (Washington, D.C.: NIHCM Foundation, March 29, 2002), http://www.nihcm.org/spending2001.pdf.

30. J.M. Zito, D.J. Safer, S. dosReis et al., "Psychotropic Practice Patterns for Youth," *Archives of Pediatric & Adolescent Medicine* 157 (January 2003): 1–25.

31. E. Goode, "Study Finds Jump in Children Taking Psychiatric Drugs," *New York Times* (January 14, 2003): A21.

32. G. Harris, "Debate Resumes on the Safety of Depression's Wonder Drugs," *New York Times* (August 7, 2003), 1. A subsequent study reported that Zoloft was effective in treating childhood and adolescent depression. However, while the study found that 69 percent of those ages six to seventeen receiving Zoloft had their depression relieved, so, too, did 59 percent of the children receiving a placebo! K.D. Wagner, P. Ambrosini, M. Rynn et al., "Efficacy of Sertraline in the Treatment of Children and Adolescents with Major Depressive Disorder," *Journal of the American Medical Association* 290 (August 27, 2003): 1033–41.

33. Harris, "Debate."

34. This is probably most surprising to people in the case of caffeine; see E.C. Strain, G.K. Mumford, K. Silverman et al., "Caffeine Dependence Syndrome: Evidence from Case Histories and

Experimental Evaluation," *Journal of the American Medical Association* 272 (October 5, 1994): 1043–8.

35. 2002 Monitoring the Future Study, Table 1.
36. Ibid., Table 2.
37. Ibid., Table 8.
38. Ibid., Table 9.
39. Ibid., Table 8.
40. Ibid., Table 9.
41. Ibid., Tables 8 and 9.
42. S.T. Ennett, N.S. Tobler, C.L. Ringwalt et al., "How Effective Is Drug Abuse Resistance Education?" *American Journal of Public Health* 84 (September 1994): 1394–401.
43. D.P. Rosenbaum and G.F. Hanson, "Assessing the Effects of School-Based Education: A Six-Year Multilevel Analysis of Project D.A.R.E.," *Journal of Research in Crime and Delinquency* 35 (1998): 381–412.
44. D.R. Lynam, R. Milich, R. Zimmerman et al., "Project DARE: No Effects at 10-Year Follow-Up," *Journal of Consulting and Clinical Psychology* 67 (August 1999): 590–3.
45. K. Zernike, "Antidrug Program Says It Will Adopt a New Strategy," *New York Times* (February 15, 2001): 1.
46. C.E. Werch and D.M. Owen, "Iatrogenic Effects of Alcohol and Drug Prevention Programs," *Journal of Studies on Alcohol* 63 (September 2002): 581–90.
47. H. Wechsler, T.F. Nelson, J.E. Lee et al., "Perception and Reality: A National Evaluation of Social Norms Marketing Interventions to Reduce College Students' Heavy Alcohol Use," *Journal of Studies on Alcohol* 64 (July 2003): 484–94.
48. College Alcohol Study, "Link Found Between High-Profile, Well-Funded Social Norms Marketing Programs and Increases in Some Measures of Student Drinking," press release (Harvard School of Public Health, July 24, 2003).
49. The U.S. Department of Education Office of Safe and Drug-Free Schools distributes drug and alcohol prevention funding to state educational authorities. As a condition for accepting these funds, states certify that they're in compliance with applicable laws, that is, prohibition of use and possession of illicit drugs and of alcohol for those under twenty-one years of age. See http://www.ed.gov/fund/data/report/contracts/rfp/00r0045/ED00R0045SOW.doc.

50. "Hard Line on Needle Exchanges; Whitman Says AIDS Program Encourages Drug Use," *New York Times* (February 2, 1999), B1.

51. Institute of Medicine, *No Time to Lose: Getting More from HIV Prevention* (Washington, D.C.: Institute of Medicine, 2000).

52. Division of AIDS Prevention and Control, *New Jersey HIV/AIDS Report* (Trenton: New Jersey Department of Health and Senior Services, December 31, 2002), http://www.state.nj.us/health/aids/qtr0212.pdf.

53. S. Peele, C. Bufe, and A. Brodsky, *Resisting 12-Step Coercion* (Tucson, AZ: See Sharp Press, 2000).

Index

About the Author

STANTON PEELE, Ph.D., J.D., is a psychologist and lawyer who is recognized as a leading expert in the addiction field. He is an adjunct professor at the New York University School of Social Work and a senior fellow at the Drug Policy Alliance. Beginning in 1975 with the publication of *Love and Addiction*, he has written a series of well-received books that forcefully present new approaches to addiction. Other of Dr. Peele's books include *Diseasing of America* and *The Truth About Addiction and Recovery*. As interest in alternative approaches to addiction has grown, more and more books appear that refer to his work.

Dr. Peele has received the Mark Keller Award from the Rutgers Center of Alcohol Studies and the lifetime scholarship award from the Drug Policy Alliance. He lectures nationally and internationally and is often called on to comment on controversial developments in the addiction arena. He also writes popular magazine and newspaper articles, many of which have been reprinted in collections for college students. He maintains an active Web site, www.peele.net, in which he answers questions about addiction from readers around the world.